Stéphane
Dion

Also by Linda Diebel

Betrayed: The Assassination of Digna Ochoa

Stéphane Dion

Against the Current

Linda Diebel

VIKING
CANADA

VIKING CANADA

Published by the Penguin Group

Penguin Group (Canada), 90 Eglinton Avenue East, Suite 700, Toronto, Ontario, Canada
M4P 2Y3 (a division of Pearson Canada Inc.)

Penguin Group (USA) Inc., 375 Hudson Street, New York, New York 10014, U.S.A.
Penguin Books Ltd, 80 Strand, London WC2R 0RL, England
Penguin Ireland, 25 St Stephen's Green, Dublin 2, Ireland (a division of Penguin Books Ltd)
Penguin Group (Australia), 250 Camberwell Road, Camberwell, Victoria 3124, Australia
(a division of Pearson Australia Group Pty Ltd)
Penguin Books India Pvt Ltd, 11 Community Centre, Panchsheel Park, New Delhi – 110 017, India
Penguin Group (NZ), 67 Apollo Drive, Rosedale, North Shore 0632, Auckland, New Zealand
(a division of Pearson New Zealand Ltd)
Penguin Books (South Africa) (Pty) Ltd, 24 Sturdee Avenue, Rosebank, Johannesburg 2196,
South Africa

Penguin Books Ltd, Registered Offices: 80 Strand, London WC2R 0RL, England

First published 2007

1 2 3 4 5 6 7 8 9 10 (RRD)

Copyright © Linda Diebel, 2007

Author representation: Westwood Creative Artists
94 Harbord Street, Toronto, Ontario M5S 1G6

Manufactured in the U.S.A.

ISBN-13: 978-0-670-06744-2
ISBN-10: 0-670-06744-X

LIBRARY AND ARCHIVES CANADA CATALOGUING IN PUBLICATION

Diebel, Linda
Stéphane Dion : against the current / Linda Diebel.

Includes index.
ISBN 978-0-670-06744-2

1. Dion, Stéphane. 2. Liberal Party of Canada—Biography.
3. Canada. Parliament. House of Commons—Biography.
4. Cabinet ministers—Canada—Biography. 5. Legislators—Canada—Biography.
6. College teachers—Québec (Province)—Biography. 7. Québec (Province)—Biography.
I. Title.

FC641.D56D53 2007   971.07'3092   C2007-901569-7

Visit the Penguin Group (Canada) website at **www.penguin.ca**

Special and corporate bulk purchase rates available; please see
www.penguin.ca/corporatesales or call 1-800-810-3104, ext. 477 or 474

For my hardworking fellow political reporters, who get the story first

CONTENTS

"HELLO, MY NAME IS STÉPHANE DION"

J AMIE CARROLL saw it all right, saw it clear as day. He, better than most among potential members of Stéphane Dion's leadership team, saw the considerable hurdles that would lie ahead. It was one thing for Janine Krieber to tell her husband on the night Paul Martin announced he would step down, "Stéphane, you—you should run for leader,"[1] and quite another for a savvy guy like Carroll to be coaxed into a leadership campaign for a man who thought being the best candidate with the best ideas should be enough.

Not that, weirdly, it wasn't.

Carroll was there when running was just an idea. Dion was environment minister when the Liberals lost the election to Stephen Harper's Conservatives on January 23, 2006. Three days later, Carroll was among a group of environment ministry staffers who, alongside their outgoing boss, were packing up their parliamentary offices. Dion and Carroll were an odd pair, the tall, thin Quebecer, fifty, so pale and serious, and the burly Maritimer, twenty-seven, with his shaved head, goatee, and fast lip. Carroll cracked open the liquor stash he'd been saving. Why not? It was probably the last time he'd be working for Dion.

The group began tossing around the question of who would succeed Martin. Frank McKenna? John Manley? Allan Rock? Dion shook his head at each name, sipping his scotch, and suggesting that perhaps someone else was needed. He didn't say who. Carroll could see the train coming, as he later described the question he knew Dion had waited to ask: "What do you think about me running for leader?"[2]

Everyone thought it was a grand idea.

Carroll burst out laughing.

Naturally Dion was hurt. "Don't you think I'd make a good leader?" he asked.

"Not the point," replied Carroll. "It's *getting* there that's the problem." He ticked off the obstacles: no money, no organization, no cross-Canada network, no caucus chums eager to climb aboard, *no money,* and, to be blunt, not the faintest idea of how a leadership campaign works, let alone a convention. "You just finished an election in the third most winnable Liberal riding in the country and you're still $6,000 in debt," he told Dion.[3] Besides, Carroll thought Dion should have begun his campaign six months earlier. "Didn't you notice all that stuff Paul Martin was doing over five years?" he asked, refer-ring to Martin's long-term leadership manoeuvrings against his former boss, Jean Chrétien. "Why do you think he did that?"

Dion seemed offended. "It shouldn't be about money," he insisted.

Carroll threw up his hands and put it to Dion: "Okay, how do you think you become leader of the Liberal party?"

The answer burned itself into Carroll's brain.

"Well, we'll all go to the convention. I'll give a big speech—I'll give my *best* speech—and everyone will vote for me."

So that's how it was going to be.

Carroll promptly switched to bourbon.

WHAT'S STUNNING IS THAT, with a variation or two, that's pretty much what happened. Sure, there were many bleary-eyed, bone-grinding hours put in by a small and dedicated staff that included Jamie Carroll. Dion didn't just float to victory eleven months later at the Liberal leadership convention in Montreal. But he beat the odds. Every step of the way, the smart money bet that he couldn't do it. He wasn't sufficiently well known in English Canada, his English wasn't good enough, and, having brought in the federal Clarity Act, he could never win Quebec—and everyone knew the Liberals were all about winning.

"Even Dion might run," scoffed an early headline in Montreal's ascetic daily *Le Devoir*.[4] Even Dion. How ridiculous was that?

And yet, there he was, shortly after 6 P.M. on a bitter Saturday in Montreal, having just won the most thrilling Liberal leadership convention in a generation. Not since Pierre Elliott Trudeau triumphed on the fourth and final ballot in April 1968 had there been a truly open convention, with character development, plot twists, and cliff-hanging suspense. Delegates made their choice, not the power brokers of the Liberal party. Many of these same delegates had started the year demoralized by the 2006 election loss, stung by the tortuous drip-drip of the sponsorship scandal in Quebec, and weary from feeling their voices weren't being heard by the party establishment. Indeed, eleven months of authoritative pronouncements about the outcome—Michael Ignatieff, Bob Rae; Bob Rae, Michael Ignatieff—showed how completely the country's elites had failed to comprehend the grassroots revolution that elected the fifty-one-year-old former professor from Montreal.

At the Palais des Congrès on December 2, 2006, delegates chose the candidate who, though twice appointed to the federal cabinet, managed to present himself as an outsider to power politics—and that wasn't a stretch. Oblivious might be the better word. As importantly, he was seen as outside the warring camps of Chrétien and Martin. Liberals had had enough of that, thank you very much.

Dion pulled it off. He defeated Ignatieff on the final ballot and the room erupted into a sea of delirious Dion green. Supporters wept, hugged, cheered themselves hoarse, and pressed in to congratulate the new leader. Janine Krieber was at his side, teary-eyed, her wild hair loose, as was Jeanne, their beaming eighteen-year-old daughter. Dion would later say that in the moment of triumph, he was thinking about his acceptance speech to come.[5] The previous night, he'd been cut off, left sputtering into a dead microphone as the music swelled, missing the big Canadian unity ending he'd practised a couple of dozen times. When that happened, his campaign chair, Mark Marissen, had thought it was over. Marissen retired to his room at the Place d'Armes Hotel across the street, poured himself a double scotch, and contemplated throwing himself off the roof.[6]

It wouldn't happen to Dion a second time. As he made his way to the stage that Saturday, he tried to acknowledge every smiling face with that funny birdlike head bob of his. He peered through his spectacles and grinned shyly. For all his later insistence about how collected he was, he looked fairly stunned on stage, even comical as a tiara of red streamers settled on his head. He couldn't wait to deliver the opener he'd worked on with his staff earlier in the afternoon, when it was clear the day would be his. He needed exactly the right phrasing in English so that everyone would get the joke. His thin shoulders shook with mirth as he kicked off with, "It looks like you really wanted to hear the rest of my speech."

It's not as though he hadn't expected to win. That's the thing. He had always refused to grasp the ridiculous odds against him. On Carroll's recommendation (and it was advice from a friend, nothing more at that point), Dion made some three hundred phone calls in February 2006 to test Liberal waters, insisting each time he wouldn't run merely to enliven the field.

Marissen, not yet on board in February, received one of those calls at his home in Vancouver. He'd been federal campaign manager in British Columbia for the Liberal debacle of an election the month before and had actually managed to pull off some gains. Marissen was a political shark in the guise of jovial, round-faced innocence. He remembered the formal, French-accented voice.

Dion: "Hello, my name is Stéphane Dion. I am calling because I am considering to run for the leadership of the Liberal party. You were very involved in the last campaign, and I am calling to get your views about this, and your views about the race."

Marissen: "I haven't decided who I am supporting yet, but I think it would be great for the party if you ran."

Dion: "But I would not run only to animate the debate. I will run to win!"

Marissen: "Of course you would."[7]

DION DIDN'T KNOW many of the folks he was calling—party people, organizers, fundraisers, provincial officials, riding presidents. How could he? He'd never been much of a backslapper.

"During ten years as a minister, I don't think he ever bought an MP a beer," Carroll remarked. He didn't mean it snidely. It was simply an affirmation of the odds against the campaign as it came together. "We're not the biggest but we have the biggest heart," Dion kept saying. As he might express it, that was the good spin.

But, in a sense, Dion did manage to float through the race. There was about his victory a magical quality, where what the candidate didn't know—for example, how a leadership campaign worked—wouldn't hurt him. He thought he was going to win. He believed and he made others believe. He was like Chauncey Gardiner in *Being There,* except really smart.

He was used to tough odds and comfortable swimming against the current. The late political scientist Léon Dion had taught his son to think for himself, and that ability shaped his life. So did Stéphane's exceptionally close relationship with his father, a respected scholar well known in academic and political circles. Both political scientists, both professors, both federalists (each in his own way), the two men

shared a bond that was psychoanalyzed by the media, especially in
Quebec. Indeed, Léon's sudden accidental death in 1997 has been the
lowest point of his son's life.

STÉPHANE DION WAS a good leadership candidate for the same
reasons he had succeeded in other areas of his life. He was a quick
learner and took advantage of the fact that people underestimated
him. "It has worked for me," he told reporters in Montreal after
winning the leadership.

He remained, above all, an individualist in his approach to life
and politics. He had often drawn from Alexis de Tocqueville in the
body of his academic work and, in his political speeches, turned to
Sir Wilfrid Laurier for inspiration. Dion was a federalist who believed
in decentralization and lived in a very different era from Laurier's.
But he ran for leader with the hope of making the same contribution
in his Canadian century as Laurier did in his.

The leadership was an endurance test, and there was ample time
for new staffers to come to know Dion. He could appear to be the
absent-minded professor, head in the clouds. But he listened. "When
you're talking to him," said Marissen, "he's genuinely interested in
what you're telling him—to the point that he's actually listening to
you more than you might be listening to yourself."

He was funny, although not always intentionally so. His English
could be a source of merriment. He talked about "urban *ghee-toes*"
and failed to master the use of gerunds during the campaign. But his
English had improved markedly from the post–1995 referendum
days when he went to Cleveland to deliver a speech about his role in
a united Canada. "Every day," he informed his audience, "Quebecers
wake up to *huge cleavages.*" Dion stood puzzled while the audience
howled.

He lost weight during the race, looking ever more frail and wispy.
But the image was misleading. A strong and athletic man, Dion took

time whenever he could to go with his family to his refuge in Quebec's northern Laurentian Mountains. There, he could fish for hours or take marathon walks with his new pup, Kyoto, a Siberian husky mix he acquired after the election defeat.

He could be obtuse, bull-headed, and exasperating during the campaign. He was demanding, occasionally short-tempered, and annoyingly pedantic. Ever the professor, he couldn't help correcting people. He never got it through his head during the leadership race that his thinly spread troops couldn't possibly provide the research services of a full-fledged ministry. As a federal minister, he'd never understood that a department couldn't whip out handy comprehensive reports in a couple of hours before Question Period. He was a stickler for detail, always holding the Cartesian view that there must be an answer for every question. *So please find it.* He was educated by Jesuits; *ergo* he loved to argue with his staff. It's like the old joke:

Q: "Is it true that a Jesuit always answers a question with another question?"
A: "Who told you that?"

But Dion had another quality that became important during the long, unpredictable leadership campaign: he inspired loyalty. Adam Campbell, a loquacious Scot and leader of the federal Liberals in Alberta, became a Dion supporter and friend in 2006, and described Dion's gift: "He has a very endearing quality, a nervous quirkiness. You feel like you want to help him make this happen."[8]

Jamie Carroll felt the power of that gift. Even knowing what he knew in the beginning, he essentially dedicated a year of his life to Dion. He ended up as deputy campaign manager after Marissen took the top job. He worked twenty-hour days throughout the eleven months of the leadership race, as did others, for weeks at a time without pay. Carroll stayed because, as demanding as Dion was, he

was no less demanding of himself. It may be that nobody worked
harder than Stéphane Dion. At Marissen's home, where he stayed
whenever the budget-strapped campaign landed in Vancouver, he
would be up and in front of the computer at 4:30 A.M. There is a
wonderful anecdote in Eddie Goldenberg's *The Way It Works* about
Dion's years with Jean Chrétien. When Dion was intergovernmental
affairs minister, his deputy, George Anderson, asked him how late he
could call him at home one night. Dion replied: "The state never
sleeps."

("The state may not sleep but the deputy minister goes to bed at
eleven o'clock," Anderson told his boss.)[9]

The Dion inner circle included staffers who had been with him
for years. André Lamarre left Radio-Canada in 1996 to work with
Dion in Ottawa. His official campaign role was media director, but
he was much more: right hand, loyal friend, and confidant. Victory
night in Montreal proved emotional for Lamarre. As Dion passed
him on the way to the podium, Lamarre's knees gave out. He sank
to the floor in front of the stage that jutted out into the hall like
the prow of a ship. He was at the very tip. He was an elegant man,
a former clothing designer always immaculately put together, but
that night he didn't care. "I just sat down on the floor and I couldn't
get up."[10]

Lamarre sat marvelling at how life had turned out. Three years
earlier, in December 2003, Dion, the former star of Jean Chrétien's
cabinet, had found himself locked out of Paul Martin's. Dion had
thought he might be included. Martin, after all, hadn't said no during
a phone conversation a week earlier. He'd only suggested it wasn't
likely.[11] The new prime minister and his cabinet were to be sworn in
on December 12 at Rideau Hall. The night before, Lamarre picked
up Dion to take him to dinner with a couple of other friends across
the Ottawa River in Hull. He kept his phone on, in case the Prime
Minister's Office called with Martin on the line.

They waited for the phone to ring. And waited. Finally, around 10:30 or 11 P.M., Lamarre took Dion home to his Ottawa apartment, knowing the call wouldn't come.

"We all felt very sad for him," Lamarre explained.[12] "It was over, it was the end of an era ... Most of us had worked for [Dion] for many years, and all of a sudden [we were] seeing all the great things he had done for the country just going up in smoke because some people didn't like him. They thought he was a liability because he was supposedly the most hated man in Quebec." He paused. "To see a guy who has brought so much to this country, and still had so much to bring, just brushed aside as if all he had done was completely irrelevant ... And all the things you do over the years—who cares?"

The next morning, as the new cabinet was being sworn in, the outgoing minister of intergovernmental affairs was in his office packing boxes. "There was," said Lamarre, "this faint little hope that someone was going to call [and say], 'We just realized we made a mistake ...'"

An ordinary MP, Dion no longer had a driver. He turned to Lamarre and, referring to a day eight years earlier when he had come to Ottawa by bus to give a speech and had ended up being invited by Chrétien to 24 Sussex, he told him, "I came to Ottawa by bus and I'll leave Ottawa by bus."

Lamarre wouldn't have it. "I said no, absolutely not, there is no way you're going to take a bus home tomorrow." The next day, he drove Dion to Montreal. Janine was at the door to greet her husband. "She was very strong," remembered Lamarre.

After assuring Dion he was "never more than a phone call away," he got into his car and drove away.

Lamarre was thinking about all that and more as he sat on the convention floor unable to speak on December 2, 2006.

CHAPTER ONE

THE HOUSE ON LIÉGEOIS

STÉPHANE MAURICE BERNARD DION was born on September 28, 1955. For proof he was "not an easy child" (as he later would come to understand), one need look no further than an early wrenching encounter with a priest. He was ten and a student of the Oblate fathers at Saint-Cyril, a private boys' school in Quebec City. One day, a nun told the class: "If you start having the problems of young boys, speak to the priest about it."

Stéphane, younger than the others, was perplexed. He had no idea what the "problems of young boys" might be. But he was a thoughtful child and turned the phrase over in his mind. He queued up for the confessional, waited his turn, and stepped into the box.

"Well, *mon père*," he said, "I need to tell you something … I'm beginning to question my faith."

"*Que dites-vous là?*" the priest demanded in a loud voice. "What are you saying?!"

"*Non, non, non, non, non,*" the boy stammered. "I-I-I just wanted to say I was not nice to my brother. Er, ah, I lied to my mother."

He scrambled, grasping for examples of ordinary misdemeanours. He'd done this, he'd done that. "Because," he would remember some four decades later, "what do you do when you go there? You invent things."

The priest pretended he hadn't heard what Dion had said. "You will repeat ten Ave Marias," he began, ladling out a routine portion of penance for the transgressions of childhood.

And so, at a tender age, Stéphane Dion learned something important about life: that it was not wise to reveal the secrets of one's innermost heart to a priest. Little boys did not go around questioning the existence of God. Not out loud, anyway. He would not communicate such thoughts again.

At home, it was different. Dion's freethinking parents, bohemian in their views, encouraged their five children to express themselves. They were not raising conformists. They valued original thought, imagination, and healthy skepticism. They had faith but did not believe in the dogma of the Roman Catholic Church. One did not go to hell for missing mass. Babies were not cast into limbo. Non-Catholics were not doomed to eternal damnation.

That day with the priest, Stéphane saw in a flash that society was not comfortable with those who would shake its foundations, whether of church, state, or the accepted wisdom of the age. He saw hypocrisy writ large.

Even so, he clearly felt the thrill of being at the centre of attention. That he didn't mind. He was too slight and bony to be a sports hero. Perhaps he had found his calling.

It was a good lesson for one who would grow up to be an iconoclast. He'd opened his heart to religion and found an unimaginative man at the door. "I'm not a ritualist. I understand why it's important in every religion but I don't like it," he would say years later as an adult. He went further: "I hate it!" It wasn't religion he despised, merely the trappings. "The substance of the message is love. I believe in it. Is it a message that is coming from a god? Are we able to have love without God?" He paused. He had ideas but preferred to keep them to himself. It had been enough to shock a priest.

No, he was not an average child. But then, he didn't have average parents.

IT WAS THE BRIGHT WORLD of the 1950s, and Sillery was the future. The war had been over for almost a decade when Léon Dion and his wife, Denyse, bought a house on Liégeois Boulevard in the upscale Quebec City suburb in 1954. Sillery was on the St. Lawrence River, southeast of the province's capital city, and in those days, it was practically in the woods. The modern bungalow was perfect. It sat on a lot overlooking the river, the foundation was solid, and, most important, it was close to Laval University in nearby Sainte-Foy. Léon was a promising academic in the social sciences department, an intellectual who, his wife was convinced, would someday leave his mark upon the world of scholarship.

Léon and Denyse wanted a big family and thought they would move to a larger place someday. Instead, they would renovate. The house on Liégeois would be their only home, and Léon's study—an addition in the early 1960s—would become its most important room. It held awe and mystery for his children, the place where their father disappeared from dawn until dark. There were bookshelves that reached to the ceiling, large windows overlooking the St. Lawrence, and soundproof padding to provide the peace Denyse knew her husband needed. He was of unsound constitution, frail, and given to migraines. Safe in his sanctuary, he wrote and wrote and wrote, his black ink filling the pages. Often he worked from his armchair with a plank laid across its arms for his papers. His second son, Stéphane, described his strongest image of his father: "Working hard," he said. "Working very, very hard."

SILLERY WAS REALLY quite posh. It was home to the Old Quebec bourgeoisie: affluent professionals, politicians, established Lower Canadian families of commerce, and professors like Léon, who could afford a down payment on a house in Sillery. They were privileged people, comfortable in their opinions, conservative in their values, and religious in their attendance at mass on Sunday. The overtly pious went every day. (How gums would flap about *la famille* Dion on that score!)

Residents of Sillery were not, however, unenlightened in their political opinions. Voters in the old provincial riding of Quebec West felt disdain for the particular brand of ultraconservative, anti-intellectual populism espoused by the Union Nationale government of Premier Maurice Duplessis. They prided themselves on being progressive and voted UN only once during his long years in power, and they were quick to fix that in the next election.[13]

Duplessis held the province in his fist in 1954 and would do so for another five years. He had no use for intellectuals. Everyone knew he called them *des pelleteux des nuage:* shovellers of clouds.

IF SUCH A DESCRIPTION might be applied to Léon Dion in 1954, it most certainly did not fit his force-of-nature wife, Denyse. She couldn't wait to move out of their little apartment on Cartier Street in Quebec City. She'd grown up in a cramped apartment in the less-than-chic nineteenth arrondissement of Paris, sharing a bedroom with her sister, Paule. She was much younger than her two siblings, barely twelve when the Germans occupied Paris in 1940 and the City of Light went dark. The occupation lasted five years and marked Denyse Kormann forever. How could it not?

Denyse lived in a time when French Jews were being deported for extermination by the Third Reich. The Vichy government of Marshal Pétain collaborated with the Germans and Charles de Gaulle was far away. It would take the invading might of the Allies to liberate France. Political dissidents were being shot, random killings were common, and spies scuttled about looking for signs of resistance.

The adolescent girl in the nineteenth arrondissement could cope with being hungry and having no heat in the winter—some of it was a lark to one so young—but not with the brutality of war. And not with having her family torn asunder.[14]

Denyse's father, Émile, a factory worker, was a communist, her sister a Gaulliste, and her brother, Jacques, a Pétainiste. Jacques was shipped to Germany under the compulsory work program (*Service du travail obligatoire*), ended up in a concentration camp after a fight with a German soldier, and escaped to Switzerland. But when World War II was over and Denyse danced in the streets of Paris, she didn't know if her only brother was alive or dead.

War was her life lesson. "What marked me most was that someone you saw today, you might not see tomorrow," she explained many years later in the house on Liégeois. By then she was 78, slim, with deep-set eyes and the good bones that hold beauty. "It was the people disappearing. The Germans would block off a street and shoot the first ten people they encountered ... What that gave me was that I was never able to stay angry for very long with anyone. I always had the idea that I might never see them again."

After the war, Denyse made a vow. Politics and religion would not be discussed in her house, or at least not at her table. "I don't like politics. It divides people. Politics poisoned my adolescence," she said. "Whatever your ideas on religion or politics, they're not important. It's humanity that's important! I detest chauvinism in any form. I detest the idea that 'I'm right and everyone else is wrong'... The family is stronger than politics and stronger than religion."

WHILE DENYSE LIVED in Paris during the occupation, Léon Dion was going through an occupation of a different sort: the stifling years of Quebec under Duplessis. Tough, charismatic, the Huey Long of Quebec politics, Duplessis had founded the Union Nationale in 1935 and became premier a year later. Apart from a five-year interregnum during World War II, he governed Quebec until his death in 1959. The Roman Catholic Church dominated Quebec, and Duplessis manipulated the Church. He liked to boast, "The bishops eat out of my hand."[15] He dispensed the grants to university rectors, making them come to his office cap in hand, and vetoed the appointment of professors who weren't sufficiently devout or subservient.[16]

But Duplessis' hold on Quebec was slipping. The Quiet Revolution that would electrify the province in the 1960s had roots in the very campus where Léon Dion would study as a young man.

He grew up to advise the rich and powerful. Their presence was part of life on Liégeois Boulevard. There were two elegant French provincial chairs in front of the living room window. One was Léon's, the other was for a succession of Quebec premiers and cabinet ministers (Jean Lesage, Robert Bourassa, Paul Gérin-Lajoie), federal politicians (Maurice Lamontagne, Jean Marchand), and intellectuals (Claude Ryan, André Laurendeau), who sought the counsel of the acclaimed political scientist. Bourassa telephoned so often that the children would answer the phone and whine, *"Papa, c'est encore BouBou."* (Papa, it's BouBou again.)

Léon's own beginnings, however, were humble. He was born in 1922 in Saint-Arsène de Rivière-du-Loup, a village on the south shore of the St. Lawrence River where it opens to the sea. The family could trace its history in New France back to Johan de Guyon in 1634. He was part of an expedition of settlers led by Robert Gifford, who would become a wealthy *seigneur*.[17] Dion was not an uncommon name in French Canada, and, by the twentieth century, Quebec undoubtedly was sprinkled with a good number of prosperous and well-educated descendants of *Monsieur* de Guyon. But Léon's family was not among them. His father, Thomas, was a carpenter who died when Léon was fifteen, leaving his widow with seven children. He was the first in his family—the first generation—to go to university; Alice Dion had wanted her son to be a priest.[18]

Léon arrived at the Catholic university in the late 1930s, taking his place at the oldest French-language institution of higher learning in the Americas. (Laval began as a seminary in 1663.) There, he came under the tutelage of a remarkable Dominican Father, Georges-Henri

Lévesque. Père Lévesque established the department of social sciences at Laval (as Léon and his colleagues would do for political science thirty years later) and educated a generation of Quebecers who would light the spark of the Quiet Revolution. He valued empirical knowledge and encouraged his students to be passionate about equality. Years before the term became fashionable elsewhere, he was a true "liberation theologist," who supported the rights of the people against blind authority. He stood with the miners and their union in Thetford Mines during the bloody Asbestos Strike of 1949 that became a symbol of opposition to Duplessis.[19]

Père Lévesque didn't mind when his former students were on different sides of a debate over nationalism that had raged in Quebec since the Plains of Abraham. "On the contrary, I am happy. I am happy because each one is carrying his own stone. And what is going to happen, I don't know," he told an interviewer before the first referendum on separation in 1980.[20] When he died in 2000, federalists and separatists hailed him as the "father of Quebec's rebirth." Stéphane Dion, then federal minister of intergovernmental affairs, said Père Lévesque's greatest gift had been the idea that "freedom also comes from God." He added: "That simple saying transformed Quebec."[21]

DENYSE AND LÉON became pen pals in 1947, the feisty Parisian sophisticate and the cerebral hayseed from rural Quebec. What were the odds?

He was planning to do some research in Europe and, at the suggestion of his sister, thought it might be fun to correspond with a French girl, the friend-of-a-friend-of-a-friend. He wrote his first letter as a joke and passed it around, laughing, to his friends and his brother, Marcel.[22] Denyse Kormann loved it. He was twenty-five, seven years older than she and a political science professor who was expecting a grant through the university for study abroad.

"Should we correspond?" he inquired.

"Ça ne me dérange pas," answered Denyse. "Sure."

A year later, Duplessis, as was his wont, shut off grants to Laval, punishing Père Lévesque for something or other. His social sciences faculty was full of dangerous ideas.

"I can't come. I don't have the money," wrote Léon. "Should we keep writing to each other?"

"Mais oui," she replied. *"Oui, oui."*

Another year passed and he wrote: "I'm not sure if I can come at all."

"Listen here," said Denyse. "I don't want to be corresponding my whole life. *I want you to come."*

Léon borrowed three hundred dollars and set off to study at the London School of Economics—and to see what would develop with Denyse Kormann. Her letters were intriguing; she was also very pretty.

They would meet in a park in Brussels. It was June 1950. Denyse, who had studied child psychology in Paris, was working with Jewish adolescents who were being reunited with their relatives after the war. Their parents had given them up to save their lives during the Holocaust and most had no recollection of their real families. Denyse, scarcely older than the teenagers she was helping, felt she was contributing something of value.

The meeting with Léon did not go well.

He was skinny, awkward, and something of a bumpkin. He didn't understand "the French approach to life," that much was clear to her. They had talked about everything under the sun in their letters, even marriage, and wound up staring like tongue-tied strangers.

Two weeks later, Léon was back in London, and Denyse returned to Paris. But the correspondence continued and rekindled its warmth. Léon's grant money was on-again-off-again, and at Christmas he came for a visit. She took one look at him and proclaimed: "This doesn't make any sense. Why, you're dying of hunger! You must come and finish your studies in France."

Marie-Thérèse Biroulès, Denyse's mother, was a wonderful cook. She was from the south of France and her savoury dishes soon filled out Léon's skeletal frame. He was not unattractive. Far from it. He had a strong jaw, hair combed back from a high forehead, and a sweet smile.

They talked of marriage again, but he wanted to wait another year until he turned thirty. Léon was preparing to travel to Germany to work on his doctorate on Adolf Hitler's National Socialism, and when he asked Denyse to go with him, she readily agreed. Her parents were scandalized.

"But you're not married!" gasped Maman.

"*Ben*, no," said Denyse with a shrug.

Marie-Thérèse wouldn't budge. "What do you think your father is going to say about this guy?"

To please her parents, they were married in a civil ceremony June 4, 1951. A year ahead of schedule for Léon. The next day, they left for Germany and, in 1952, sailed for Canada.

"Well," her mother had said, "if you're happy, there's no problem."

She was, and would be for the rest of her life with Léon Dion. *Un mariage d'amour.* "Listen," Denyse said, laughing, more than a half-century later, "we must have married for love because he didn't have a cent and I'm no longer beautiful."

"They had a kind of intellectual partnership," said their good friend John Meisel, the distinguished Canadian political scientist and Companion of the Order of Canada. "They were at ease with one another. By no means did they always agree, but they had affection, respect, and love. Even late in life, they were very much in love," he said. "If Léon had a streak of timidity, Denyse has no streak of that whatsoever. She's a very strong person ... She took complete charge of his life."[23]

IN THE FALL OF 1952, Léon was back at Laval and Denyse was making a home and exploring the old capital. Its skyline was defined by the copper turrets of the Parliament buildings and the Château Frontenac that guarded the St. Lawrence gateway. The city belonged to generals Wolfe and Montcalm, who died a day apart on the Plains of Abraham; to Frontenac, who defended New France; and to Champlain, the greatest of the first nation-builders. Like Montcalm, Champlain lay buried there.[24]

Denyse was part of Léon's world of ideas and, as the years passed, his writing as well. She typed everything he wrote. "I never felt inferior to my husband even if he was much better known ... I helped with the books. I'm not saying I wrote the books for him, but we certainly discussed everything."

She recognized Père Lévesque was ahead of his time and was fond of her husband's friends at the university. These were heady times in intellectual circles in Quebec. Léon's colleagues made her feel welcome, crowding around and making a fuss over la petite Française. "But what is this you've found in France?" they would ask Léon in mock surprise.

The social sciences department became Denyse's adoptive family. They were good to her. Over the years, she would repay their kindness. "She's the most generous person I've met in my life," said her son, Stéphane. "If somebody's in difficulty, you go to see Denyse—she'll do her best to help."

At first the family struggled financially, but they didn't mind. "Having money wasn't important, not for Léon, not for me," Denyse said. "There's no snobbism in my family and I don't think my kids are snobs either. We have never chosen our friends from a social or monetary perspective ... My father was a factory worker, Léon's dad was a carpenter. They were workers, they weren't the same as those guys in the bourgeois French clubs."

Denyse even adjusted to winter. During her third year in Quebec, she tossed aside French fashion and put on a real winter coat. By then the babies had begun to arrive, Patrice in 1953 and Stéphane in 1955, Georges ten months after Stéphane, Francis in 1959, and her only girl, France, in 1961.

Things weren't all rosy at Laval. "When I arrived in Canada, it was so Catholic. Ah, it was absolutely dreadful," Denyse recalled. She had grown up with a religion that seemed to know its place. Her French Catholic Church welcomed souls for baptism and burials and otherwise didn't intrude. She suddenly found herself in a society where the gossips kept track of attendance. And soon, the rigidity of Catholic dogma would take its toll on Léon's work at the university.

By 1954, the year they bought the home on Liégeois, Léon had finished his PhD on Nazism and was pleased when a French publisher wanted to publish his dissertation as a book jointly with Laval's university press.[25] But Laval authorities balked at the idea, according to Denyse, claiming that the thesis had not met the standards of Catholic Church dictates on Thomas Aquinas. There was nothing Père Lévesque could do. The book was never published, and Denyse would never get over her fury. Years later she fumed: "It wasn't published because there was this old cleric[26]—I hope he's burning in hell! (See how bad I am!)—who said it wasn't *Thomiste.*"

Léon was worried. If he pushed to get it published, "they could throw me out of the university," he told his wife. Patrice was a baby, Stéphane would arrive the next year. They had student loans, a mortgage. How would he support his family? "It was hard, very hard, on Léon," remembered Denyse.

Léon had been put in his place; he was a mere shoveller of clouds. It was a tough time in his career. They knew change would come; Duplessis couldn't live forever. Léon and Denyse were plugged into a network of dissent. Pierre Trudeau, Gérard Pelletier, and Claude Ryan were writing against stodgy, Church-run nationalism for the influential political journal *Cité libre,* which they'd started in Montreal. Père Lévesque's former student Jean Marchand had led the asbestos strikers. Economist Maurice Lamontagne opposed Duplessis at Laval. Léon Dion and Maurice Lamontagne were very close; his second son's middle name honoured him.[27]

What they couldn't see was how quickly and dramatically that change would come in Quebec when Duplessis died. It was like the fall of the Berlin Wall. Change seemed to happen overnight, bringing with it the new era of the Quiet Revolution (*la Révolution tranquille*), the wonderful oxymoron that describes the awakening of Quebec. The Catholic Church imploded, Jean Lesage's Liberal party formed the provincial government, and, in 1964 with the passage of Bill 60, Quebec had its first secular ministry of education. Education no longer existed just to turn out good Catholics. "Certainly, one mustn't exaggerate the break of 1960 and the myth of 'The Great Darkness,'" Stéphane Dion, political scientist and federal minister, cautioned in 2000. Nevertheless, he observed: "One could never measure enough the profound repercussions the clergy's loss of power had on the everyday life of francophone, French-Catholic Quebecers."[28]

Even the gossips of Sillery changed their tune. "I remember neighbour kids who said, 'You Dions are going to burn in hell because you aren't attending mass each Sunday,'" he wrote. "Then, suddenly, one Sunday morning, they were out on the ski slopes with us."[29]

Léon's career would blossom and he would become a prolific writer (as would his son). It must have given him no small degree of satisfaction to have the new education minister Gérin-Lajoie consult him about legislation, or to later chronicle the decline of the Church and the evolution of Bill 60.[30] His reputation as a scholar was growing, as Denyse always had faith it would.

STÉPHANE WAS A HEALTHY BABY (like all the Dion children), and Denyse dressed him in smart berets and little French frock coats. He sprouted like a beanstalk, always tall for his age (on his way to six foot one), *"Le grand Steph,"* kids called him. "Big Steph." He had his father's high forehead, a long, angular face, and heavy-lidded eyes.

But he had his mother's irrepressible energy. The problem was, he couldn't channel it. In another age, he might have been diagnosed with attention deficit disorder and given a handful of prescriptions to calm him down. His big brother, Patrice, shone academically and would become a microbiologist of note at his father's alma mater. But the second son didn't do so well in his early years. Stéphane started school at four and could read at five, but he was bored and lacked discipline. They tried one school after another, including the stint with the Oblate fathers of Saint-Cyril. Nothing worked. "I was difficult," Dion would later observe. "I was at war with everyone."

Given their views, it was not surprising that his parents thought the problem lay with the schools and not their bright boy. "The main difference between Quebec and France then was that in France, one was critical and here, *non*," Denyse said. She remembered having seen a production of Racine's *Andromache* as a twelve-year-old and imperiously spouting her opinions in class. Her teachers must have found her amusing, ridiculous even, she would later surmise, but they didn't tell her she was wrong. "Here, when you had the misfortune to criticize, everybody closed right up. You couldn't be too critical."

Just as another mother might have taken pride in a flair for art or talent for the violin, Denyse Dion boasted about the streak of stubbornness running through her children. They got it from her. "All my children are the same—all obstinate!"

Ultimately however, Léon and Denyse put their foot down with Stéphane. He needed discipline to anchor his life. They enrolled him at the Collège des Jésuites in 1968 when he was going on thirteen. Quebec City had nothing finer to offer the children of its elites than the school founded in 1634 as a seminary by Jesuits. In 1968, it still followed the classical curriculum (*cours classiques*) of private Catholic high schools. Though it would adopt a secular curriculum in 1970, its academic rigour remained.[31]

It took only a week for Stéphane to get into trouble. He spent his first Saturday in detention for acting up in class. "Look," his father told him. "It will be five years in this college. We will not move you. So learn discipline for once." Stéphane buckled down but didn't excel. His school friend Laurent Arsenault remembers him being a "bit of a daydreamer."[32]

Léon never lost faith. "One day, one day I know you will *débloquer* [unblock] and you will fulfill your potential," he told his son. "I know that, I know that."

He would be proven right. Stéphane had been devouring history and historical fiction at home since childhood—*Les trois mousque-taires,* by Alexandre Dumas, along with other books his mother gave him—and the link between his studies and what he was reading for fun finally came together during his last two years before university. At CEGEP Collège François-Xavier-Garneau,[33] he became the student his father always knew he would be. He developed confidence in himself and his own ideas; other students would soon come to think he'd always stood at the top of his class.

THE BOND BETWEEN father and son would be very intense, but it grew slowly. "It was very dry with him," Stéphane would recall of his early childhood. "I felt a kind of distance from him."

Stéphane Dion insisted he didn't learn his love of work from his father. Léon hadn't made it look like fun. Instead Stéphane said it was instinctive once he settled down. When he was running to be Liberal leader in 2006, he declared: "I am unable not to work hard! If you are lazy and you have to convince yourself to work [hard], then you have a lot of merit. I am not lazy and so it has no merit for me."[34]

And yet the child's admiration for how his father worked was evident in the man, and in the stories he told of the book-lined study and all that happened within. It may be that Stéphane Dion was not naturally lazy, but a love of work (which for his father, after all, constituted acquiring and sharing knowledge) did come from Léon Dion, whether he realized it or not.

When Stéphane was twelve, he asked Patrice why the industrialized northern hemisphere was rich and the southern hemisphere was so poor.

"Let's ask Dad," said Patrice.

"Dad, *why?*"

"Because it's his job to know the answer."

Léon was in his study. The boys knocked gently on the door.

"Can we interrupt you?" they asked. Stéphane was sure he would say no, but Léon waved them in.

"He was so pleased. He explained to us the theory of Max Weber, the link between Protestantism and industrialization and so on. It was so fascinating for me." It was a magical moment. Stéphane would later draw on the theories of the nineteenth-century German social and political thinker in his own writing.[35]

The two began to communicate more easily as Stéphane grew into his teens. The disagreements would come later. For Stéphane, it was enough to feel somewhat closer to his father. Their relationship would work itself out in the end. "There was a distance between us, but over the years it disappeared ... because he accepted me."

The truth is, father and son were very much alike: thinkers and worriers about existential what-ifs. Stéphane even had his father's headaches. Léon was hard on his son. "My father was very demanding but he helped me to improve myself ... Never my father told me, 'You're good enough.' It was never good enough."[36]

But Léon also took enormous pride in him and his son knew it. When Stéphane was thirteen, he accompanied his parents to a play in the old city. Sitting in front of them was the Union Nationale premier of Quebec, Jean-Jacques Bertrand. "One of my sons has a theory he'd like to explain to you," announced Léon, gesturing toward Stéphane. "I don't know what kind of theory I had [that] my father wanted me to explain. I tried … I'm not sure I was very clear." He bumbled along until at last Bertrand snorted, "Pffft! I don't know," and, mercifully, it was over. Whatever it was, Léon had wanted his boy to share it with the premier.

Denyse Dion saw the tightness of their bond: "Stéphane was much closer to his father than to me. As an adolescent he spent a lot of time with his father. I think it was Stéphane, of all my children, over whom his father had the greatest influence."

IT SHOULD NOT be thought this childhood was sombre. There was lots of fun in the Dion household. It was full of reptiles, birds, animals, insects: Trotsky the turtle, a parrot taught by Stéphane to say *id-é-o-lo-gie,* Rusty the Beagle, Bracque the beautiful German pointer, tadpoles and minnows and frogs from the pond in the yard. No wonder Léon's study door was closed. Denyse Dion was hesitant to open any door or cupboard for fear of something jumping out. Stéphane kept busy collecting butterflies, observing animals, and bird-watching. As he would later concede, there was a downside to these particular hobbies: "I was colour-blind so I was not very good at recognizing animals."

Denyse and Léon were mindful of their children's cultural education. They enjoyed opera and symphony orchestras at the Palais Montcalm Theatre in the old capital and, at home, listened to classical music. Stéphane would grow up to be a fan of opera, leaning to the sentimental, like Verdi. But it wasn't all highbrow entertainment. On Sunday night, the family would watch *Papa a raison* (*Father Knows Best*) and Léon would race around the house with his children on his shoulders before bedtime. And once a week, Stéphane would settle in for his dose of Robin Hood riding through the glen with his merry men, in *Les aventures de Robin des bois.* He also liked going to the movies. One of his favourites was *La Mélodie du bonheur (The Sound of Music)*. The adult Stéphane would call it "a beautiful movie."

There were annual summer vacations to visit Léon's relatives in Saint-Arsène, with the whole family packed into a sedan called Cunegongue, singing French songs and telling jokes. Léon would smoke, and Stéphane would get carsick. Once in Saint-Arsène, which in those days was a four-hour drive southeast from Quebec City, Léon would leave the family for two or three months and go off to study at the Sorbonne in Paris or at Harvard University in Cambridge. There were fishing trips to Lac-Saint-Jean or Lac Trois-Saumons, where Stéphane practised a sport that would become a lifelong passion. In the summertime, too, they spent long afternoons at beaches near Quebec City that were open for swimming in those days.

The summer Stéphane was twelve, Léon and Denyse took the kids to France. They saw relatives and visited castles with a tourist guide. Stéphane was a brat. He convinced his little brother Francis that every castle belonged to him. "I was awful ... I told him to ask the guide, 'Where is our Francis de Dion castle?' And he and I and Georges had a contest to see who could be closer to the guide. The one closest won. It was, 'Me! Me! No, me!' ... For our parents, it was not easy."

Denyse Dion wanted her children to know France and her culture. It was who she was. "What's she like?" her fourth son, Francis, was asked about his mother in 2007. "*Elle est française, madame* [she's French]—that should explain everything."[37]

Denyse had arrived to a French Canada that hadn't shaken off an inferiority complex about the *français de France* accent, just as English Canadians of the time genuflected to plummy British vowels. They wanted to imitate accents they thought were better than theirs. This too would change with the Quiet Revolution, when people would start to value *joual*, the rich language of ordinary Quebecers. *Les Belles-soeurs* and other plays by Michel Tremblay were a cultural turning point for Quebec, and there would be a growing tendency to regard a French accent as pretentious, snobby, and condescending, rather than something to be emulated.

The part of Stéphane Dion that was French encompassed more than berets and frock coats, a Parisian inflection in his speech, or the occasional *Ooo là là* (as in "*Ooo là là* my tooth hurts"). His self-assurance, his propensity to correct (as much a Parisian as an academic trait) sometimes would be taken for arrogance in his home province.

"I am abandoning my French nationality but I am keeping my little know-it-all air," said a 2006 year-end spoof of Dion in *La Presse*.[38] At the time he'd just won the Liberal leadership and controversy was swirling about the French citizenship he inherited from Denyse.

His feelings were hurt. "I know I'm not like that but this image was repeated so much everywhere that, at the end of the day, you are afraid you will believe in it yourself," he said during a night flight to Edmonton early in 2007.[39] He ticked off reasons people assume he disagreed with them. "Oh, because he's arrogant! He thinks he's more intelligent than everybody else. He's so proud of himself ... Who does he think [he] is?" He threw up his hands. It hadn't always been easy for him knowing what people thought.

THE DION HOUSEHOLD was very French. On Sunday, the midday meal stretched interminably for children aching to go outside and play. There was a cheese course, and his parents would linger over their wine. When it came time for dessert, Léon would ask the children about their weekly resolution (*les résolutions de la semaine*). Had Stéphane cleaned his room? Been nice to his sister? Each child had a turn. Denyse and Léon offered praise or disappointment at a broken resolution and set new ones for the coming week. It was a ritual, part of being a Dion.

Mark Marissen ran smack up against Liégeois tradition in 2006 when he was managing Stéphane Dion's leadership campaign. It was the lead-up to the Winnipeg candidates' debate and "we were running late ... We were supposed to have lunch first before we did the debate prep and instead we all had to pile into the van and they were all handing out sandwiches. And Stéphane takes the sandwich in his hand and he says to me, 'Next time, respect my culture—and on a day like today, let's have a proper lunch.'"[40]

Respect my culture?! Marissen didn't quite know what to say. Similarly, Dion's staffers on Parliament Hill would get a kick out of his repugnance at the cheese served in the parliamentary lounge off the House of Commons. "They serve it cold!" he would exclaim constantly, as if discovering the sad fact for the first time.

YOUNG STÉPHANE LOVED SPORTS. He fell under the spell of hockey, which naturally meant that he was a fan of *Les Canadiens*. He was eleven at the start of the 1966–67 season. Goalie Gump Worsley wasn't playing that year, and his uncle Marcel made a strange comment: "We will not win the Stanley Cup this year because Rogatien Vachon is not the name of a goalie."

Sure enough, on May 2, 1967, the Leafs beat the Habs in the last game of the playoffs at Maple Leaf Gardens and won the Cup. Expo 67 was about to open in Montreal and fans had been expecting the Canadiens to deliver the trophy to the Quebec Pavillion on Île-Notre-Dame. Instead, it was sitting in a convertible parading down Yonge Street. "It was a disaster, the year of Expo and the Stanley Cup was in Toronto," moaned Stéphane Dion forty seasons later. Some hurts never go away.

He was hockey mad. On Sunday, April 6, 1968, Pierre Elliott Trudeau was on the verge of winning the leadership of the Liberal Party of Canada. The Canadiens were set to play game two of the quarter-finals against the Boston Bruins at the Montreal Forum that night, and he was parked in front of the TV waiting. "I remember on the fourth ballot I was crying, 'I hope he will win!' because the hockey game was starting … It was not possible to switch [channels] at the time [in 1968]. And we missed the first period because of Trudeau! But not the second, because he won on the fourth ballot."

So did the Habs. They took the series in four straight games and went on to defeat the Chicago Blackhawks in the semi-finals and the St. Louis Blues in the playoffs to win their thirteenth Stanley Cup. Fans were delirious when Captain Jean Béliveau, with a broken ankle, swung his way on crutches out to centre ice to accept the Cup.

Big Jean Béliveau was Stéphane's hero. Stéphane was too young to have witnessed the great Maurice Richard in his heyday. He was only six when the Rocket retired. But his life intersected twice with the hockey legend.

Stéphane Dion was born the year of the Richard Riot of March 1955. That year, English-speaking officials in the NHL had suspended Richard for the season, and outraged fans rioted in the streets of Montreal. It's been said that the Rocket played hockey with the pride of French Canada on his back. The violence was seen as a political act of defiance, another sign of the pent-up nationalism that would transform life with the coming of the Quiet Revolution.

It was tough for Dion when, as federal intergovernmental affairs minister, he was booed by separatists at the Rocket's funeral in 2000. Richard's passing was a big event and he was honoured at a state funeral at Notre-Dame Basilica in Montreal. Dion wasn't booed by a lot of people, just a handful, but it wounded nevertheless. They didn't see Stéphane Dion, passionate, lifelong hockey fan, Canadiens fanatic. Those few saw instead the tall, cold and most despised representative of *le gouvernement du Canada* and author of the Clarity Act.

STÉPHANE DION HAD one other boyhood passion: baseball. He took after his father. Léon Dion had an "affection for baseball," as his son would put it. Father and son would sit together in the house on Liégeois and listen to baseball on the radio. Their team was the Montreal Expos. They were destined for sorrow. They both shook their heads in disbelief when Rusty Staub got traded.

"I think he must have played baseball when he was a kid," Stéphane said of his father's feel for the game. "It's the most collectivist sport and individualist at the same time. You're alone when you're at the bat—you're alone in life—but there's almost nothing except a home run that you can do alone. You need the others … And when there is a mistake, it is easy to identify the individual who made the mistake, more than in any other collective sport. So my father was a baseball man."

A baseball man. It was a nice image of his dad. But Stéphane didn't leave it there. Instead, like the little boy in the confessional, he searched for the metaphysical in Leon's love of baseball. There had to have been more. "But at the same time he had this sense of the team, of the institution. The University of Laval for him was the institution. He wanted the University of Laval to succeed; he wanted political science to succeed, for Canadian political science to succeed." Baseball … political science … life. Stéphane had insisted on closing the circle. Sometimes though, as he would discover in life, baseball was just a game.

CHAPTER TWO

"WE CANNOT BETRAY OUR ANCESTORS"

IT WAS INCESSANT, night after night, two, three, four hours of verbal jousting between father and son on Liégeois Boulevard. Léon and Stéphane didn't quarrel exactly. Léon was too sophisticated to engage emotionally with a combative son seeking to score points. But they discussed endlessly—at the dining room table, in Léon's study, in the downstairs family room. Denyse Dion would be fed up, as would his brothers and sister.

Beginning when he was about seventeen, Stéphane Dion devoted himself to proving he was the brainy equal of his distinguished father. "And each time, he destroyed my arguments—but very politely," the adult son recalled looking back. "He respected me. I was very aggressive with him ... he was never aggressive with me."[41]

Perhaps young Stéphane needed the outlet because, in all the important aspects of his life, he followed the wishes of Léon Dion. Stéphane had wanted to study history when he entered Laval University in the fall of 1974, but his father said no, choose political science, it's more rigorous. He went along. "I thought if he says it, he knows what he's talking about." His career path had always been set. "It was obvious that I would be a professor. It was obvious I would have a PhD and obvious I would be a professor at a university." Like his father. He even took courses from Léon at Laval. The first year it had been compulsory. He sat in an auditorium with some three hundred other students for his father's introductory course on the history of political movements. But that was it, he promised himself; after first year he would take no electives from the other Dion.

Léon was devastated when he saw Stéphane's second-year course list. "Dad is very mad at you," Patrice told him. "You didn't choose his course." Did he think his father was a bad professor? Stéphane gave in. He always did. He wore his hair long and his beard bushy, and he affected the plaid flannel shirts and work boots of the proletariat. But he was the obedient son. He signed up for Léon's class on political interest groups and studied with his father for the rest of his undergraduate years at Laval.

Léon was *un vrai maître,* a real master in the true sense of the word. His classical, one might say paternalistic, approach would seem antiquated in another generation. He had studied under his own master and treated his graduate students like his loyal disciples. He seemed old, weighted down by the world, even when he was in his early forties. He would always be a shy man, rather gauche, who could be awkward in social situations. He was idiosyncratic; he would deliver his thoughts with a little cough, a stutter, and an air of gravitas.[42]

But Léon was a good teacher. "He was really sure of himself—you know, *the* professor. He looked like that," said Janine Krieber, who took a course on political movements with Léon Dion before she met his son. "And you never really challenged him. He was so logical, so organized, so thematic, there was almost no room to challenge him."[43]

Stéphane challenged his father, of course, in private. It was his rite of passage into adulthood. "I did it to try to make sense of things with my father. I wanted to be as strong as him." He tried on political theories like new suits of clothing. "I first tried Marxism, then, within forty-eight hours, I was a Trotskyite. Trotsky was a kind of hero for me." He thought Leon Trotsky, not Vladimir Lenin, triumphed over greater odds in the Russian Revolution of 1917. He'd named his pet turtle after him. "But my father told me Trotsky was a terror as much as [Joseph] Stalin, and so on ... After forty-eight hours I changed my mind ... I was a little ashamed of myself to not be Marxist in forty-eight hours."

Over the years, Stéphane tried other streams of communism, republicanism, federalism—any "ism" he could find. Nothing clicked.

STÉPHANE'S EARLIEST political memory was the funeral of John F. Kennedy in November 1963. He watched it on television with his family. Kennedy was the first Catholic president of the United States and very popular in Quebec. The nuns at school said he was like a saint. Holy Kennedy, they called him.

His first memory of a heated political conversation on Liégeois came in 1967, when French president Charles de Gaulle visited Quebec. Denyse Dion had once been delirious with joy seeing him pass, so tall and impressive, along the Champs-Élysées in the liberated Paris of 1945. Everyone looked forward to his arrival. But the general stood on the balcony of Montreal's City Hall and intoned in his deep voice, syllable by crescendo-ing syllable, *"Vive le Qué-bec LIB-re"* ("Long Live Free Quebec!") and thousands of Quebecers were ecstatic; Léon Dion was furious. Stéphane recalled his father saying, "Who is this Frenchman to tell us what to do in our own country? He doesn't know what he's talking about!" Léon reminded his children that Canada rescued France in two world wars. "Why is he coming here and trying to break up the country? ... *It's none of his business!"*

Lester Pearson, the prime minister of the day, protested and de Gaulle cut short his trip and returned to France.[44] It was the only time Stéphane had seen his father erupt with such anger. The next big political crisis of his youth brought only regret and sorrow.

In October 1970, the Dions, like Quebecers and Canadians everywhere, were shocked by the kidnapping of British trade commissioner James Cross by radicals from the Front de Libération du Québec, the FLQ. A week later, the sombre voice of a Radio-Canada announcer broke into regular Saturday programming: "*Mesdames, messieurs, bonsoir.* The minister of labour and immigration, Mr. Pierre Laporte, was kidnapped earlier this evening …"[45]

Cross would be freed, but Laporte was found strangled with his rosary chain in the trunk of a car. He had been tossing a football with his seventeen-year-old nephew, Claude, at his home in Saint-Lambert when men with machine guns grabbed him.[46] Stéphane was haunted by dreams of the poor boy almost his own age. He couldn't stop thinking about Claude Laporte and how helpless he must have felt. (Quebecers shared his sympathy, including Claude Laporte's future wife, Dominique. How awful for him, she thought at the time. "Poor young man," and later, "Whatever happened to him?")[47]

The events of the October Crisis were seared into the minds of a generation of Canadians: the War Measures Act; federal troops deployed to Quebec; Pierre Trudeau saying "Well, just watch me!" when asked how far he would go in combating the FLQ. There were mass arrests, protests, and the first modern-day debate over the suppression of civil liberties using protection of the common weal as justification.

Gérard D. Lévesque, intergovernmental affairs minister in Robert Bourassa's cabinet, lived across the street from the Dion family. When soldiers were moved in to protect Lévesque's residence, the Dion kids were unimpressed. They threw snowballs at the soldiers. Denyse Dion, her memories of occupied Paris still vivid in 1970, hated seeing guns and helmets on her block. But she had no sympathy for the FLQ. Nobody could be so sure of their political beliefs, she told her children, to justify killing someone. She opposed capital punishment for the same reason.

Stéphane would recall both parents talking in grave tones. "Some of our friends may have had as a reaction a kind of romanticism, but my parents were very clear. There is nothing romantic about this. They are killers. Period."

MANY YEARS LATER, when Stéphane was a political science professor in Montreal, he met Claude Laporte at a party and they became friends. He was finally able to banish his image of the horrified teenager frozen on his uncle's front lawn. They talked about their families and their work and played golf together. In December 2006, Laporte would be a delegate for Dion at the Liberal leadership convention at the Palais des Congrès. He was standing on the floor with another Dion buddy, Laurent Arsenault, when the results of the final ballot were announced and they shouted with joy for their old friend.

BY HIS TWENTY-FIRST BIRTHDAY, on September 28, 1976, Stéphane Dion had found his political niche. Or so he thought. His conversion had begun some years earlier on the day Claude Charron sauntered into his CEGEP and began to talk about Quebec independence. Charron wasn't much older than the students. He was like a gnome—with a baby face, a corona of fuzzy hair, and a merry giggle. But when he opened his mouth to speak, he held the kids spellbound. He was a firebrand in the separatist Parti Québécois, which was founded in 1968 under the leadership of René Lévesque. The PQ wasn't doing badly for a fledgling party, having won seven seats in 1970 and six in 1973.[48] Charron had taught in the CEGEPs and was a natural to join the handful of PQ members of the National Assembly (MNAs) assigned to find recruits among the students.

Stéphane wanted to believe in something. He didn't feel Canada was his country. Sure, if he'd been asked as a boy he would have said he was Canadian. He saw Canada as "the country of the big bears, big mountains—everything was big." But it was picture-book stuff. He wanted to belong, and he found a home in the Quebec nationalism of Claude Charron. "He was very impressive and I never missed a speech. I was taking notes and I would try his arguments with my father."

He wasn't alone in embracing the PQ's brand of separatism in the early seventies. It was a generational thing. The Parti Québécois wasn't about the prissy, inward-looking, Church-approved nationalism of his parents' generation. Instead, Péquistes were young, hip, and part of a revolution of shout-out-loud pride in everything Québécois (not French Canadian) in the arts, publishing, language, cinema, business, education, and sports. Stéphane finally had an "ism" he was sure his father wouldn't be able to demolish: separatism.

On Liégeois Boulevard, the dialectic began. Stéphane thought a European approach would appeal. "Look, in Europe they are building a union but they are all countries. We are only a province," he said. Why didn't Quebecers have a country?

Léon was not impressed. Canada *was* a country.

What about pride? "We need to be loyal to our ancestors. They would have asked us to become a country if they had the opportunity ... *We cannot betray our ancestors.*"

But they did feel *Canadien*, Léon insisted. Besides, *la Nouvelle France* was a colony. Don't forget that.

Stéphane switched to education, his father's domain. "McGill must be French," he proclaimed of the English-language university on Sherbrooke Street in Montreal, where wealthy Anglo merchants had built their stone mansions.

What about linguistic freedom for others? Léon rebutted. You don't support that?

Stéphane felt ashamed.

"I tried each of the arguments, one after the other with my father," Dion would say later. "None of them worked!"

LÉON HAD GOOD REASON to challenge Stéphane. He was dedicated to exactly the opposite course for Quebec. By the time he was being confronted by his son, he was in his early fifties and had made an enormous contribution to the memory of his ancestors. Léon had been director of research for the Royal Commission on Bilingualism and Biculturalism. For the better part of the 1960s, he commuted weekly between Ottawa and Quebec City (a far more arduous journey in those days), arriving home Friday evening at around seven and hurrying back on Sunday night. Sometimes he would miss the Dion Sunday resolutions. It was a sacrifice. The commute wore him down and his absence may have been a factor in the distance with Stéphane. His workload at the B&B commission was onerous. "I was doing a little slice and Léon was looking at the big picture," said Peter Russell, the University of Toronto political scientist (later emeritus) who worked on the Supreme Court committee for the commission. "Léon was a strong federalist when I met him. He was a wonderful man, a great colleague."[49]

In early 2007 a poll for Radio-Canada by the polling firm CROP found that eighty-one percent of Canadians supported bilingualism. The public yawned. *Et puis?* But Canada was a different planet in the 1960s, before the passage of the Official Languages Act, before there were real options for French-language education outside Quebec, before the shake-up in hiring practices that would transform the federal bureaucracy, and before head offices in Montreal woke up and started promoting Francophones.

Back then, Quebecers didn't own their province or share its wealth. It was before Hautes études commerciales became the place to go for an MBA[50] or the Caisse de dépôt et placement du Québec took over the management of a few billion dollars in provincial pension-fund money. In 1961, commission research showed that English speakers earned thirty-five percent more than French speakers. In Montreal, the wage gap was fifty-one percent.[51]

It was also about pride. French Quebecers lived with discrimination as part of daily life. Clerks in the finest shops in Montreal couldn't speak French. Fathers had to speak English when the boss called at home. Often it was a struggle. Children would listen and feel the humiliation. Even the Rocket was treated like a child by anglophone sports writers. (*"Je me souviens,"* say licence plates in Quebec: "I remember.") Speak white, as Pierre Vallières put it in *White Niggers of America.*[52] Old wounds were still raw. People still talked about conscription at the dinner table. *In the Boer War!*

One incident cut deep. In November 1962, Donald Gordon, president of the Canadian National Railway (his salary paid by taxpayers), was asked at a House of Commons committee about francophone hiring at the public corporation. Quebec Créditiste MP Gilles Grégoire listed the president, seventeen vice-presidents, and ten directors, pointing out "not one of them is French Canadian."

Gordon was smug. He said the CNR promoted people on merit and he didn't care if they were "black, white, red, or French." He said he was sure that the railway's university recruitment program would have French Canadians in senior management ranks over the next decade. And he qualified even that: "As long as I am president, promotions are not going to be made because the person is French Canadian. He has to be something else as well!"[53]

His comments hit a nerve. "The incongruity was obvious: a high-school dropout [Gordon] was suggesting that it would take ten years before Quebec university graduates would be ready for executive positions in the state-owned railway whose headquarters was in Montreal," wrote Graham Fraser in *Sorry, I Don't Speak French.*[54] Gordon was burned in effigy; there were protests in Quebec and on Parliament Hill, and there were increasing calls for government to investigate the state of bilingualism. Pearson saw support for federal Liberals slipping away in Quebec; he had already lost a couple of Quebec ministers to scandal (including Maurice Lamontagne), and

Quebec Liberals had come to power on the nationalist slogan, *"maîtres chez nous"*: "masters in our home."

Pearson acted. He authorized the commission in 1963, and it would deliver sweeping recommendations. Its co-chairs were André Laurendeau, publisher of *Le Devoir* and a good friend of Léon Dion, and A. Davidson Dunton, president of Carleton University. Two years later, in 1965, Pearson would reach outside his caucus to bring in the "three wise men" from Quebec—Pierre Trudeau, Gérard Pelletier, and Jean Marchand—much in the way Jean Chrétien would invite Stéphane Dion and Pierre Pettigrew to Ottawa during the separatist crisis of 1995. "I remember January 1965 as if it were yesterday," said Russell, who heard about the Pearson appointments over lunch in the university cafeteria. He felt the excitement; times were changing.

Certainly, it can't be said that the bilingualism and biculturalism commission was born in altruism. Pearson had faced hard political realities. And yet its sweeping recommendations in 1969 helped usher in change across the country. For the first time, there was indisputable empirical proof of inequality for much of francophone Canada. The Official Languages Act became law, and New Brunswick, the province that had banished Acadians two centuries earlier, became bilingual. There would be real opportunities for French speakers in Canada, including in Quebec. It was not independence—and those who had fought for that ideal would continue to fight. But in a post–B&B world, scholar Stéphane Dion would find reasons to oppose Péquiste arguments he had once espoused, albeit shakily.

His relationship with his father was complicated—and always would be—and the issue of separatism and federalism lay at its intellectual core, as it did in many Quebec families. Peter Russell, who would get to know both Dions, the son better than the father, watched the gradual evolution of their views over the years. "Both formidable," he called them. Léon Dion's vast body of work gave him a better understanding of modern Quebec.[55] He invited Léon to speak to his classes at the University of Toronto so his students could grasp Léon's analysis of how the province had gone "from a rural, Catholic, priest-ridden society to a secular state where there was a new kind of Quebec nationalism that would have to be dealt with." Stéphane would make his mark later, but, as Russell saw it, Léon laid the foundation. "Stéphane gets his understanding of Quebec nationalism from his father."

In 1976, however, that understanding meant a poster of René Lévesque on his bedroom wall and a PQ membership card in his pocket.

A SURPRISE WAS in store that year. On November 15, 1976, the Parti Québécois won the Quebec election. The mood was extraordinary at Paul Sauvé Arena in Montreal's north end. Ecstatic PQ supporters swayed back and forth to Gilles Vigneault's haunting "Gens du Pays."[56] It was the anthem of the Parti Québécois, of Quebec nationalism, and those who were there that night would never forget. The flickering flames of thousands of lighters illuminated tear-streaked faces. It was like a rock concert. On stage were the party stars, among them, Claude Charron, Lise Payette, Camille Laurin, and René Lévesque. They were leaping for joy and hugging each other. Nobody could believe it. Lévesque broke down a couple of times. "I never thought I'd be as proud of being Québécois as I am tonight."[57]

Stéphane Dion celebrated with his friends in Quebec City. "We were together at my house and we threw a big party," said Guy Lévesque, a husky Quebec City lawyer who would become a Liberal and laugh at his youthful enthusiasm for independence. "During those years—and we were still in our second year of undergrad—it was normal for everyone to be happy with the result. The Quebec government was very unpopular, if you remember Bourassa, and it came like a surprise. That election for the province was like a big, big explosion of joy ... We were in the living room ... and I remember we were shouting."[58]

Quebecers would grow to love René Lévesque, though a bumpy road lay ahead of him in dealings with the rest of Canada. He was a short man who smelled of cigarettes and had a bad comb-over. His fingers were permanently stained yellow with nicotine, his voice was always hoarse, and he always looked rumpled, as if he'd just dragged himself out of bed or away from a blackjack table. But he was one of the most magnetic political leaders of his time—of any time—and, on November 15, he made Ottawa very nervous.

The Aislin cartoon in the *Gazette* the next day nailed it. Lévesque was standing with a cigarette burning in his outstretched hand: "Okay, everybody, take a Valium."

LÉON DION WAS MORE CONCERNED over his son's separatist leanings than he let on. When Stéphane was still a teenager, he'd asked John Meisel, his friend and fellow political scientist, to speak to him. "Stéphane was quite *indépendantiste* and Léon wanted him to meet an Anglophone who knew a lot about Quebec ... who wasn't a monster," said Meisel. "I don't know how much impact I had on him exactly. He was extremely polite, but maybe he thought I was just a crazy Anglo."[59]

Léon was going through another rough period at Laval in the 1970s. He was not in vogue. "He was not Marxist and he was not separatist, so he had difficulties with some students," Stéphane remembered. Classes brimmed with young Quebecers full of fervour for a separate Quebec, preferably a separate Marxist Quebec. Léon Dion would discuss Marx with students who didn't know the first thing about Marx, and yet doubted their professor. Léon was a liberal, "but he taught me to always be aware of other views," said Stéphane. "Always be open to change your mind if you hear a good argument. But don't change your mind because you are alone."

But it was not Léon who turned his son off separatism. It was the demon rum.

Stéphane was a canvasser in the 1976 provincial campaign, going door to door in Quebec City. One man opened his door and said, "Oh, you're a *séparatiste*! I want to talk with you."

It was about 7:30 P.M. The man's wife trundled in with a tray of rum and Cokes, then another and another ... until Stéphane lurched out some three hours later.

"I came out of the house completely drunk." As he was leaving, he swayed around on the step and said to the man: "Well, maybe you're right."

He didn't know how he got home. He was sick all night and "since then, I'm not a *séparatiste* anymore—and I am not able to look at a rum and Coke."

THE ANECDOTE WOULD sound pat in later years, an easy way, perhaps, for the federal politician to eschew his separatist past. But it was true, at least as metaphor. At some point that night or gradually over subsequent years, Stéphane realized he preferred the role of scientist. He wouldn't be a political player; he would be the cool observer. His father had introduced him to liberal thinkers and chroniclers of the modern Western state from John Stuart Mill to Alexis de Tocqueville, who wrote about bustling, broad-shouldered democracy in a young America with its focus on capitalism and the individual.[60] Ultimately, Stéphane decided, he was "a universalist more than anything else."

He wouldn't remember when he let his PQ membership lapse. But as a newly hatched "universalist," he turned his clinical attention to the Parti Québécois for his master's thesis at Laval University.[61] Looking at the history of the PQ over three elections, he addressed the contradiction of political societies: the desire for victory in the short term versus longer-term goals and aspirations. The raison d'être of the PQ since 1968 had been to achieve the province's independence. Hardliners wanted it made clear to the public that a PQ victory would bring an immediate announcement of separation from Canada. Not so fast, said the pragmatists, including René Lévesque, who argued for a step-by-step approach—*étapisme*—in order not to scare away voters. And they defined independence as *souveraineté-association*—sovereignty plus an economic association with Canada. The pragmatists would win.

From campaign to campaign, the PQ changed its focus from independence in 1970 to independence plus good government in 1973, to a change of government and not a change of country in 1976. Robert Bourassa had to be defeated, Jacques Parizeau would make the best finance minister, and independence would come only after a referendum. "We have seen how, in order to come closer to power, the PQ put its independence project on a back burner and focused instead on more reassuring aspects of its electoral program," Dion wrote in 1979, three years after celebrating November 15 as a PQ militant.[62] It was a lesson in how political parties can prefer winning over moral victory.

"I'm not sure I would write the same today, but for a young person of twenty-four years old, I guess it was good since I had the MA," he would say of his first analysis of how power works within an organization. The topic would continue to fascinate him, remaining the central theme of his research. Many years after completing his MA, his power analysis of another organization, the federal bureaucracy, would save a rookie minister from being eaten alive by the mandarins of Parliament Hill.

Léon was proud of Stéphane's work. No longer was he telling his undisciplined son: "You need to wake up!"

STÉPHANE WAS STILL WORKING on his MA in 1978 when his life changed profoundly. On a warm May evening he was at his desk in his basement bedroom when big Guy Lévesque came pounding down the stairs with his girlfriend, Céline Tremblay. They wanted Stéphane to go to a birthday party.

Girls were a late addition to Stéphane's life. He'd always had lots of friends, but he'd never really noticed girls until his CEGEP went co-ed in the early 1970s. "We were very curious," said his school chum Laurent Arsenault. "We were growing up … Stéphane was no exception."[63] He remembered when *La Presse* asked quirky questions of Liberal leadership candidates in 2006 and Stéphane Dion was asked for his favourite word. *"Femme,"* he replied: "woman."

But he hadn't had a serious relationship by 1978.

Guy and Stéphane burst out laughing when they saw each other that evening. They both looked like skinned rats. Without telling each other, they'd shaved off their beards and cut their hair.

"Stéphane, let's go," shouted Guy. "We need to get out, we need to have some fun. *We need to have a drink!"*

"Noooooo, I have too much work," Stéphane replied, as usual. The couple wouldn't listen. Guy pulled Stéphane physically out of his chair and dragged him up the stairs.

"If he had not done that, I would not have met her," Stéphane Dion would say many years later.

There were a couple of hundred people at the barbecue, but "her" was Janine Krieber. It was the first time he noticed her, although she was a fellow poli-sci graduate student. Janine was 23, nine months older than Stéphane, a dynamic girl with a heart-shaped face and curly hair. She had a dazzling smile and spoke so softly he had to lean in to listen.

"We felt well together," he said. "Maybe because we were both of European background."

Janine was from Alma in Saguenay, the wild and beautiful Precambrian north coast of the St. Lawrence, where whales swim each summer and porpoises chase the tourist boats. Her father, Hans, from the Corinthian region of Austria, had been conscripted by the

Wehrmacht in World War II and sent to the Eastern Front. He said his own father had been shipped to Dachau, but Janine never knew the details. Hans Krieber was a photographer who, after the war, got a job in Alma, where he met and married Thérèse Gagné. They had three children, Janine, Michel, and Edith.

Janine was a quiet child, a voracious reader who dreamed of adventure and enjoyed swimming, camping, and sailing on nearby Lac-Saint-Jean. The region was a child's paradise. She was educated by the nuns of the Congregation of Notre Dame (a female equivalent of the Jesuits), studied fine arts, and, after the family moved to Quebec City, enrolled at Laval. She specialized in international relations and did her postgraduate work on revolutionary groups. A professor had asked her to translate a German newspaper article on the kidnapping of industrialist Hanns-Martin Schleyer by the terrorist Baader-Meinhof Gang.[64] Intrigued, she developed the question at the heart of her MA thesis. The idea was simple: "How normal people like you and me—nice students from large universities, middle class, well educated, well cultured—can turn into killers overnight."[65]

Janine was working on her thesis in the late spring of 1978 when she met Stéphane. She was developing her theory that ordinary kids become killers by militarizing their world and seeing themselves as soldiers fighting a war. She would undoubtedly have shared her ideas with him that evening. They found it easy to talk about everything.

"He had something original about him." *She* had noticed *him* and immediately liked his altered appearance. "He was so cute without all that hair ... I fell in love with him."

It was the same for Stéphane. "We fell in love during the party." They left together. Although both would continue to live at home for another year or so, it was the beginning of a life together. That summer they travelled to the Gaspé; soon they would travel the world.

"They are very different but, at the same time, they're very complementary. The best proof lies in how long they've been together," observed their friend Jean-Philippe Thérien, almost a quarter-century after they all became friends in Paris in 1982. "Janine is someone who shares Stéphane's very pronounced taste for intellectual questions. This is a woman who did her PhD at Sciences Po in Paris—so this is not just *anyone*."[66]

There was something else about Janine Krieber that would have appealed to Stéphane Dion. She came from a family where girls were treated the same as boys. She had initially wanted to be a pilot but chose a path that would lead her to become an internationally recognized specialist on terrorism. Janine was a strong woman—and he was most comfortable with strong women.

Just as Denyse Kormann had taken charge of Léon Dion's life, Janine Krieber would take charge of their son's. They would be partners in everything, and it is difficult to imagine Stéphane Dion's successes in life without Janine Krieber by his side. And vice versa.

"What separates them from one another is that Janine is more concrete than Stéphane," said Thérien, a political scientist at the University of Montreal who was studying in Paris when he met the Dion-Krieber pair. *Concrete*. This was Thérien's delicate way of contrasting his friend Stéphane, who could be rather inept about day-to-day life, with Janine. "The intellectual with his head in the clouds and the practical wife," was how he put it. What did Janine know that Stéphane didn't? Well, Thérien began, "How to cook, decorate a home, take care of the car, *change a lightbulb,* manage a household ... "

Thérien recalled when Stéphane and Janine, both young professors, helped him move into a new apartment on Hutchison Street in central Montreal. "They brought me boxes, an indication of the level of our friendship! But it was clear when it came to moving day that it wasn't Stéphane who brought the boxes. And when we arrived at the house, Stéphane wasn't the one who asked, 'Where do I put these boxes?' ... This is someone who doesn't have a lot of practical sense;

I think he would agree with me on that. There are many things in daily life in which it's Janine who's in charge."

DURING THEIR LAST MONTHS as students at Laval, Stéphane and Janine completed their MAs and talked of the future. Both wanted to go to the prestigious Institut d'études politiques in Paris, the famed Sciences Po. Janine planned to study with German specialist Alfred Grosser, while Stéphane hoped to work with French sociologist Michel Crozier, who had pioneered the analysis of power in organizations and taught half the year at Sciences Po and the other half at Harvard University. He met Crozier for coffee in Quebec City's Quartier Latin and it went well. Crozier said he would expect him.

Léon Dion always stressed the importance of choosing the right mentor. It was a maxim for him, along with, "You have to start to publish young. Otherwise, it's a trauma." But Léon didn't mean for Stéphane to find his mentor in Paris! He was not happy with the idea. "He wanted me to be truly bilingual—and that I've never been able to be because I'm still struggling with the [English] language," Stéphane would say soon after winning the federal Liberal leadership in 2006. "He also told me that in the [academic] network—whether English-speaking Canada or the United States—if you went to France you were out."

Stéphane didn't care. He thought Crozier was the best. He would worry about his English later.

He and Janine left for Paris in September 1979 and would be gone for more than four years, until December 1983. Shortly before their departure, Janine's father was killed in a car accident. Her love of photography came from her father: he was the storyteller in the family, the keeper of legends, and she would miss him terribly.

She needed Paris.

THE CITY WAS EVERYTHING Janine hoped it would be. Even her workaholic boyfriend couldn't ignore the excitement, mystery, and romance of Paris. "Ah, my memories," said Janine with a dreamy look, as she sat smoking and remembering in their Montreal townhouse in 2007. "That was a life without responsibility. We went to Austria and Germany a couple of times. We travelled France from south to north ... I think the best memories are of friendship ... We were alone, didn't have the family—the mothers-in-law on both sides," she laughed. "You have to solve your own problems with your friends."

They rented a little apartment in Montmartre for a song from a woman who had retired from the United Nations. Montmartre was diverse and full of colour. They lived near Place Pigalle and the red-light district. The can-can girls of the Moulin Rouge were neighbours. There were apartments worth millions and cold-water flats in decaying buildings where drug dealers plied their trade. "There were call girls just a few blocks from the richest people in Paris," she said. "You'd turn a little east, and there was the poorest street in Paris, la Goutte d'Or."

They didn't have much money—Janine had arranged small grants for both of them from the Research Council of Canada—but they managed. They walked everywhere or took the bus. Who cared? It was Paris. Janine felt carefree. One morning, she was walking to the bus to Sciences Po, moving past the bars and the lounging prostitutes, when a man called out: *"On engage, mademoiselle?"*—"Shall we?"

She laughed. She thought it was a lark.

Stéphane and Janine couldn't afford restaurants, but that didn't matter either. There were invitations from Stéphane's French family, and they often had dinner with his great-uncle Lucien Biroulès, who'd been in the wartime French Resistance and was president of his local veterans' association.[67] Everyone always said how much Stéphane looked like his grandmother Thérèse-Marie.

And Janine loved to cook. She pulled out her Paul Bocuse cookbook or whipped up her mother's recipes. Her specialty was Cipaille du Lac-Saint-Jean, a stew with plump morsels of chicken and light-as-air pastry. She made lovely omelets with sautéed potatoes and garden greens and served trays of cheeses and wine at the informal parties they threw.

Paris was full of Quebec expats pining for home while talking about the issues of the day: the state of the Cold War, the reunification of Europe, the close victory in 1981 of Socialist François Mitterrand over incumbent president Valéry Giscard d'Estaing from the right. Janine liked what François Mitterrand was doing, nationalizing the banks and increasing social assistance payments. "When you're young and you're a student of political science, you are leftist and you believe in social progress."

EACH YEAR, JANINE had to queue for her papers in order to live and study in France. It was a chore that Stéphane, with his French passport, could avoid. But everybody knew he was Canadian the moment he opened his mouth. It was the accent. "When people learned my mother was from Paris, they were very surprised." Ah yes, *le snobisme*. "It's difficult to convince French people to take you seriously because of your French-Canadian accent," he explained. "The first time they are not listening to what you are saying. They are only listening to the way you are saying it."

And Parisians, believing they had a superior French to provincials, could be horrible. After a time, it got better for Stéphane at Sciences Po. He was a good researcher and he was studying with the highly respected Crozier.

"But at the beginning, it was only, '*Ohhhh, it's so charming, the way he speaks!*'" One thing would never change. Always, *always*, the French would correct his French. "But I knew it would be like that."[68]

To say stéphane worked hard was an understatement. His PhD supervisor, Michel Crozier, had established the sociology of organizations as a discipline and set out a template for their analysis. His seminal work, *The Bureaucratic Phenomenon,* describes an organizational culture that expands because people fear face-to-face encounters and set up a complicated bureaucracy to avoid it.[69] Those at the top are protected as the bureaucracy grows more inflexible.[70]

But Stéphane found Crozier's sociology optimistic. It was about power, and "power is a part of life and it's not something bad or wrong," he explained. "The use of power is what makes human societies different from animals who act on instinct. Humans are always sizing each other up. I don't know what you will do, you don't know what I will do. That constant jockeying for power is what makes life interesting."

He had already decided his thesis would be about France. "Many Quebecers make the mistake when they go to France [of asking] French professors to supervise their dissertations on Canadian or Quebec topics," he said. "And French professors know nothing about this."

It was a smart move. His friend Denis Saint-Martin said his decision to study under Crozier in the first place ran "against the current" and proved that Stéphane Dion was "the archetype of underdog."[71]

Many years later, in his political science office at the University of Montreal, Saint-Martin described how most people did it. Francophone intellectuals from Quebec in the 1970s and 1980s went to France to study with the sociologists on the left. But Michel Crozier was not a left-wing individual. "That's not to say he was on the right, but he wasn't on the left. He also was a critic of the Paris Spring of 1968, the student revolution in France.... All the left said, 'Oh wow, this is wonderful!' So it shows that Dion was not someone who likes to be part of the mainstream, *hein?*"

Jean-Philippe Thérien, who would also become a political science professor, admired Dion for having had the "self-confidence to go to

France and explain to the French how French politics work." He called it "audacious … very much in line with his personality."

UNDER CROZIER'S GUIDANCE, Stéphane chose the study of the communist and socialist communes that ringed Paris. In the early 1980s, communists districts were losing power under Mitterand's Socialist government. He interviewed people about their daily lives: how they worked, how they found solutions to problems, how they reconciled their ideological differences. And his resulting study would find the characteristics of most political systems: cronyism, patronage, tokenism, and people just trying to get by.[72] His work, as he would later say, "has been a good school of life."

"Why are you studying that," Quebec friends would ask Stéphane. Why not choose something more interesting? The Middle East, perhaps? Big topics.

Stéphane always demurred. "I was seeing these small debates in suburbs where nobody wanted to go because they are ugly, if you compare with Paris and such … To me it was really fascinating to do. If you go to a country, it's to study the country and not to pretend that the country will help you to study your own country."

In those same suburbs, he saw growing anti-immigrant attitudes in the suburbs that would explode more than twenty years later in racial riots in the fall of 2005. "I saw a lot of racism and anxiety among the workers who saw their way of life under threat by a large immigration and new religion," he said. "It was more difficult for them than for the people in the beautiful paradise of Paris. I saw how Parisians didn't understand. I saw communists when they were beginning to lose their faith in communism."

STÉPHANE WORKED SO HARD he almost died, literally.

"Janine, I don't feel well," he said one day at their apartment. But he kept working. He'd been taking pills for stomach pain for days, more and more pills, but nothing worked.

"Okay, now I cannot work anymore," he told her. "I need to take a rest for five minutes."

He couldn't get out of bed.

"We need to see a doctor," she told him.

Janine took him to the hospital, where it was discovered his appendix had burst. He survived after emergency surgery.

FINALLY, HE FINISHED his thesis and delivered it to Michel Crozier. Two weeks later, Crozier invited him to his office. "It's marvellous," he said. But he went on to tell Stéphane it was only the beginning. He expected his student to complete the more advanced PhD, the *thèse d'état*, or state-sanctioned thesis. In France, there were two PhDs, the ordinary one and the exceptional one. "We have an additional year to go," said Crozier brightly.

"But why?" moaned Stéphane. "Look, it's time for me to go home. We're really short of money." Besides, he continued: "Nobody in Canada knows about the *thèse d'état*. You have your PhD or you don't. Nobody knows the difference!"

He figured it didn't really matter even in France. The last thing people with an ordinary PhD wanted was for anyone to know there was a more prestigious model. Why was everything also so complicated in France, he wanted to know. "If my PhD is good," he told Crozier, "then give me my PhD!"

"Not at all. We will not miss this opportunity," said his professor, unfazed. "Now, this is what I suggest to improve it ..."

Dion stayed yet another year.

HIS WORK PAID OFF. In April 1983, he successfully defended his thesis (in sociology) in a half-day session at Sciences Po. That year, he won the bronze medal from the Centre national de la recherche scientifique. It was the highest honour a student could have for a thesis. The gold medal was for a professor's lifetime body of work; the silver medal went to the best book of the year.

His parents were there to witness their son's success. Léon and Denyse would stay in Paris for a year, taking over the apartment from Stéphane and Janine. Léon would study at the Sorbonne.

Crozier wrote a preface to the published version of Stéphane's dissertation, saying he was impressed people spoke so frankly with him about their complicated problems, "particularly in a period of great tensions." His student, he said, had shown "no attraction for left-wing ideology," and yet people opened up to him because he showed a sympathy for their lives that was "more profound and more human" than political sympathy alone and had gained their confidence and their friendship. He continued:

> Stéphane Dion is Québécois. His origins and his culture provide him vis-à-vis France with an interesting perspective that is a mixture of proximity and distance. He understands all our passions and their nuances. But at the same time he is truly North American, sufficiently distant to keep on the other hand an insatiable curiosity for his subjects of observation, no matter how trivial their activities can be. His strong sociological and political background helped him discover in these tiny bureaucratic disputes of the "little French idiosyncracies"[73] underlying problems of administration and politics that have preoccupied all political thinkers since Machiavelli.[74]

THROUGHOUT THEIR FOUR YEARS in Paris, Stéphane Dion had felt removed from events at home. He had laid aside the separatism of his early years and become the cool scientist he sought to be. That quality had stayed with him through the biggest event to occur in Quebec during his absence, the referendum of May 14, 1980.

Quebecers voted on the question of whether or not to give the Parti Québécois government a mandate to negotiate separation from Canada, and sixty percent had said No. In Quebec City, Léon Dion, the federalist who had worked for the B&B commission voted Yes. It was, as his son said later, "for strategic reasons" to give Quebec bargaining power with the federal government.[75] Léon explained his reasons in a book published on the eve of the referendum.[76] He hadn't become a separatist—far from it—but the ground was beginning to shift in his thinking on federalism and Quebec's place within Canada.

Stéphane remained aloof. He and Janine went to the Canadian embassy on Avenue Montaigne, and later to the Quebec delegation on Rue Pergolèse. "My friends were crying because the Yes lost. We were a very nationalist network, as you can imagine in social sciences in France," he said. "I was analyzing. I was proud to have no strong emotion. I was not pro-Canadian or pro-separatist."

He knew what he *wasn't* politically. What he didn't know yet was what he *was*.

CHAPTER THREE

ONE DION WAS ENOUGH

T HE DOME of Saint Joseph's Oratory against the sky is both familiar and comforting to Montrealers. Seen at a certain time of day, the view could be of Florence. It's the light of late afternoon, with the same soft, pinkish hues of Italy. The oratory is inspiring, and it's fitting that it crowns the Montreal district that houses the sprawling campus of the University of Montreal. The pavilion at 3200 Jean-Brillant Street looks across the headstones of Notre-Dame-des-Neiges Cemetery and up to the glorious sight of the oratory.

Côte-des-Neiges Road winds up the side of the mountain from downtown Montreal towards the university. The neighbourhood is dynamic and full of life, one of the many reasons Montrealers wouldn't live anywhere else. The school's political science department is on the fourth floor of 3200 Jean-Brillant. The building itself is rather ugly but, when a class lets out, students fill the outside patio, even in winter, chatting and smoking cigarettes. There are lots of cheap restaurants and coffee shops, a metro station, and residential streets with a mix of charming old homes and low-rise apartments. At noon, the bells of Notre-Dame-des-Neiges begin to chime, drowning out all but the traffic.

The department of political science was at the centre of Stéphane Dion's world for six years in the 1980s. After a sabbatical year away, it would be his world again in the 1990s, but everything would be different then. He wouldn't be the same unassuming professor of public administration who wanted simply to find his niche in a discipline dominated by his famous father, and who shied away from the drama over Quebec and Canada. He would be at the centre of a gathering political storm and, for the most part, relishing the role.

THE YOUNG PROFESSOR didn't have that fabulous view of the oratory from his little fourth-floor cubbyhole. Instead, his office in the political science department looked out through thin, vertical slits of windows to a brick wall with rows of more thin windows just like his. His door opened into a long, narrow corridor that was somewhat dark. In fact, it seemed the architecture of the building had been designed to keep as much natural light as possible from the learning process within.

But the professor kept his door open to his students. His office was filled with books and cluttered with piles of papers, but he was organized. And he was accessible. Not all professors were. He lived in a small apartment in nearby Outremont with his partner, Janine Krieber, and would often invite his postgrad students for dinner or a glass of wine in the evening. Janine taught in the political science department at Laval University and took the 250-kilometre commute to Quebec City in stride.

They'd returned to Canada from Paris the winter before, and Dion had accepted a short-term teaching stint in January 1984 at the French-language University of Moncton. There had been some confusion about his application for a poli-sci position in Montreal because his PhD, although the *ne plus ultra* of French academia, was in sociology. But once he met with members of the hiring committee at the University of Montreal, they were so impressed they waived the routine assessment period and hired him on the spot.[77]

Dion had turned twenty-eight in the autumn of 1984. He had shaved off the beard of rebellious youth and cut the bouffant-like hair of Paris. He looked appropriately professorial in the round, oversized glasses of the day. He wore jeans and boots and carried a knapsack. Suits always seemed big for him and hung on his bony frame.

He was under the impression he'd begun to get the knack of teaching during his six months at Moncton. His "Introduction to Political Science" course had been no picnic. "For these first hours we will have together, I will introduce you to the pioneers of political science, the great thinkers of the past," he said, before zooming through Plato and Aristotle and skimming over Karl Marx and Max Weber.

The next week, hands went up.

"I tried to find the things you spoke about—that Machiavelli, is he Scottish?" a student wanted to know. Asked another: "Marx Weber, who is that?" He realized he needed to slow down and *teach*. On the blackboard he wrote *"Dé-mo-cra-tie"* and began again.

"I think I am a clear person and I owe a lot to my first students," he later summed up. "I was convinced I was a good researcher. I wanted to become a good professor."[78]

His style wasn't a hit with everyone, however, especially considering he had big shoes to fill.

DION BROUGHT ENTHUSIASM to Montreal. Although he always saw himself as having three tasks—professor, researcher, and internationally recognized scholar—being a good teacher was closest to his heart, and it always would be. Ten years after leaving the profession, after becoming a cabinet minister, a member of Parliament, and leader of Her Majesty's Loyal Opposition, he would remain sensitive to any suggestion he wasn't.

In January 2007, the talented, French-born journalist Benoît Aubin wrote a lengthy feature about Stéphane Dion for *Maclean's* magazine. It was a positive piece from the fresh angle of a political marriage. But it contained the comment from former MA student

Denis Saint-Martin: "His lectures got ratings closer to C– than to A+."[79] It wasn't meant to be a negative review. Saint-Martin stressed that public administration was, after all, an "arid" topic.[80]

But, oh, how Dion chafed. Janine, who was included in the article, liked it; she admired anyone who could write with ease in two languages.[81] But it bothered Dion. So many things had been said and written about him by that time in his life—nasty things, such as how he was a traitor to Quebec. Cartoonist Serge Chapleau from *La Presse* drew him as a rat. But it wounded Dion to think students might have considered him dull. In actual fact, Denis Saint-Martin was a huge admirer of Stéphane Dion, a point that was crystal clear in the article. But he couldn't say Dion was Mr. Charisma, and who could quibble with that? "He was a good professor who explained clearly what he had to say, but he didn't have any more charisma than he has today," said Saint-Martin not long after the article appeared. That was a *good* thing. "There are other professors who don't have interesting things to say, but they are very charismatic with lots of expression. Stéphane wasn't like that."[82]

Public administration focuses on bureaucrats and wasn't the most popular class, particularly among first-year students. Dion taught three or four hundred of them in the amphitheatre, struggling to keep their attention. Even in smaller classes, he could be awkward. "When I had my first course with him, he was shy, he was shy, he was shy…. He was a little bit gauche, but kind," said Saint-Martin, who would become Dion's MA student, his research assistant, and, ultimately, a professor of public administration.

They also became friends. "He was very sensitive, very warm, but obviously if intellectually I had produced work he didn't like, I don't think we'd have the same dynamic. It's not a secret—everyone knows he's a very cerebral person. There isn't a lot of chitchat with Stéphane."

His teaching style was straightforward, like the man. He would describe the objective of each class, how it would be divided—into A, B, C, and D—and students who depended on detailed notes were content. "Stéphane was very good at making the material very clear. So, he was a good pedagogue," said Saint-Martin. "I imagine growing up in a professor's family it was natural enough for him."

Word had gotten around the campus quickly in the fall of 1984 that Stéphane was Léon Dion's son. Some fifteen master's degree students showed up for his first class, shopping around. By the second week, there were seven. "What scared them off is that Mr. Dion was very, very rigorous … demanding,"said Patricia Bittar. "We knew in his class we would have to work hard." She said she worked harder for him than for any other professor.

Dion was keen to practise the "strategic analysis" approach of his mentor, Michel Crozier, and he taught his students to analyze how power works in the organizations they were studying. With Bittar, it was the refugee claim system. "He was very, very present." He expected her—and all his students—to be hands-on, to get out and interview people and see how things operated. Later, when he represented the suburban Montreal riding of Saint-Laurent-Cartierville, Bittar worked in his constituency office, often dealing with the problems of a large immigrant population.

"He would always ask, 'What happened with that case? … Could you do something for that madame? … Could you do something for that man? Did he get his children here in Canada?'" In 2004, Bittar was elected a city councillor for the same area of Saint-Laurent, often having to come to grips with the same issues. Essentially, she credited Dion with teaching her how to think strategically and to focus. "He taught me the most, you know, of all the professors I've had."

André Bélanger could be sparing in his praise for an original idea. He'd been teaching in the political science department for more than three decades in 2007 and felt one good, original idea a year would be more than enough for any university. Stéphane Dion, in his opinion, was an original thinker. "His research was very focused and what he focused on was often very original. He was the one who told me that Canadian federalism was not a centralized type of federalism. On the contrary, it was one of the less centralized. I was convinced of the opposite, not because I had really looked at it but because it was so common to think that way. He had gone against what all Quebecers thought. He can go counter and that's his strength. He's one of the few men I've known who concentrates and then brings something out of that through thick and thin—what seems to him obvious is not necessarily so to those listening to him."

WHILE DION'S HEART may have lain with being a good teacher, it wasn't his only purpose in the 1980s. Most people have to establish their name. He had to establish his Christian name. Not just Dion, but *Stéphane* Dion. Moreover, by the time he turned thirty, he was intent on not following the example of his father. He was beginning to see drawbacks to being Léon Dion.

The political scene was full of change. Brian Mulroney was in Ottawa, René Lévesque was out of power in Quebec, Robert Bourassa was back in, and the country was about to plunge into "constitutional wrangling," as the media shorthand put it, over the failed Meech Lake and, later, Charlottetown accords—and all the various hand-wringing permutations thereof.

The tables had turned completely on the partisan son and the father who had once concentrated on the thoughtful application of academic research to public policy, as in his work for the B&B commission. Léon Dion began the 1980s by voting Yes in the Quebec referendum as a strategic move and, by the decade's end, was becoming more and more entangled in the angst of the Quebec debate over separation. Léon wanted something different for his son.

"My father had been handicapped by his involvement in the Quebec–Canada relationship to the point that he didn't have the international career he was dreaming of for himself," Stéphane would say later. Looking back on his many discussions with his father over the period, he most remembered Léon urging him not to get involved in the Quebec–Canada politics.

Father and son agreed: *"One Dion was enough."*

His father's academic aspirations were lost. It was a revealing thing to say about someone whose career had always been deemed so successful. Léon had been a beacon.

"I'm not sure he made a choice," the younger Dion would observe. "I think it's a result. Because he always tried to come back to research but it was so demanding to play the role of Léon Dion for the Quebec–Canada issue."

In other words, there was no way out.

"And I was resolute not to do that and to focus on my own role as a professor of public administration." His research would be solid, the organization theory well applied, and the name *Stéphane Dion* would be respected far from the hurly-burly—and hurtful—world of politics.

AND SO STÉPHANE DION avoided politics. He had switched his vote from the Parti Québécois to Bourassa and the Liberals, and he voted Liberal federally, but he didn't like to talk about the subject. He was attempting to be apolitical at the most politically intense university in Quebec. The departments of law, political science, and sociology had played a significant role in the intellectual development of the Quiet Revolution and had an even greater impact on the formation of the Parti Québécois. There were always PQ-related events on campus, and, in the early 1980s, the workshops were held there for the PQ convention after Pierre Trudeau and the other premiers signed a constitutional agreement in 1981 without René Lévesque and Quebec.

Denis Monière was director of the political science department. He had founded the Parti indépendantiste, a more hard-line separatist party than the PQ. He thought PQ policy was weak and regarded the failure of the Patriote rebellion in 1837 as a death knell for Quebec. Yet he hired Stéphane Dion. And so, as Denis Saint-Martin pointed out, "We see that Stéphane could not have been involved in the questions of Quebec and Canadian politics ... If he was a federalist back then, it would have been much harder!"

While there were professors and students in the federalist camp, the vast majority at the University of Montreal believed in independence for Quebec. Conversation in the cafeteria, in hallways, and on the concrete patio outside Pavilion 3200 Jean-Brillant examined the ins and outs of how to separate, when to separate, the benefits of separation, or lack thereof, and the timing of another referendum. As Graciela Ducatenzeiler, a political science professor who would later become director of the department, remembered, "Everyone could discuss their opinions frankly and the atmosphere among professors was very civilized."

But Stéphane didn't want to discuss politics. His classes were about public administration and political theory, not the intense debate over the future of Quebec. He preferred the more general discussions of the day's news—although news in Quebec dwelled heavily on federal–Quebec struggles—and the latest on the Expos and Canadiens. In his class, politics was strictly forbidden, according to Ducatenzeiler. "He said you could have whatever political opinion you wanted, but not in the classroom."[83]

DION WORKED, TOO, on his own research projects. His father had warned him that a French postgraduate education wasn't worth much in North America, meaning the *American* academic community. He had to build his name first in Canada, so he wrote for the *Canadian Journal of Political Science* and other academic publications, and, with his colleague and mentor André Blais, began work on a project that would be published as a book in the United States in 1991. Its title, *The Budget-Maximizing Bureaucrat,* was a neat twist on its theme.[84] Conventional wisdom said bureaucrats were always trying to increase their budgets because more resources meant more power. But the Blais–Dion research showed that bureaucrats do what their political superiors tell them to do. Denis Saint-Martin was one of Dion's research assistants. "I think the Americans liked it because it was like this big balloon in the neoconservative rhetoric went *pop!*"

Gradually, there would be invitations, to Pittsburgh, Toronto, and, ultimately, to Washington. The name Stéphane Dion was becoming known in political science circles, just as his father had hoped it would be.

DION HAD ANOTHER research project, a personal one. He and Janine had been trying to have a baby without success. They saw doctors and discussed whether they should consider the options of medical science. "I think we were scared by the ultra medication and all those hormone therapies, and we said that was much too unnatural for us," said Janine. "And there are a lot of babies to be adopted all over the world ... so why not adopt?"

They had been friends with Graciela Ducatenzeiler since their return from Paris, going skiing at her chalet in the Eastern Townships south of Montreal or having dinner at their apartment, or hers, in Montreal. She was from Argentina and, through her Latin American connections, knew about adoption in Peru. They decided to go ahead. There would be long hours spent in early 1987 at Graciela's apartment in Notre-Dame-de-Grâce while she went back and forth in Spanish on the telephone to Cusco, Peru. Stéphane would remember drinking cognac and waiting, waiting.

Things were looking positive. Finally, word came through of a child in Cusco, a girl. She was about a year old and was living with a lawyer and his family. She'd never been in an orphanage. They were nervous. The adoption of a boy had already fallen apart in the early months of 1987. Janine vowed she wouldn't look at a photograph this time, not until everything was certain.

First, though, they had to marry in order to adopt from Peru.

"We didn't feel we needed a contract. It's a question of generation, *our* generation," Janine explained. There had never been pressure from either family. It felt nice to make the decision for such a compelling reason.

By now it was springtime; they had to pick a date. Stéphane's sense of humour tended to the absurd. Janine's was simply goofy. She liked slapstick, and her wedding would be no exception. She seized on the idea of marrying on April Fool's Day. But Good Friday fell on April 1 that year and municipal services were closed. "So I said, 'Get me the day after that!'"

They were married on Saturday, April 2, 1987, at city hall in Old Montreal. Almost April Fool's. They celebrated with friends and family crammed into their Outremont apartment—his parents, Denyse and Léon, her mother Thérèse, an assortment of brothers and sisters and friends. They cut a wedding cake with meringue on top and were one step closer to a baby.

SOON AFTER, STÉPHANE set out alone for the old Incan capital of Cusco in the Andes Mountains. Janine stayed in Montreal and worked on the adoption. "It's a full-time career to get everything you need for international adoption. The legal system of Peru and Quebec, going before the courts, the bureaucracy ..."

Janine's career was flourishing at Laval and, as Stéphane was advancing in his field, she was becoming known for her work on international terrorism. She decided she would go to a strategic studies conference in Europe. There was nothing more to be done in Montreal—except wait. When she returned, there was a photograph waiting and Stéphane was on the phone telling her to come to Peru. She left the next day.

Even though the adoption was far from certain, Stéphane had been caring for the child since his arrival three months earlier. He'd moved into the home of the lawyer where the little girl was living and, with some help from her grandmother, was getting to know her. He found he was very good at being a father. His friend Jean-Philippe Thérien said Dion's relationship with his child was the exception to the rule of Dion's disinterest in practical matters. "His relationship with his daughter is very, very strong," he said. "He's always busy with her in a practical way." She was sixteen months old when Stéphane arrived in Peru, and he dove right in, finding the right food, changing diapers, soothing her when she cried. And he'd been sick the whole time. He didn't have a great stomach to begin with and the combination of altitude and strange bugs was rough.

But it would have killed him to give her up. The bond was already strong between the tall, skinny gringo and the dark-eyed child. He carried her everywhere in a baby carrier.

The family came together for the first time at the airport in Cusco. Stéphane, Janine, and Jeanne. They liked the old French name, plus it was a tradition in Janine's family to give the first child of each generation some form of the name John. She was Jeanne, followed by Yessica, her birth name.

Janine, too, was in love. "She was a wonderful girl, wonderful baby ... and her dark black hair ... and she was *so small.*" Their family doctor would later show how much below normal she was on the charts. "She'll catch up in three years," she said, and she was proven right.

Janine began taking photographs of her daughter in Cusco. In all the shots, the child already has a firm little grasp on her father.

BACK IN MONTREAL, Stéphane would continue his infatuation with his daughter. He looked after her while Janine commuted to Laval, taking her to daycare before class and picking her up. He put her on his back in the carrier, and, at the university, everyone got to know her. "It was remarkable to see them," said Graciela. "The relationship was so strong, it was if they had been a family all their lives."

Dinner at the Dion-Krieber household involved, for their friends, discussions of Middle Eastern politics or the latest strike in France, with a little child squirming on Stéphane's lap. He loved it. When they made plans to go to Washington, D.C., three years later for Stéphane's sabbatical year at the Brookings Institution, they wanted to know what was available for children in the U.S. capital. He would embark on a journey that would change the course of his life and he needed a list of public swimming pools for his daughter.

Dion knew from the beginning that he would be a different father from Léon. He would have the time that his father never did. Stéphane and Jeanne played for hours together. He invented characters for her, and even homework turned into a fantasy production with Papa playing all the parts. There was Miss Pineapple, the English professor, and Madame Cartenpion, who taught everything else. "Jeanne, Jeanne," he would ask in a high, woman's voice. *"As-tu bien étudié aujourd'hui?"* ("Did you study well today?")

And there was a little boy. His name was *le P'tit Stéphane* (Little Stéphane), and whenever she wanted, Jeanne would just say: "Dad, okay, now I want you to be *le P'tit Stéphane!*" And a squeaky little boy's voice would pipe in, *"Bonjour Jeanne,* I want to play with you, my friend."

"It was as if she thought he was really existing in my body—and at her request," he would say many years later, a few days after Christmas 2006. Just about to turn nineteen, his daughter, Jeanne, sat beside him and laughed when he did all the old voices again. They remembered how Jeanne had wanted him to be *le P'tit Stéphane* when they went to the Haunted House at the amusement park at La Ronde. But once they got inside, she cried out: "No! No! I want you to be my dad!"

IN SEPTEMBER 1991, Stéphane, Janine, and Jeanne were living in Washington not far from the gothic spires of the National Cathedral on Wisconsin Avenue. They had a little apartment and, once again, were on a tight budget. But they took it in stride; they hadn't wanted to miss the opportunity of living and studying in the U.S. capital.

It was an interesting year in Washington, Janine would later reflect. A month earlier, in August, Iraqi president Saddam Hussein had invaded Kuwait, and, by mid-January, the United States would be at war with Iraq. Janine was still working on her PhD, and she would sit with a small TV set on her desk and watch the war on CNN. It was the first fully televised war, and she found it gripping to watch. "That year Washington was the capital of the world," said Janine, although that wasn't so unusual.

The conflict served as a backdrop to her own studies. Janine hunkered down and finally completed the dissertation she'd begun in Paris, examining terrorist groups in the United States, Italy, and Germany. Her husband had always urged her to finish it, and Washington appeared to be the perfect opportunity.

"I always said I was in prison [in Washington]. Stéphane just cut me off from all my friends. The military college asked me to come back and I just said no." Before she left, Janine had begun teaching at the Royal Military College, at the Saint-Jean-sur-Richelieu campus near Montreal. She would gradually expand her class load to include courses on guerrilla groups, terrorism, and peacekeeping and continue to develop an international reputation for her expertise. But from October to July of 1990–91, she worked away in their small Washington flat until, at last, she completed her PhD the day before the Fourth of July holiday. Both Janine Krieber and Stéphane Dion's careers appeared to be unfolding exactly as they had planned.

CHAPTER FOUR

FINDING HIS RELIGION

S TÉPHANE DION FOUND HIS COUNTRY, as many do, by leaving it. But he had to leave twice. The first time, when he was a graduate student in Paris, there had been little incentive to examine his own identity and political beliefs. The denizens of French academia were hardly brimming with curiosity about Canada, plus he was in his ostrich period about Canadian politics. It was very different in Washington in 1991, or rather the official Washington of the academic-diplomatic-political circuit that essentially runs from Georgetown University over to the Capitol Dome and down to the White House and the State Department. He was at the Brookings Institution, which, like other important think tanks in the capital, plays a role in keeping the shapers of U.S. policy abreast of political and intellectual currents around the globe. What was happening right next door in Canada certainly qualified as a political current. More like a river. Constitutional reform had failed and the country appeared on the brink of breaking apart. The future of Canada was a hot topic on National Public Radio and the *MacNeil/Lehrer NewsHour* on PBS (if not on CNN),[85] and would remain so into the 1990s as Quebec bore down on a vote to separate that was filled with drama, suspense, and bitterness.

"Look, something is happening in your country that I don't understand," Thomas E. Mann, director of governmental studies at the Brookings, said to Dion in the spring of 1991.[86] This was an understatement; neither did a lot of Canadians. Support for sovereignty was surging in Quebec, while the rest of the country appeared to have gone sour on the province and its perceived demands. Mann asked the three visiting Canadian scholars, Stéphane Dion from the University of Montreal, Andrew Stark from Harvard, and Keith Banting from Queen's, to shed light on the issue.[87] "Can you give us a backgrounder in a couple of weeks?" he inquired. They acquiesced and set a date in May for a "brown bag" seminar over a lunch hour. "How can you say no to somebody who's giving you an office and a year at Brookings?" asked Dion.

He had avoided politics since his early flirtation with the Parti Québécois other than, over the course of the 1980s, casting a vote twice for the federal Liberals and once for Robert Bourassa's provincial party. He hadn't paid particular attention to constitutional talks and didn't pretend to be an expert. But Mann had made him think. He sat down at his computer at the Brookings at around 11 o'clock on the morning of the event and was finished writing by noon when Keith Banting popped by his office and, seeing him printing out his comments, urged him to hurry. In the elevator, Dion told Banting that when he reread his remarks, he'd suddenly realized he was a federalist. "This clearly surprised him a bit," Banting would recall.[88]

The seminar hall was packed with congressional staffers, officials from the White House, diplomats from embassies up and down Massachusetts Avenue, people from the Paul H. Nitze School of Advanced International Studies across the street and the Canadian Embassy over on Pennsylvania, other academics, and assorted politicos working in the world's most powerful capital. "The Brookings did it big," Dion said. The week before he'd delivered a lecture about his research in public administration and fifteen people showed up, all fellow researchers. At the May seminar, they covered the topic from the perspective of Quebec (Dion), of English Canada (Stark), and of potential scenarios for North America after Quebec separation (Banting). Mann was pleased. Later, he pulled Dion aside and asked if he and the others would care to write a monograph. Unfamiliar with the English term, Dion tossed off, "Sure, why not?" The others were a bit startled, he recalled, to have been so airily committed to a book. They asked R. Kent Weaver, a specialist on Canadian affairs at the Brookings (and an American), to become editor and began a project that would take a year to complete.[89] *The Collapse of Canada?* was launched with a big splash at the Brookings in the spring of 1992.[90] The question mark in the title was added at Dion's insistence. As he remembered, he was more optimistic at the time than his colleagues about the future of Canada.

The book created quite the buzz. The reaction of the Canadian media to its release was "exceptional," according to Banting. "I was interviewed by the CBC using an uplink from their Washington bureau and I spent a lot of time with Canadian radio. My coauthors did the same. The name of Brookings generated the intensity. It took some time for the media to realize that this was a collection of opinion pieces largely by Canadians, and not the result of some deeply analytical study by a team of Brookings number crunchers." A CBC interviewer told him "he had had to calm down CBC central, explaining that Brookings itself was not predicting the collapse of Canada. And I kept being asked by hostile radio hosts where we got our data. If the same book had been published by a Canadian press, it would not have received anything like the same attention from the Canadian media."

It was a turning point for Stéphane Dion. Forced to think about his own country, he not only discovered he believed in Canadian federalism, but understood why. His essay laid out the reasons why federalism was working for the province of Quebec and, in the process, challenged what he would later call "nationalist myths" about Canada. "We talked about his appreciation of federalism," Andrew

Stark said in early 2007. By then, the two Brookings colleagues were old friends. "Stéphane saw it as analogous to the separation of powers in the United States and thought it was a good thing to have different power sources in the government system."[91] Just as the executive, legislative, and judicial branches were designed to keep each other in check in the United States, he believed the federal–provincial dynamic kept the players honest in Canada. It was the intellectual foundation of his federalism. He accepted the separation of powers described in the British North America Act,[92] but he was a classic federalist for whom strong provinces equalled a strong country, and he would return to that theme often in speeches when he was a cabinet minister. "Our federation is decentralized. That is very clear when you compare it with the other major federations," Dion said in a speech at the University of Ottawa in 1998. "And that's a good thing ... At the same time, however, the provinces cannot behave as ten inward-looking republics, and there are broader responsibilities that are the purview of the federal government."[93] Dealing with the intrinsic push–pull tensions of the Canadian dynamic would be his struggle for a later day.

Dion called his essay for the Brookings book "Explaining Quebec Nationalism" and began by examining a world of ethnic tensions. The Soviet Union had collapsed over a weekend in August 1991 and it didn't appear as if other nations, such as Yugoslavia and Ethiopia, would remain intact. He argued the Canada–Quebec conflict was different because Canada was different. "Created in 1867, the Canadian Confederation is not a decaying, totalitarian regime, a new democracy, or an unstable third world country; it is a wealthy modern welfare state." By the latter, he was referring to social services provided to the Canadian population by both layers of government. Canada was a liberal democracy with free speech and voting rights.[94] Repeatedly during the course of his political career, Stéphane Dion would revisit the theme of Canada as beacon. "We need to give the good signal to the world," he would say, the slightly awkward English phrasing becoming a trademark, like the knapsack he would always carry. If Canada couldn't make it, then which country could?

It was obvious that Stéphane Dion understood in his bones Quebec's fear of losing the French language in the English sea of North America, and that he saw that fear as the root cause of political conflict in the province. Writing at another time for a U.S. political review, he expressed it this way: "The history of Quebec is haunted by the fear of Anglicization, obsessed by examples of Louisiana and parts of Canada where the French presence survives only as folklore."[95] In *The Collapse of Canada?* he described a dichotomy in the rising support for sovereignty in his home province. On one hand, nationalism was fuelled by confidence in the economic and cultural rebirth that came with the Quiet Revolution and led to the sense Quebec could go it alone. On the other, it surged because French Quebecers felt rejected by the collapse of the Meech Lake constitutional deal in 1990. The agreement was named for the retreat in the Gatineau Hills where it was negotiated between Brian Mulroney, the Progressive Conservative prime minister, and ten premiers, including Robert Bourassa. For Mulroney, the impetus of the Meech Lake round had been to right the wrong of having a constitutional pact without Quebec, and its recognition of Quebec as a distinct society was critical. Once the accord had been signed in June 1987, the clock began ticking for ratification by the provinces, and when that clock ran down on June 22, 1990, without the required votes, the deal was dead. Dion looked at the poll numbers showing surging nationalist sentiments in Quebec and wrote in his Brookings essay: "I do not think they are strong enough to create the first welfare state collapse in history, but I may be wrong."[96]

THE STORY OF QUEBEC'S EXCLUSION from the Constitution is in itself a dichotomy of conflicting emotion over the same event, an example of the eternal Canadian dilemma of whether to rejoice or mourn. The event was the 1981 constitutional conference hosted for the premiers by Pierre Elliott Trudeau in a grand old railway station in Ottawa that had been transformed into the Government Conference Centre. Trudeau wanted to amend and repatriate the BNA Act from Britain and enshrine it with the Charter of Rights and Freedoms. Talks were deadlocked until, overnight on November 4, 1981, three politicians worked out a deal in the kitchen of the Château Laurier where the premiers were staying, with the exception of René Lévesque, who was across the river in Hull. The politicians were Jean Chrétien, the federal justice minister, and his two provincial counterparts, Roy McMurtry and Roy Romanow, the attorneys general of Ontario and Saskatchewan. It was called *la nuit des longs couteaux* (the night of the long knives) because the next morning, nine premiers and Trudeau signed a deal *sans Québec*. The agreement had been kept secret from a sleeping René Lévesque, who found it beside his place setting at breakfast the next morning. Great care had been taken to keep him out of the loop. He was devastated and felt betrayed. Lévesque had agreed earlier that year to a different pact with the so-called Gang of Eight premiers (minus Ontario and New Brunswick), who had found common cause in trying to stop Trudeau from unilaterally repatriating the Constitution. In a gesture of good faith to find an amending formula to please everyone, Lévesque had given up what he saw as Quebec's birthright of a veto over constitutional change (in exchange for easier terms for opting out, as well as financial compensation for doing so).[97] That agreement was now defunct, but it was more than that. Lévesque saw Quebec losing power over language rights in the new constitutional agreement.

The BNA Act would be brought home from Britain the following year, in 1982, and Canada would at last be a truly independent country after 115 years and would have a Charter of Rights and Freedoms.[98] There was euphoria and immense pride. Nine premiers talked about the "historic" day and how proud they felt to be Canadian. John Buchanan from Nova Scotia quoted *King Lear*.[99] They congratulated one another, and the "kitchen cabinet" re-created the scene for the CBC's Mike Duffy. Meanwhile, Lévesque was isolated. He would die six years later almost to the day. But that morning at the Government Conference Centre, he wore his death mask.

DION APPEARED TO HAVE no illusions about what had been done to Lévesque. His isolation, he wrote in his Brookings chapter, was "to say the least, unfair, and is so perceived ten years later."[100] Dion took pains to explain the rationale behind language legislation in Quebec, beginning with the controversial Bill 101, which Lévesque's Parti Québécois government passed nine months into its mandate in 1977. The PQ government (and not just the PQ) was worried because immigrants were sending their children to English-language schools and Péquistes looked ahead to a dwindling French-speaking population. Bill 101 made it mandatory that "Allophones," or those Quebecers whose first language was neither English nor French, would be educated in French.[101] Dion didn't oppose Bill 101 and agreed with the view that it was "an important factor" in the defeat of the separatist side in the 1980 referendum on sovereignty. The law would be challenged under the provisions of Canada's new Charter of Rights and Freedoms (as Lévesque had foreseen at the constitutional conference in November 1981), and Dion wrote, "Never has a law enacted in Canada been so contested in the courts."[102]

Throughout the chapter he wrote for the Brookings book, Dion showed his understanding of Quebec. He looked closely at the popular wisdom surrounding the Royal Commission on Bilingualism and Biculturalism and the 1969 Official Languages Act, and concluded of the latter: "The achievements are undeniable ... But this federal policy did not make the English-speaking provinces effectively bilingual and it did not stop the assimilation of French-speaking communities outside Quebec. Federal policy did little to change the aspirations of the French-speaking population in Quebec—and Montreal in particular—which are to live daily lives in French and to secure the same French environment for future generations."[103]

Despite court challenges and the backlash over language issues that erupted in Quebec and in other parts of Canada, polls of French Quebecers during the 1980s showed no great desire for another vote on separation. The 1980 referendum had been significant. But the failure of the Meech Lake Accord made French Quebec throw up its hands as if to say, "*Les Anglais* do not want us any more."[104] Dion argued that the minimum for Quebec in any new constitutional deal should be a clause giving its legislature "the duty to protect the French-speaking character of the province."[105] It was, he wrote, "a remarkably modest demand from a francophone political scientist Quebecer ... And I cannot imagine that it would be considered excessive by the rest of the country after a reasonable examination."[106] (With time, he would come to consider it just that—excessive. As leader of the official Opposition in 2007, he looked at federal legislation passed in the 1990s and no longer saw the need for such a provision. Of the opinion in his Brookings essay, he said simply, "I don't agree with myself.")[107]

Peter Russell, the Toronto political scientist who edited a collection of the speeches of Intergovernmental Affairs Minister Dion, considered *The Collapse of Canada?* required reading in order to understand Dion's thinking. "It laid out in specific terms why he thought Quebec nationalists didn't need to separate in order to achieve what they were after.... and it showed he was never going to be disdainful of Quebec nationalism as Trudeau was," said Russell, whose work for the Royal Commission on Bilingualism and Biculturalism was completed when Trudeau was prime minister. "Stéphane was Pierre Trudeau's equal as an intellectual, but [Dion] was the better scholar."[108]

Dion was not able to appreciate his essay through Russell's admiring eyes, even with the passage of time. He was hard on himself. "It's always the case, I'm never satisfied and I am always thinking I have to improve myself," he said.[109] But he did recognize one aspect of that particular work: "Of all the things I wrote that were much better than that, it has been quoted everywhere and afterwards it would never stop."

STÉPHANE DION HAD BEEN like a visiting scholar in his own country, but no longer. He returned to the University of Montreal for the fall term in 1991 and began to develop a public profile as an analyst on the Quebec–Canada question. He turned thirty-six at the end of September that year and would soon be a prolific contributor to newspaper opinion pages and a regular commentator on respected television public affairs programs such as *Le Point* on Radio-Canada. The country was caught up in yet another tangle of constitutional talks, this time leading to the Charlottetown Accord, which was signed in the Prince Edward Island capital and rejected by Canadians in a national referendum in October 1992. It, too, recognized Quebec as a distinct society. (No wonder Thomas Mann at the Brookings had commented he didn't understand what was happening in Canada. Keeping track of constitutional innings over that period required diligence—and a scorecard.) Dion would vote in favour of Charlottetown, although he didn't agree with holding the vote in the first place: "I thought it would be interpreted as mutual rejection, which it was. It was like playing Russian roulette with the future of the country."[110]

There was an increasingly bitter mood as the 1990s ticked by in Quebec, and, in a new development, provincial Liberals appeared to be moving towards the same support for a referendum on independence as the Péquistes. In 1991, Bourassa's Liberal government endorsed the recommendation of the Bélanger-Campeau Commission on Quebec's political future, which called for a referendum the following year.[111] That vote ended up being rolled (roughly speaking) into the Charlottetown referendum and was defeated. But another referendum was coming; everybody could feel its looming presence just over the horizon. The Quebec Liberal government also approved the recommendations of another study in 1991 by the Allaire Committee, which said Quebec needed a massive transfer of powers from Ottawa. Though Bourassa would later distance himself from Allaire, it gave Quebecers another reason to resent Ottawa. Into these roiling waters dove Stéphane Dion, headfirst and almost always on the opposite side of conventional wisdom.

It began for Dion in February 1992 with a speech at York University's Glendon College in Toronto. He took on the two biggest shibboleths of the Parti Québécois: that Quebec needed massive new powers from Ottawa (upon which Péquistes and Liberals appeared to be in agreement) and that Quebecers were paying for a duplication of services and, thus, would be better off on their own as an independent country. *Un gouvernement de trop,* as the PQ claimed. One government too many. That speech put Stéphane Dion on the map. It would be excerpted in the mass-market daily *La Presse* and in *Le Devoir,* the slim little paper that considered itself the opinion leader. Dion said Quebecers weren't preoccupied with gaining more powers. What they cared about was being rejected as a distinct society by English Canada, while English Canadians fumed because they thought Quebecers wanted special treatment from Ottawa. "That's how two populations rose up against each other, because of judicial abstractions strongly charged with symbolism."[112]

Dion insisted that the federal and provincial governments were not providing the same services. "The myth at the time was if you have a deficit of $30 billion at the federal level, it's because governments are duplicating themselves ... And that was at the core of my expertise." He kept hammering away at the subject, surprised at first that people didn't accept his research and thank him. "We should not think the grass is greener on the other side or believe in Santa Claus when it comes to public finances," he wrote two weeks before the Charlottetown referendum in 1992. "To save billions, one must severely cut services to the population. And if we choose independence we must know that we can't finance it by eliminating duplication because there are few savings to be made in that fashion."[113]

Dion didn't make a dent; the common wisdom prevailed. In a debate during the election campaign of 1994, PQ leader Jacques Parizeau accused Liberal premier Daniel Johnson of hiding the true costs of duplication. There were secret reports, he said, and he would release them once he was in power. "But there were no studies—you see how far myths go, eh?—and when [Parizeau] came to power he discovered nothing and he released nothing," Dion said scornfully in 2007. He would remain frustrated all those years later that his scientific research in his area of expertise had been insufficient to change people's minds. Dion argued that duplication was a myth the same way he would say there was no "fiscal imbalance" between Quebec and Ottawa more than a decade later when he was Liberal leader. At that time, he thought that pointing to the example of a budget surplus in Ottawa as "fiscal imbalance" was ludicrous. He would deny the existence of such an imbalance even as others clamoured to fix the supposedly historic problem of Quebec being shortchanged by Ottawa.

It didn't take long for Stéphane Dion to be perceived as *the* federalist champion in Quebec. "The media were looking for a French-speaking intellectual defending the Canadian cause," he said looking back. He rarely appeared on television alone. "You may be perceived as neutral if you are a separatist. They will invite you as a 'neutral' commentator. But if you are a federalist, you need to have a match. You need to have a separatist intellectual with you." He became a fixture on *Le Point* during the referendum campaign of

1995, often paired with Laval political scientist Guy Laforest. Behind the scenes at Radio-Canada, technicians referred to them as Pixie and Dixie, after the cartoon mice in *Huckleberry Hound*.[114] Dion felt overwhelmed, trying to work on his own research in public administration while ready to leap into the Quebec–Canada fray. "So it was a double life. It was crazy." During the referendum campaign of 1995, he would take breaks from teaching a class to check his voice mail and find fifteen or twenty messages waiting for him, often from around the world, all wanting comment on Quebec.

His predicament sounded familiar. What was it he had said about his father? That Léon hadn't been able to fulfill his dream for his own career? That it had been "too demanding to play the role of Léon Dion?" And, in another era, there was his son increasingly distracted from his research by the same Quebec–Canada struggle that had occupied his father. Léon had struggled to be the moderate, the political scientist who supported federalism but believed in the nationalist argument of special status for Quebec. As Stéphane morphed into federalist hero, Léon appeared increasingly frustrated with English Canada. Before Christmas of 1990, Léon Dion presented a brief to the Bélanger-Campeau hearings in Quebec City. He advised caution before holding another referendum. The stakes were high. "Reason must prevail over passion," Léon warned. "One must take the time to reflect. Don't act out of exasperation ... If we lose this referendum, then where will we find ourselves?"[115] Léon urged that English Canada be given one last and absolutely final chance to accept Quebec as a "distinct society." If it failed, Quebec must be prepared to separate. In his brief to the commission, he offered the bleak opinion that "Canada will not give way unless there's a knife to its throat, and even that is not assured."[116]

They were fateful words. "He was sorry [for having said it]," said his son. "I told him he made a mistake." Stéphane Dion thought it was unfortunate that the line would become, for many, his father's

legacy when he did "so much for political science and for the relationship between the two solitudes. It was sad." Léon would describe
himself as a "tired federalist" after the Bélanger-Campeau hearings.
Soon, Stéphane would be spoofed as the "tiresome" federalist. In
reality, his father never wavered, Stéphane later insisted. Léon "always
believed in Canada. He never changed his mind about Canada."[117]

OCCASIONALLY THERE WAS praise for the tough positions of
Stéphane Dion. "How refreshing it is to hear a speech that breaks
away from what almost all of Quebec's political class is parroting on
the subject of sharing powers," said *La Presse* editorial writer Marcel
Adam, taking his own gutsy stand. He lauded Dion for his courage
and for having exposed the ways in which the "Quebec nationalist
intelligentsia behave like mindless sheep."[118] And Lysiane Gagnon,
who delivered astute analysis in both *La Presse* and *The Globe and
Mail*, shared Dion's view on the transfer-of-powers issue. She argued
it was a well-kept secret that no federal politician would admit (for
fear of backlash from the West) that Quebec already had more than
its fair share of powers in most areas named by the Allaire report.
Gagnon cited Dion's assertion that debate on the issue showed little
understanding of the actual services being offered to Quebecers,
exclaiming, "How true!"[119]

Mostly though, they told him he was wrong. The duplication argument was particularly galling. There were studies, didn't he know?
There was a *consensus*. "So it was the first time in my life, but not the
last time, I was against the consensus," he would recall. "Nobody else
was making the argument so I convinced myself that if I didn't speak
out, nobody will, for whatever reason. It was so obviously wrong." He
continued to argue from a scientist's point of view. "You cannot
separate the country for something like [the duplication argument].
It was not 'I love Canada,' and so on, eh? It was only an argument, a
scientific argument against something that I found completely wrong."

He was his father's son, yes, but his entry into public discourse also showed how much he was Michel Crozier's protégé. The French sociologist believed above all in individualism and the power of individuals to effect change. His intellectual core ran counter to the Marxist theory that human beings were swept along helplessly by large historical trends. That school of thought argued that when an immensely powerful human being did emerge, a Napoleon Bonaparte for example, he was a product of the mass psyche fulfilling its own need.[120] In contrast, belief in individualism was a current running through Dion's intellectual development, said Denis Saint-Martin. "Stéphane believes that we decide. Humans shape their own history. Neither our ethnic or social origins nor our history determine who we are."[121] That foundation shaped his view towards the independence of Quebec. "It's not just political, it's philosophical ... he's against its reasoning." Dion rejected the theory held by nationalist-minded intellectuals during the last forty years: that every people has a right to its own state and that there has been a movement pushing Quebec inexorably towards independence since the 1837 rebellion of the *patriotes* against British colonial power.

Dion certainly didn't need the exposure of the media. "Not at all," said Saint-Martin. "There are people we always see on the CBC, on Radio-Canada, with a little title that says 'university professor,' but when we look at their C.V., there's nothing there. They haven't written a book, never written an article ... whereas Stéphane began to appear in the media because he felt he had a duty to do it, the intellectual's duty ... and obviously it made him a lot of enemies."[122]

By the mid-1990s, Dion had grown into a recognized public intellectual in Quebec, a role more highly prized in French Canada than in its English counterpart. In French society, as in other Latin cultures, it is perfectly acceptable to talk about being an intellectual or to reflect on the lifestyle of the intellectual in a way that, in an English milieu, might sound pretentious. In a video clip for his leadership campaign website in 2006, Dion talked with nostalgia about living in Paris. He had slipped easily into the ritual of reading the influential newspaper *Le Monde* every day, knowing that everyone else would be reading it too. Undoubtedly over the course of the day, an article would come up in conversation and people would have thought about it and would have an opinion. "There's not really an equivalent here [to] the very, very deep intellectual life one can have in Paris," he said. When he was preparing to leave Paris, friends asked how he would survive without his *Le Monde* in the morning.[123] It's true that filmmakers like Luis Buñuel (a Spaniard after all) spoofed the intellectual elites of Paris, making them seem most pretentious and snotty indeed.[124] But Stéphane Dion didn't seem that way in the video clip, not with his body language of little shrugs and birdie-bobs. And he didn't act like a snob. (He defined an intellectual as "somebody who is good with ideas," and the only person he referred to as an intellectual during a discussion on the topic was François Goulet, his good friend and fishing partner. Their families got together at the Dion cottage in the Laurentians over Christmas 2006. Goulet also was his government chauffeur for many years.)[125]

BY 1995, THE YEAR of Quebec's second referendum on independence, Stéphane Dion was taking a serious pounding for his political analysis. The Yes forces had failed in 1980, and this time Premier Jacques Parizeau and the Parti Québécois government thought they could win. Dion kicked off his tough year in January by chiding the provincial Liberals at their General Council meeting in Quebec City. "Your party committed a terrible error by seeming to ally with the Parti Québécois following the failure of Meech Lake," he said, referring to the Allaire report and its push for more powers for Quebec. "You wanted to accompany Quebecers in the growth of their nationalist fever but, in so doing, you drove many into the arms of the enemy— in other words, you fuelled a fire you don't know how to control."

Liberal leader Daniel Johnson, a former premier, the son of a premier, the brother of a premier, didn't bother to hide his pique: "From his university position, Mr. Dion didn't have to trouble himself with the circumstances and imperatives of the Liberal party during that time."[126]

Writer Michel David was acidic in a column in Dion's hometown paper *Le Soleil.* Under the headline "The Impertinent One," he mocked father and son. While he characterized Léon Dion as being possessed by that "deep old ambivalence that has characterized our collective history," he found "no trace of ambivalence in the son." Stéphane Dion was "becoming at all costs the intellectual darling of the federalists." He said people were "sickened by Mr. Dion's arrogance." Had he even been invited? No matter. He wouldn't be again.[127] In *Le Devoir,* Pierre Graveline was mordant. "The spiritual son of Pierre Trudeau is born," he announced, mining the deepest nerve he could find. Trudeau was loved and *hated* in Quebec depending on where people stood on independence. Wrote Graveline: "The new guru feels forced to come down from his ivory tower to teach a lesson to his poor population of dunces who decidedly don't want to understand anything."[128]

It was rough enough in January, but it would get rougher as the months passed in 1995. After Dion won the leadership of the Liberal party more than a decade later, the political cognoscenti would talk about how it would be so difficult for him in Quebec—as if it were a new thing. But it was hard to imagine how anything could have been more stressful than 1995, when so much was at stake for Quebecers on both sides. "You have no idea what it was like in Quebec" during the 1995 referendum, Liberal organizer Yves Picard commented on an August day during the leadership race. He was sitting in a restaurant in the capital's Old City, not far from the stone ramparts and the Plains of Abraham, the site of a battle that was far from over in Quebec. "In those days," he said, "it took real guts."[129]

The worst for Dion came in March of 1995. "Awful," he would say later. A date for a referendum still hadn't been set, but potential separation scenarios were being devised by think tanks and seminars, just as Canadian political scientist Keith Banting had worked out the restructuring of North America for his chapter in *The Collapse of Canada?* (Fifteen years after its publication at the Brookings Institution, Banting still believed that Canada would not be well positioned if Quebec decided to separate, adding the observation that Canada was "no closer to having sorted out how it would govern itself.")[130] Admittedly, separation issues were sticky. What would happen to Quebec's share of the federal debt? Could Quebec continue to use the Canadian dollar? Would there be an economic downturn in an independent Quebec? What would the Canadian government do?

Stéphane Dion attended one such seminar on separation sponsored by the C.D. Howe Institute in Toronto in March 1995 and ended up being denounced by Jacques Parizeau and a goodly portion of the Yes forces of Quebec. The controversy erupted over a comment at the seminar by Stanley Hartt and supported by Stéphane Dion. Hartt, an English Quebecer and former adviser to Brian Mulroney, apparently had urged English Canada to "make Quebec suffer" if the Yes side won. *Faire souffrir.* Parizeau was in high dudgeon. From Quebec City, he called the remarks "odious" and "appalling" and was astonished that Quebecers would go to Toronto to betray their own. (Michel Bélanger, chair of the Quebec No forces was also supposed to have agreed with Hartt.) It was theatre at its most absurd. Dion took the brunt of the attack. He was accused of being the shady mastermind behind a plot to engineer hardship for his own people. Except that's not what was said, at least not in that context.[131] And certainly Dion wasn't the original speaker. Hartt, who was, wrote an op-ed article for *The Gazette* in Montreal stressing that he had merely been trying to point out that the more things went badly in Quebec post-separation, the more support for independence would fail. Not *make* them suffer. "Let us get one thing straight: Dion does not have the power to create a recession in Quebec; not even the C.D. Howe Institute can do that."[132]

Stéphane Dion didn't know what had hit him. He was scrambling to explain what he *had* said at the seminar. "I said that if after a Yes victory, economic difficulties hit Quebec, support for sovereignty could fall below fifty percent," he insisted to the Presse Canadienne. "But I never proposed provoking economic difficulties."[133] He would remain in a state of semi-shock years later, unable to get over feeling thoroughly pummelled for a sentiment he hadn't expressed. He was treated like a traitor. "It was a storm against me. The office of Parizeau was against me. The journalists were after me. And it was not me. I didn't say it. This storm was the first crisis of this magnitude and it was the worst one because we were alone," he recalled in December 2006.

By then, he was Liberal leader and had twice been in the federal cabinet, with all the staffing and logistical support provided to ministers that made it easier to cope. During the passage of contentious federal legislation on the rules of secession in 2000, Dion had required protection from the Royal Canadian Mounted Police. But even that was not as difficult to handle as the C.D. Howe brouhaha of 1995. "When you are a minister, there are people helping out. A professor is alone. People were almost attacking me [physically]. And I had no support, no psychological help … I repeated and repeated and repeated *it's not me* … I found that awful, awful …" The outcry in March 1995 was made worse by the fact that, a couple of weeks earlier, Radio-Canada had reported that Dion, the champion of federalism, was doing research work for the federal No forces, having signed several contracts worth about $14,000. His critics argued that he had a conflict of interest, but Dion pointed out that nobody objected when separatist academics routinely accepted contract work from the PQ government in Quebec City.[134]

The date for the Quebec referendum was finally set for October 30, 1995. The Parizeau government released the ballot question in August: "Do you agree that Quebec should become sovereign after having made a formal offer to Canada for a new economic and political partnership within the scope of the bill respecting the future of Quebec and the agreement signed on June 12, 1995?" The No forces immediately criticized the question as complicated and confusing, among them Stéphane Dion, who stepped up his output of newspaper columns against separation. After criticizing the question in *La Presse,* he wrote: "It must be said to these sovereignist leaders by looking them in the eyes, that if they feel diminished in Canada, it's their problem, but the majority of Quebecers are proud of their belonging to Quebec and Canada."[135]

The June 12 reference was a reference to Bill 1, a tripartite agreement on the mechanics of separation signed on that date in Quebec City by the three leading advocates of independence, Quebec premier Parizeau; Mario Dumont, leader of Action démocratique du Québec (ADQ); and the new boy on the separatist block, Lucien Bouchard. It bound Quebec to trying to negotiate an economic and political partnership—in other words, sovereignty-association—with Canada after a Yes vote, but stipulated that Quebec would separate unilaterally if no such deal had been struck in a year.

If Dion was the darling of the federalists, Lucien Bouchard was his far more magnetic separatist counterpart, and animosity would soon deepen between them. Bouchard had been a close friend, Laval University law classmate, and political colleague of Brian Mulroney, who, as prime minister, had chosen him for the choice diplomatic post of ambassador to France in 1985. After Bouchard was elected to federal politics in 1988, Mulroney brought him into his cabinet and was devastated two years later when Bouchard abruptly quit and went on to become leader of a new federal party dedicated to the separation of Quebec. The Bloc Québécois emerged as a force to be reckoned with in the battle for an independent Quebec, winning fifty-four of seventy-five Quebec seats in the 1993 federal election. Bouchard appeared to have inherited the mantle of René Lévesque.

Bouchard had a charisma that Parizeau lacked and, in late 1994, a bizarre twist of fate added to his mystique. He lost a leg to necrotizing fasciitis, the flesh-eating disease, and went into the referendum campaign with a cane and a stoicism that won him support and, in 1996, helped make him premier. In the face of the strong separatist alliance and an energetic and well-organized push in the last three weeks of the campaign, the federalist forces were faltering. As the day of the vote grew closer, the polls showed the Yes side steadily gaining strength.

In mid-October, Dion and colleague François Vaillancourt, a University of Montreal economics professor, took an unconventional approach to the coming referendum. With opposing views on independence, they decided to write an article together. Vaillancourt, like Dion, was an out-of-the-box thinker who didn't back away from controversy. A separatist who'd cheered for the PQ on election night in 1976, he'd nevertheless offered up interesting commentary appealing to federalists over the years. In 1982, he addressed the founding meeting in Montreal of the English rights group Alliance Quebec with a speech about how bilingual Anglophones played a critical bridging role for francophone society with the rest of North America. "If you don't have [bilingual Anglophones], you'll be isolated."[136] Vaillancourt believed an independent Quebec would take an economic hit, at least in the short term and, one day in early October 1995, talked about his opinions over lunch with Dion and other professors in the university cafeteria. "That's very interesting. We should do something together," he remembered Dion telling him. "We talked, we went to Stéphane's office, and, in a few hours, we had the outline of what we were going to say."

The joint article appeared in *La Presse,* the separatist and the federalist elucidating twelve points on which both the Yes and No sides could agree. "I was interested in doing it because I thought the worst thing would be to vote for sovereignty without understanding what could happen," said Vaillancourt. "It was very dishonest in my opinion to promise that the gates of paradise would open to Quebec with sovereignty." They described shared principles, including that Quebec has greater autonomy than any other province in key areas, that Quebec would always remain a minority within Canada, and that "Quebec sovereignty is, and will remain, a legitimate goal." It was not based, they wrote, on xenophobia but on "democratic and liberal values." They listed the consequences of a Yes vote, among them short-term economic disruption, an increase in the Quebec debt, an exodus of 250,000 people, the loss of the Canadian dollar as currency, and the consolidation of the French language in Quebec.[137] Both found the experience rewarding. Vaillancourt considered Dion "very rigorous," and the two would remain in touch. Dion would often telephone Vaillancourt seeking economic advice, including during the 2006 Liberal leadership campaign. "I'm not much of a flag waver," said Vaillancourt. "I'm more a right-wing separatist," and he laughed. "Better make that a market-economy separatist."

But such a collaborative spirit, praised by people on both sides of the independence divide, offered only a brief peaceful interlude in a very acrimonious struggle. On October 30, 1995, the country stood still to watch the nail-biting battle on referendum night. For most of the evening, it was unclear who would win, and, in the end, there were only 54,288 votes separating winner and loser. The No side won. The final vote was 50.58 percent against separation and 49.42 percent in favour. It couldn't have been more suspenseful it if had been written by Hollywood scriptwriters. Parizeau angrily denounced "money and the ethnic vote," blaming Anglophones and Allophones on Montreal Island and in the Eastern Townships for stealing victory from the

Yes forces. Parizeau was intensely criticized for his comment and would resign the next year, to be replaced by Lucien Bouchard.

There would be no great joy on the federalist side either. The vote had been too close. It had merely served to show how they had stood on the brink of losing. Dion would say a Yes win would not have brought independence but confusion. The question itself was ambiguous, and he was dismayed by polls in the final days showing a majority of Quebecers believed that separation wouldn't mean a loss of their Canadian passports or the Canadian dollar. It was no wonder people felt that way; it was what Bill 1 had led them to believe would happen. The document signed by the three separatist leaders in Quebec City had been reassuring to Quebecers considering a Yes vote, assuring them that unemployment insurance cheques and child tax credits (which came under federal jurisdiction) would continue to arrive. Moreover, Bill 1 talked about changes to international agreements involving Canada, such as the North American Free Trade Agreement (NAFTA), as if they would be a small and insignificant matter. "It was very scary. It didn't feel like victory," said Geoffroi Montpetit, who would begin working for Dion in Ottawa the following year. "I remember a friend in Montreal telling me he had voted Yes just to signal he wanted more power for Quebec. He didn't know what was at stake."[138] Montpetit was special assistant to Foreign Affairs Minister André Ouellet in 1995 and said, "A lot of people from embassies were calling to ask in bewilderment, 'What the hell are you guys doing?'" Dion hated the "soft" nationalist approach that characterized the No side, the idea that it would make things worse to challenge separatist assumptions or to point out that a vote for independence would have serious consequences. To many federalists, the timidity of the No side in Quebec was exemplified by Premier Daniel Johnson, who was loath even to allow the word "Canada" to pass his lips. He referred most often to an "economic union." He had gotten into that habit during the 1994 election campaign, which he lost to the Parti Québécois. When Jacques Parizeau had insisted during a leaders' debate in 1994 that Quebec could save $3 billion by eliminating the duplication of services, Johnson had shot back: "Are you willing to replace all the benefits of economic union with the creations of the PQ?"[139] Yes, indeed, on the hangover morning after Quebec's second referendum on separation in fifteen years, there was angst and finger-pointing on the federalist side and, in Ottawa, a vow by Prime Minister Jean Chrétien that he would not allow such a vote to occur on his watch again.

CHAPTER FIVE

A WALK IN THE SNOW

S TÉPHANE DION had a decision to make in December 1995 and not much time to make it; in fact, he had until the Feast of the Epiphany on the sixth of January, the day that celebrates the story of the three kings who followed the Star of Bethlehem to the Christ child. It had always been a lucky day for Dion. More often than not, he got the little king figurine in his slice of the traditional *galette des rois* (kings' cake) during family festivities on that day.[140] But the January deadline in 1996 held no particular holiday significance. It simply fell on the first Friday of the new year and was the agreed upon day for Dion to make up his mind about an intriguing offer from Jean Chrétien. That weekend, the prime minister was leaving Canada on a two-week trade mission to China and Pakistan and he needed an answer.

On November 25, Chrétien had asked Dion to join his cabinet and play an important role in the unity battle. The decision was a big one for Dion. His reaction had first been negative and then positive, while his wife, Janine Krieber, had changed her mind in the opposite direction. At Christmas that year, Dion went home to see his family and talk privately to Léon Dion. Father and son went for a walk in the snowy streets of Sillery. They chatted as they walked, Léon's short legs working to match his son's long strides. Stéphane asked his dad what he thought: should he accept Chrétien's offer?[141]

"No, no, no," replied Léon. "You are making a mistake! You're forty years old. Your career is very, very promising. It's likely you will have tenure [at the University of Montreal]." Besides, he continued, "If you go into politics at forty, forget it! For the rest of your life you will be an academic for the politicians and a politician for the academics." It was a blunt warning and Stéphane would mull over it on another winter's night eleven years later. On the Thursday before Christmas 2006, he would find himself on an airplane flying from Winnipeg back to his Ottawa home. It was almost midnight and he wouldn't see his bed before at least two in the morning. He had become the Liberal leader in December 2006 and would have to give up much of the coming holiday week to his work. "He was right," he said of Léon's prediction. "That's what happened to me."

CHRÉTIEN'S INVITATION had come out of the blue. On the morning of November 25, Dion was at the home of friends in Ottawa, having come to the capital by bus from Montreal in order to give a speech at Carleton University. The referendum on independence had occurred just a month earlier and was raw in everyone's mind—on both sides. The No forces had won by the slimmest of margins, and the topic of Dion's talk was how the federalist forces had blown the referendum campaign. They had been too timid. He was preparing the speech, which was for that afternoon, when Janine called from their Montreal apartment to say she'd just received a phone call. The woman on the line had told her, "*Le premier ministre* wants to talk to Professor Dion."

"Which *premier ministre?*" Janine asked, since in French it means both premier and prime minister.

"*Monsieur Chrétien, cette affaire.*" It concerned Chrétien.

Dion thought it was a student prank. It was easy to imitate Chrétien, and, as he dialled the number, he was doubtful about who would answer. But he got through to the PMO switchboard quickly and realized it was no joke. Within seconds, the raspy voice of Jean Chrétien was on the line. "Where are you?" he asked Dion, and, when he said he was in Ottawa, Chrétien wanted to know why. Dion told him about his speech and that he planned to criticize Chrétien himself. "Well, come to see me," said Chrétien. "Come to Sussex. You can explain that to me."

It was Aline Chrétien, whose opinion was much respected by her husband, who had drawn his attention to Stéphane Dion. She'd often watched the Montreal political scientist defend the federalist cause on Radio-Canada's *Le Point*, and, the night before when he'd been on again, she beckoned to her husband to "come and see this guy." Chrétien was impressed and asked his wife if she thought he should meet with Dion. "That would be a very good idea, Jean," said Aline Chrétien. Wheels were set in motion, and the very next morning Stéphane Dion received his phone call.[142]

Dion had spent most of the 1990s as the federalist champion but still had to ask his friends how to find 24 Sussex Drive. They told him the city's most famous residence was not far away and that he could walk over in twenty minutes. When he arrived, Chrétien was ready and asked first to see a copy of the talk he would give that afternoon. Dion would remember that, after reading it, Chrétien wanted to know one thing only: "Do you think it's possible to make sure another referendum won't happen?" Dion didn't think that it was. But he did think that Chrétien could say he wouldn't accept the results of any provincial referendum in Canada unless the question was clear. In his opinion, the Quebec referendum had fallen far short of that prerequisite.

As Chrétien and Dion chatted, Aline Chrétien stuck her head in to ask, "How's it going?"

"I'm trying, I'm trying," said Chrétien.[143]

Chrétien asked Dion to stay for lunch and, over their meal, invited him to come to Ottawa. Dion would never forget how Chrétien put it: "I would be very honoured if you would accept to sit at my cabinet table."

Dion demurred. Politics wasn't what he wanted in life and not what his wife wanted. He talked about how important academia was to him, telling Chrétien he would be more influential in that role than as a politician. "I was very surprised he did not kick me right out of there, right then," Dion would recall. "It was so arrogant to say that, so pretentious. I don't know, but it was the way I felt at the time. I had been trained by my father to think there was nothing more important than to be a university professor ... I was convinced of that."

But Chrétien insisted otherwise. "It's a good life," he said. "Politicians can make a difference ... You can help me with the unity of the country. You have some very strong ideas."

When Dion recounted the story of that meeting a decade later, it sounded sentimental, corny even, to believe the two men had talked that way about Canada, about *saving* the country. "No, it was really about that," said Dion. "The key point was that the prime minister of my country was asking me to be part of his cabinet table when, in fact, I was not even a member of the party, with no experience at all in politics and he had never met me before—maybe once when we were interviewed at the same time and we shook hands, but we had never had a conversation."

In his effort to win Dion over, Chrétien told him it wasn't his style to ask people to join his cabinet like that. If somebody was interested in the role, he'd always been clear with them: "You want to run for me, I will not tell you that you will be at the cabinet table." Nevertheless, Dion wasn't swayed. As they sat looking out over the Ottawa River from the official residence, he told Chrétien he had a friend, Pierre Pettigrew, who wanted to be in politics and was the perfect person for Chrétien. Pettigrew had been a foreign policy adviser to Pierre Trudeau and a candidate for the federal Liberals in an election (albeit unsuccessfully) before becoming an international trade consultant. "Maybe, maybe," he remembered Chrétien saying. "But I'm talking to *you* now!"

Dion knew he could not simply turn down his prime minister and saunter out the front door. "Okay, I will take the time to think about this," he said. Chrétien was pleased. They shook hands, and Chrétien's parting words were, "I hope you will accept."

Back in Montreal, Janine thought her husband was telling her an early April Fool's joke. "You have never been involved in politics whatsoever," she remarked in astonishment. "Why would he ask you to accept?" But she liked the idea. She reminded him of all the risks they had taken: how they had gone to Paris together for their PhDs without knowing each other very well and without much money; how they had gone to Washington, again almost broke, when Janine preferred to remain in Montreal; how they had adopted a child without any experience as parents. They had survived all those things and they were solid. "We took risks," she told him. "Why don't we take an additional risk? We are that kind of people. We are not afraid to take risks."

In early December, Dion left for Belgium, Spain, and Germany, where he was scheduled to give a series of speeches on Canadian unity. "I met with friends of mine in Spain who believed it was good to be Catalan and Spaniard and European at the same time, and in Germany, I saw the same mentality of *one people*," he said. "I changed my mind. I began to think that [unity] was not an issue only for Canadians but an issue for the world ... We have a duty to show that it's possible to build strong states, strong countries, with people of different languages." The transition marked his third evolution. He'd gone from separatist to federalist and from political observer to activist academic. As 1995 was drawing to a close, he was ready to enter politics. "I changed my mind," he told his wife. "I think you're right, Janine. I think we should go to Ottawa."

Meanwhile, she'd changed her mind. "I don't think we should go because the separatists are so pissed off they have lost the referendum," she told him. "They are awful, they are mean ... If you run, they will be after us. Our life will be a nightmare." He remembered the discussion and her concerns about their daughter, Jeanne. They'd already been through a rough referendum year in Quebec. But she said she would support him. He needed to talk with his father. What's more, he told her he would only be going to Ottawa for a short time.

As they walked in the snow at the end of December, Léon was still insistent that he should decline. Stéphane knew very well that Léon had said no to many politicians himself over the years. But he reminded his father how different they were and how different Janine Krieber was from Denyse Dion. Janine would accept whatever decision he made, while his mother had not wanted his father to get involved in politics.

"*Écoutez,* let's not exaggerate," Denyse would exclaim in 2006 when it was suggested she had kept her husband out of party politics. She laughed the big boisterous laugh that punctuated her conversation. "If he had wanted to do it, he would have." She said he had used his wife as an excuse for things he didn't want to do, saying how sorry he was. "Léon was not made for politics," Denyse explained. "When Stéphane went into politics I asked him a question, 'What are you going to do when you are going to vote white and all the others are going to vote black?' And he said, 'I will do everything I can to convert them to white.' I asked, 'And if that doesn't happen, what will you do?' And he said, 'I will wait and see.' And I said, 'Go into politics.' Because the same question to Léon, he would have said, 'I will resign!' You see the difference?" A traditional politician, she said, works to change hearts and minds. "With Léon, it was 'This is what I think, if you don't agree, *bonsoir.*'"

It was tough trying to convince someone with such strong convictions to understand his perspective, but that was exactly Stéphane's intent during the long walk in the snow with his father. An hour earlier, they'd been sitting in the house on Liégeois Boulevard and Léon had been praising an academic paper that Stéphane had just completed. And suddenly he saw his son's career in academia going up in smoke. Léon kept shaking his head. But Stéphane persisted until he finally found the argument to make his father come around to say he would help and support him. "Look, in other circumstances, I would say you are right," said Stéphane. But when Léon was asked to go into politics, circumstances in Canada had been normal. "I have been invited to enter politics when the country is at risk and, wrongly or not, the prime minister thinks that I'm the one … And you know what, Dad? I think I'm the one too. If I don't do it, then nobody else will."

CHAPTER SIX

THE MINISTER OF UNITY

T HERE HAVE BEEN many theories about why Queen Victoria chose Ottawa as the capital of Canada in 1857, but none has ever hinted that it was a joke on obstreperous colonialists who couldn't decide among themselves whether they preferred Kingston, Quebec City, Toronto, or Montreal. The young queen considered the town's location on the Ontario–Quebec border and was much taken with scenic renditions of the landscape.[144] Whether she knew how cold Ottawa could get in the winter was not recorded, nor whether she had a giggle at the thought of her royal subjects shivering at its inauguration on the last day of December 1857. Ottawa can be a deep freeze. The wind whips down O'Connor and Metcalfe streets from Parliament Hill and makes walking a challenge in winter, especially when it gets dark at 4:30 in the afternoon. It was into the path of these wintry winds that Stéphane Dion arrived in January 1996 as the new minister of intergovernmental affairs, setting up shop on the eighth floor of the federal building at 66 Slater Street near the corner of Metcalfe.

The job title defines the workload: Dion was the intergovernmental conduit for the prime minister with the premiers, and the premiers with the prime minister. But his real mission for Prime Minister Jean Chrétien was to establish a plan for dealing with a future Quebec referendum that would put Ottawa ahead of the curve with the Parti

Québécois government, instead of scrambling to play catch-up as it had the last time. The so-called soft nationalist approach to Quebec hadn't worked, and Chrétien was ready for the ideas of the tough Quebec political scientist who challenged separatist arguments and wasn't afraid to puncture myths about the Canadian federation, no matter the personal cost.

Dion wasn't afraid to tell people they were wrong, and frequently did so. The new minister was expected to play hardball on the unity issue: to talk openly about the potential consequences of separation for Quebec and to come to grips with a plan for dealing with secession. Dion and Chrétien had discussed the need for clear rules for separation at their first meeting at 24 Sussex Drive two months earlier. And from his first days as intergovernmental affairs minister, Dion talked about the issue that drove a stake into separatist hearts: partition. "You can't consider Canada divisible but the territory of Quebec sacred," Dion told the Canadian Press shortly after his swearing-in.[145] Over the next few years in Ottawa, Dion would fight for a course of action that carried enormous risk and would ultimately set a precedent in Canada and internationally. He had come a long way from the diffident professor of the 1980s who hesitated to speak about partisan politics. Dion spent long hours travelling, even longer hours in his office, often working through the night, and he would be praised, vilified, and, above all, misunderstood. It would be a wild ride.

Chrétien shuffled his cabinet on January 26, 1996. Ottawa is a company town and had been abuzz with rumours of an impending shuffle for a couple of weeks that January while Chrétien was out of the country. The prime minister returned to appoint Stéphane Dion to Marcel Massé's former position at Intergovernmental Affairs and to move Massé over to the Treasury Board. Chrétien had great faith in Massé's judgement, and the Montreal native was both political minister for Quebec and chair of an ad hoc cabinet committee on national unity. Chrétien further ramped up the Quebec team by bringing in

Dion's friend Pierre Pettigrew as minister of international cooperation and minister for La Francophonie, the international organization of French-speaking nations. Dion and Pettigrew were dubbed *"les deux colombes"* (the two doves) by the Quebec media, a reference to *"les trois colombes"* who had flown to Ottawa from Quebec in an earlier era— Pierre Trudeau, Jean Marchand, and Gérard Pelletier.[146]

Dion was virtually unknown outside Quebec, other than in the political science circles he cultivated. The swearing-in ceremony at Rideau Hall was emotional for him and for his proud father, Léon Dion. Stéphane had invited Léon to come from Quebec City but didn't want his mother, Denyse, or his wife, Janine Krieber, at Rideau Hall. "Janine told me afterwards she was a bit offended by that, but I didn't want to make it a family thing. I thought it was only me," Dion explained. His staffers would have to push him to make himself and his family available for the requisite media profiles after he became Liberal leader in 2006. "I wanted to protect my family at the very beginning. It's the way I am. I don't want to mix my private life with my public life. You have a beautiful word in English and it's 'privacy.' We don't have the equivalent in French, but it's more than private life—I believe in privacy."[147]

With his appointment in January 1996, Dion embarked on a pivotal job and a pivotal relationship. Dion and Chrétien would become very close. Long-time Chrétien aide Eddie Goldenberg described his former boss's bond with Dion as "almost one of father and son."[148] Dion said his time with Jean Chrétien was "a good school of politics." And Chrétien would agree. "You know, maybe I was to [Dion] what Mitchell Sharp was to me," said Chrétien, speaking of the Liberal minister who had been his mentor in the 1960s.[149]

There has never been a better description of Jean Chrétien than the line by political guru Dalton Camp that he looked "like the driver of the getaway car." Chrétien liked to play the rube, with all his verbal tics and shrugs and his stock image of *"le p'tit gars de Shawinigan,"* the little guy from small-town Quebec. But he was a tough and canny political player, not to be underestimated. He liked his cabinet meetings brief and to the point, he expected staffers to boil their briefing notes down to one-page memos, and he didn't like to watch television or read newspapers. But he read biographies and history and was happy discussing comparative politics with Stéphane Dion. "I would not be in politics without him," said Dion. "I've had many arguments with him—and many times *he* was right and I was wrong."[150] Chrétien understood what he gave to Stéphane Dion. "He was a political scientist who understood the science of politics and I practised politics as an art," he said. "The art of politics has been my life."

From the beginning, Dion had privileges that nobody else had. Dion wasn't a yes man and he had stood up to Chrétien at that first meeting at 24 Sussex when he offered up criticism of the federal referendum strategy and reacted without enthusiasm to the offer of a cabinet post. In his memoir of the Chrétien years, *The Way It Works,* Goldenberg describes a cabinet meeting in which the new intergovernmental affairs minister reacted sternly when Chrétien began the session with a few jokes. "Prime Minister, this is a serious matter and we do not have time for joking around," Dion admonished Chrétien. Goldenberg writes: "No other minister would have dared to say something like that to a prime minister. Dion could get away with it."[151] Dion's lack of humour became assumed wisdom on the Hill (understandably), but he loved a good practical joke. Geoffroi Montpetit, whom Dion hired as policy adviser and speechwriter early in 1996, remembered Goldenberg telling Dion, "you're a minister now, you've got to carry a briefcase." His old blue nylon knapsack would no longer do. At his first cabinet meeting, Dion dropped his government-issue briefcase on the table, opened it, and with a flourish pulled out his same old knapsack.[152]

Dion had many privileges with Chrétien. Harrington Lake, the prime ministerial retreat in the Gatineau Hills, was off-limits to all but the closest friends of the Chrétien family. Goldenberg received an invitation from Chrétien twice in ten years. But Stéphane Dion and Janine Krieber were frequent guests. Both Stéphane Dion and Aline Chrétien were passionate about fishing and the fishing wasn't bad at Harrington; the old chief, John Diefenbaker, had loved to fish and stocked the lake with bass when he was prime minister. The couples became good friends. "If my wife hadn't been friendly, there would have been no invitations," Jean Chrétien said matter-of-factly. Janine respected Aline for having pursued her own interests (languages, music) and valued her good advice. "I think in a certain way, I took her as a role model," said Janine.[153]

Dion wasted no time diving into his job. He saw his goal literally, as did Chrétien, as saving Canada. First, he had to become accustomed to his staff and get a handle on the internal politics of power that made Ottawa run. Dion had spent a career studying bureaucracies, including the senior ranks of the civil service in Ottawa, and he was well prepared to work among gifted and strong-willed people. His deputy minister was George Anderson, a senior bureaucrat with an impressive curriculum vitae who shared interests with Dion in nationalism and the nature of political systems.[154] "So I'm told you should be my deputy minister. I don't know about that," Anderson recalled Dion saying rather abruptly at their first meeting.[155]

Dion was wary of his deputy, or rather of the bureaucratic system in which Anderson functioned. He felt that Goldenberg, Chrétien's trusted senior policy adviser, had put Anderson in the job to keep an eye on the rookie. "George was there to control me," said Dion. "I was an unknown; I was the choice of the prime minister. I needed a good, solid civil servant. He was very careful, very prudent, and [his role was to] put on the brakes. He always thought I was going too fast—and he was reporting to the PMO [Prime Minister's Office] about everything."[156]

Goldenberg had his own sense of the dynamic. "I hope I had something to do with the appointment [of] someone strong and intelligent to do an important job, not to keep an eye on the new minister," he responded when asked years later about Dion's take on his deputy minister. "I had been a great fan of George Anderson and a good friend long before I heard of Dion, and had been pushing for him for that job well before Chrétien thought of Dion for cabinet."[157]

Moreover, it was Anderson's job to report back. He was expected to keep the larger Privy Council Office (which provides support to both the prime minister and cabinet) briefed, and he did so through the secretary to the cabinet.[158] "I never took the view that my job was to keep [Dion] under control," said Anderson, looking back at their relationship. As deputy minister in Intergovernmental Affairs, Anderson had two masters: his minister and the secretary to the cabinet. He was the person who "squared the circle," as he later put it. Occasionally, he would get different signals from his two masters when Dion wanted to move fast and others, including senior ministers, were holding up a caution sign.[159]

That conflict would be the story of Dion's political career. The new boy on the Hill in 1996 was handling a sensitive file for the prime minister—*the* most sensitive file from Chrétien's perspective—and it was only natural he was going to make waves. Dion had strong and controversial opinions about how to deal with Quebec separatism (which was why Chrétien had chosen him) and would recommend actions that frankly scared cabinet colleagues, especially the Quebec caucus. Dion wouldn't always win on timing, but he would always have Chrétien's support. And he would always bristle at those in politics who couldn't take a step without first taking a poll. "How many times at the beginning when I was coming with my ideas did I hear, 'Stéphane, the political perception is not there yet. *Le terrain n'est pas là. Le terrain n'est pas bon.*' [The ground hasn't been laid.] So many times I've heard that! I think we overreact to every poll, to every event. You have to have your convictions. Handle the perception, okay, but never accept that the perception will be your master."[160]

Dion was tagged as impatient, that was true. But he also earned respect. Goldenberg, a small man with a chipmunk grin and a brain the size of Manitoba, learned to respect Dion. He'd picked Dion up on Chrétien's behalf at the Ottawa bus station on a Sunday night in January 1996 and had come away from their first dinner together not knowing what to expect. Chrétien called him from Asia later that evening to see how it had gone. "Your choice will either be a spectacular success or a spectacular failure, and nothing in between. I cannot predict which it will be," Goldenberg told Chrétien.[161] After having worked for years with Dion on Parliament Hill, Goldenberg would say he had been a success, although "he's not your typical politician, to be sure." Said Goldenberg: "He's very smart. He sets very high standards for himself and expects others to produce as much." He described a minister who always did his homework, read his briefing books (as well as everybody else's), and could put colleagues through their paces. "People say he's arrogant, but he's not. He's a very decent, very thoughtful person. Not a lot of small talk, but there's a charm ... and he's in it for the right reasons."[162]

Chrétien had set up a mixed committee of ministers, officials, and people from the Prime Minister's Office to air new ideas on how to handle another referendum. (At times it seemed there were more committees on Quebec than ministers.) Originally, the committee was referred to as G-3 after the three ministers involved, Stéphane Dion, Justice Minister Allan Rock, and Marcel Massé, but its membership expanded. The first meeting where Dion was expected to make a presentation was a rocky one.

Anderson had given him speaking points, but when chair Jocelyn Bourgon called on Dion to deliver his text, he said he couldn't because he didn't agree with the document he'd been given by his department. It gave the perception, he explained, that Canada needed

to be protected from Quebec and that the two were monolithic enti-
ties. Dion recalled that Anderson was in the room and urged him to
read the document. Instead, Dion insisted the paper didn't express
what he wanted to say as minister and explained why: "I don't want
to protect Canada against Quebec, or find ways in which we can
avoid separation by keeping Quebecers in Canada against their will.
This is not the point. The point is that if [separation] is done outside
the law and if it's not done with clarity, it will be very difficult in
Vancouver or Toronto and it will be chaos in Montreal. The problem
of separation is above all not a problem between other Canadians and
Quebecers, but first and foremost a problem among Quebecers. You
have seven million human beings in Quebec equally divided among
themselves and with no clear rules to solve their disagreement. This is
unacceptable to democracy."[163]

Bourgon, a senior civil servant, asked Dion to come back the next
week with a revised document he was comfortable reading and to
ask his staff to help him prepare it. Dion would always have the
impression that somebody spoke to Anderson after that meeting,
telling him something along the lines of: "Work with your minister.
He was chosen by the prime minister. He is not your spokesperson,
he's your minister. Work with him." Dion said that when Anderson
saw he was going to get his ideas through "despite all the efforts
[Anderson] was creating to stop me, he decided it wouldn't happen in
spite of him, but with his help … and his help was tremendous.
When he decided to stop putting on the brakes, he was very, very
good…. But we needed to learn to work together."

Anderson would have no recollection of the G-3 meeting or of any
particular growing pains with Dion. In retrospect, Anderson
appeared to be remarkably forgiving of someone who had criticized
the efforts of his staff in front of others. But Anderson used "forgiving" as an adjective for Dion. He said he saw a certain "social
awkwardness" in Dion but went on to say, "one of his qualities is that

he does not personalize things. He is prepared to have people say terrible things and the next day ... you scarcely know what had happened the day before. In six years, I have no recollection of him being abusive to anyone. I am not saying he had alligator skin but he was remarkably forgiving. I didn't hear an expletive in all the years I worked for him ... And he spoke such beautiful French."[164]

Within a short period of time, Dion and Anderson were working together as a team. That was a good thing because they were about to face gigantic obstacles.

PUBLIC CONTROVERSY BEGAN for Stéphane Dion within days of his appointment in 1996. He seemed to court it, awkward in both body language and the flaps he could get himself into. He was Inspector Clouseau. At the beginning of February that year, the federal cabinet moved its meetings to Vancouver for two days, and there, they discussed the topic on everyone's mind, a strategy for national unity. Two days earlier, Lucien Bouchard had taken over as premier of Quebec (replacing the retired Jacques Parizeau), and polls in the province showed an overwhelming majority of respondents felt that separation was simply a matter of time. Bouchard had Dion in his sights: there was bad blood between the two, and their mutual animosity would add to the friction in coming years between the Chrétien government and the Parti Québécois. Already there was speculation Dion hadn't been the right choice for the job. "The task of reconciliation now belongs to a political neophyte, a young feder-alist wolf somewhat unknown in English Canada and, let's not mince words, there is no love lost between him and Quebec sovereignists," wrote Paul Gaboury in *Le Droit,* the National Capital Region's French-language newspaper.[165] He wrote further that Bouchard and the other premiers were waiting for Dion "in the lion's den." Quebec Liberal leader Daniel Johnson hadn't forgotten how, a year earlier at a conference in Quebec City, Professor Dion had criticized provincial

Liberals for having supported the idea of another referendum in the early 1990s. Federal Liberals and Quebec Liberals didn't get along traditionally; the addition of Dion to the mix made matters worse. Dion also had a knack for getting under people's skin. Johnson said that a university professor could afford himself the luxury of not having to vet every word, "but now [Dion] is involved in active politics rather than being at the rostrum—these are two things and it makes a difference."[166]

At the Vancouver meeting, a final report by Massé's ad hoc committee on national unity was tabled, as well as a letter from Massé to Chrétien expressing the urgency of getting the federalist message across in Quebec.[167] Decisions taken by ministers over those two days on the West Coast (and specifically the recommendation that "a coordinated effort be made to increase the visibility and presence of Canada in Quebec")[168] would play a role in the creation of a scandal down the road for the Liberal party. The scandal would shake the mighty party when it broke in the new century and have ramifications for the leader who would replace Jean Chrétien in 2003. Meanwhile, in 1996, Stéphane Dion was discovering there was such a thing as cabinet secrecy, and he was expected to understand the concept without having been told. He didn't.

Ministers around the cabinet table in Vancouver discussed a two-track strategy for Quebec. The first option, Plan A, was the "renewed federalism" Chrétien had promised to Quebec before the referendum of October 30, 1995. The prime minister followed up by introducing his "unity package" to the House of Commons in November. The Canadian Parliament would recognize Quebec as a distinct society within Canada (one of the tenets of Meech Lake), grant Quebec a veto over major constitutional changes affecting the province, and transfer more powers to the provinces.[169] Nobody in Chrétien's cabinet referred to a Plan A as such because that would mean admitting there was a Plan B, and that they weren't doing. Plan B was the new realism, the hard line towards Quebec epitomized by Dion's appointment to cabinet. It was the rules-of-secession strategy. How would Ottawa deal with a separate Quebec? What were the ground rules for secession? (From the outset, the Parti Québécois government in Quebec rejected the idea the federal government could set ground rules.) There was an increasing demand in English Canada for the Chrétien government to come up with a plan in the days after the 1995 referendum. It had not gone unnoticed that the federal side had been floundering and there was frustration among Canadians who had feared they were losing their country as they knew it on referendum night.

Plan B would eventually become the basis of dramatic action by Chrétien's government. There had already been signs that something was afoot federally. Dion had said an independent Quebec could be divided, and his cabinet colleague Allan Rock had said the government's national unity plan would deal with the legality of Quebec separation.[170] Dion was taking a drubbing in the Quebec press for talking about the partition issue. *La Presse* columnist Lysiane Gagnon called his comments dangerous. "An intellectual who speaks only for himself can very well speculate on what happens post-sovereignty and play with abstract concepts," she wrote. "But there is a world of difference between the speculations of an independent intellectual and the declarations of a minister invested with political responsibility—the world that separates speculation from blackmail, theory from practice, cold logic from fiery action."[171]

Naturally, at the cabinet table, with his referendum strategy team in place—Dion, Rock, Pettigrew, Massé among others—Chrétien was eager to discuss options for Plan B. But when the Vancouver meetings broke up, Chrétien insisted to curious reporters that, really, it existed only in their imaginations. "The strategy for national unity is well known. We've been talking about it for a long time, about harmonization, simplification, decentralization, reorganizing the federation so it functions better … That's what our plan is, A, B, C, D," said Chrétien. "There's no Plan A and Plan B."[172] And then out strolled Inspector Clouseau to take questions from reporters, oblivious to what the prime minister might be saying in his own scrum. When asked, Stéphane Dion helpfully explained that Plan A was the reconciliation of Quebec and the rest of Canada and, yes, Plan B was defining "the rules of secession." The next day, the headline in *Le Devoir* said, "Chrétien contradicts Dion."

"So wow! Welcome to politics," said Dion of his first battle scar as a federal minister. Home in Montreal the next day, he saw the headline and was worried. His phone rang, and Paul Martin, minister of finance and fellow Montreal MP (LaSalle-Émard), asked Dion to come over to his home. "I was sure that he would be after me about the article but, no, he talked about [knowing] my father and after a while I said, 'But what about the article?' 'Which article?' he asked. 'The story in *Le Devoir*.' 'Which story in *Le Devoir*?' I showed it to him and he told me, 'Nobody read it. Don't worry!'"[173] While it was a lesson for Dion not to panic about every headline, he would not get over his addiction to newspapers. Like Brian Mulroney, he read every word written about him. It was a compulsion. Arriving back in Ottawa after midnight in December of 2006 after a gruelling day on the road, he was stewing in the backseat of a cab because he hadn't yet had a chance to read that day's papers. The taxi crawled through the dark streets searching for a newsstand that was open, until Dion finally gave up.

By the spring of 1996, Chrétien's government had not decided on a plan for handling another Quebec referendum. And then events occurred in which Lucien Bouchard made two critical errors in judgement, according to those working in the high-pressure atmosphere of the Intergovernmental Affairs offices at 66 Slater Street in downtown Ottawa.

There was disagreement at the cabinet table on what the next first step should be. Some wanted to seek a ruling on whether Quebec could separate at the International Court of Justice at The Hague, but Foreign Affairs Department lawyers opposed the idea. "They thought it was a sign of weakness," said Dion. Meanwhile, the Bertrand case was working its way through the Superior Court system in Quebec. Guy Bertrand was a Quebec City lawyer and former Parti Québécois activist who had tried to stop the referendum in the fall of 1995 by filing an injunction. On September 8, 1995, he was turned down. However, the court ruling offered some findings on the legality of the Quebec government's plan for separation, saying it had violated Bertrand's rights under the Constitution. That was because, in the opinion of the court, Bill 1, which set out the terms of separation, said there would have been a unilateral declaration of independence by Quebec if negotiations for a customs union with Canada (sovereignty-association) had fallen through.[174] Bertrand kept fighting. Ottawa didn't plan to get involved in the case because federal lawyers didn't see any way to win. It was all hypothetical. "We thought the court would say that without a referendum, there was no case," said Dion. "So we didn't want to intervene. And we were almost sure the Government of Quebec would argue the same thing. But No! The Government of Quebec came [to court]—it was a big mistake!—and argued that this was not a matter for the Superior Court of Quebec, it was a matter only of politics and international law, and that's it," said Dion, remembering what he considered to be a stroke of luck for the federal side.[175]

On April 12, 1996, the Quebec government filed a motion seeking to have Bertrand's claim dismissed on the basis that Canadian courts had no jurisdiction over the process of Quebec's accession to sovereignty.[176] The federal Department of Justice changed its mind. The hearing on Quebec's motion was set to begin on Monday, May 13, and, on the Friday before, Justice Minister Allan Rock announced that federal lawyers would intervene in the Bertrand case, saying that

Ottawa had to respond to the Quebec government's stance that the court had no role in Canadian unity. "This intervention by the Government of Quebec was my best ally," said Dion. "As lawyers they were upset. [They said:] 'It's wrong. It cannot be! We need to face them!'"

But then Dion's colleagues in caucus got very nervous at the idea of Ottawa and Quebec squaring off in a courtroom. Chrétien supported the idea of going to court, however, and Ottawa intervened. Dion recalled the reaction of his Quebec caucus colleagues as, *"Are you crazy?"* They especially didn't want to go to court over a case involving Guy Bertrand. He was an odd duck, a founder of the Parti Québécois in 1968 and a hardliner who had fought for years for a unilateral declaration of independence. René Lévesque called him an "ayatollah in bedroom slippers." He had apparently soured on the PQ when Jacques Parizeau became leader in 1988 and shut Bertrand out. Quebec's media and political class regarded Bertrand as a buffoon and traitor. Cartoonist Serge Chapleau from *La Presse* drew him with a clown nose and shoes.[177] Bertrand explained his conversion to federalism differently. "I think it all began when the Bloc Québécois was elected the official opposition in Ottawa," he told Barry Came from *Maclean's* over *saucisses* in a Quebec City restaurant. "I asked myself what other country in the world would permit that, the election of a party dedicated to the country's destruction? It dawned on me then that this might be a democracy worth saving." Bertrand was also touched by the outpouring of support from Canadians across the country when Lucien Bouchard's leg was amputated at the end of 1994. "I saw that most Canadians reacted to Bouchard's plight as if he were a member of the family. It moved me."[178]

Bouchard reacted with fury to Rock's announcement. He threatened to call a snap election. In Ottawa, Chrétien stood his ground. Dion summed up Chrétien's response as, "Look, if you call an election, you will lose or you will win. In either case, I will intervene in court."

On May 13, 1996, as the court convened, Bouchard held an emergency cabinet meeting in Quebec City. The day was full of suspense; the Bouchard press conference was televised and, on Slater Street in Ottawa, Intergovernmental Affairs Ministry staffers were anxious. Dion and Anderson viewed the televised press conference in the boardroom between their offices. Anderson had watched the October 30 referendum results the previous year with his heart in his mouth. "There was a period when the Yes side was leading and I kept thinking, 'Oh, my God.' For me, it was very hard to imagine Canada without Quebec." Anderson was extremely worried about another referendum because Bouchard was "riding high in the polls and we were afraid he could call a snap election…. There was a lot of nervousness," he said. Bouchard was in the power position; he was still flushed with his success the previous year in energizing the Yes vote for the referendum and he'd fashioned the Bloc Québécois into a sovereignist tactical weapon in Ottawa. Moreover, recalled Anderson, the referendum had been so close, "you could almost sense the Yes had won."[179]

Dion and Anderson listened as Bouchard kept talking and the temperature rose in their boardroom. The Quebec premier called Canada a "prison from which we cannot escape" and accused Bertrand of being "a professional agitator." Ottawa was trying to repudiate Quebec's fundamental rights, said Bouchard, by insisting that "Quebec's neighbours would not only have a say—as Mr. Chrétien likes to say— but that they have the final word."[180] On Slater Street, they waited for the punch line to come. As Bouchard's rhetoric grew more heated, Anderson became convinced Bouchard would call an election when he was at his strongest and Ottawa still didn't have a referendum strategy. And then the climax came and Bouchard announced, "I'm cancelling my meeting with Prime Minister Chrétien." He was cancelling a meeting? *That was it?* A collective sigh of relief was felt in Dion's offices in Ottawa. It was palpable. In George Anderson's opinion, Bouchard had just made a tactical error, a big one.

Dion would attack Bouchard's comments about Canada being a prison. In May, Dion would win a by-election in Saint-Laurent-Cartierville, a riding in Montreal's northern suburbs, and take his place as a member of Parliament. In a speech to the House of Commons on May 16, 1996, he admonished separatist leaders to "get a grip on themselves." He made particular mention of Canada having been compared to a prison. Dion then used his time to lay out his basic approach to separation, repeating remarks he'd made extemporaneously to his cabinet colleagues in January; he used the speech to describe his position on separation: "Now is the time to calmly set, under the law, mutually acceptable secession rules, not two weeks before a referendum ... The Government of Canada does not deny in any way the right of Quebecers to pull out of Canada, if such is their explicit wish. However, the Government of Canada does object to the Quebec government's plans to unilaterally set and change as it pleases the procedure according to which this right will be exercised and expressed. A unilateral declaration of independence would fly in the face of democracy and the rule of law."[181]

Only three days earlier, however, on that Monday afternoon in the boardroom, George Anderson hadn't thought the federal government would get any time to calmly set out rules for anything. For him, watching Bouchard was like a near-death experience. When Bouchard had finished speaking, he could have left Ottawa in the worst position possible. "[Bouchard] was never going to be in quite the position as he was at that point," said Anderson. "The fear had been that another election with a big majority would have led to another vote on separation and this time, he could have won it." Ottawa was not ready in May of 1996, not by a long shot. The two sides—Ottawa and Quebec—had gone face-to-face and Bouchard blinked. At that point, said Anderson, "it was very much Mr. Chrétien, Mr. Dion, and Mr. Rock who were in the driver's seat, and they were keen to push it. If Bouchard had called an election, he would have defined the core argument. It would have been all or nothing." A referendum, followed by the election of a popular premier, followed by another referendum would have been a long and painful process, and potentially a fatal one for Canadian federalism.

DION WAS SETTLING into his position and relishing the speeches that he was giving across the country. They were beginning to reflect a new sentiment about Canada, one he hadn't expressed before and didn't allow to enter his thinking on federal referendum strategy. "Canada is perhaps the country where human beings, no matter where they come from, have the best chance of being treated as human beings. That, more than anything, is why I love this country, and why I don't want to see it torn apart," he said in a speech in Calgary in June 1996.[182] And, in another address in Toronto that November, he said, "I'm a kid from Quebec City, now living in Montreal, and I have my own way of being Canadian. I don't have to be Canadian in the same way as somebody from Winnipeg. I know instinctively, however, that sharing this same country with that person from Winnipeg makes both of us better human beings."[183] Increasingly, he chose a more personal way of getting across the message that he was not centrist in his thinking about federalism and didn't believe in accumulating more powers for Ottawa. He was learning how to become a politician.

And yet, Dion kept so completely the mindset of the academic. In 1996, Stéphane Dion hired Geoffroi Montpetit, a young political scientist who had graduated three years earlier from the University of Ottawa, as a speechwriter and special assistant in his ministry. In March, they worked on their first speech together, brainstorming over a weekend in their offices on Slater Street. The speech was about Dion's vision of federalism; they were bouncing ideas back and forth, and, at one point, Dion insisted that they include a particular point, exclaiming, "I know the politicians won't say these things and we've got to get it right." Montpetit wouldn't remember in 2007 what it was exactly that Dion had wanted to say. But he remembered what struck him. "I thought to myself, 'I'm actually working for a minister who doesn't view himself as a politician.'"[184]

Everyone who worked for Dion over the years commented on how difficult and demanding he was about his speeches. George Anderson said bluntly: "He was impossible to write speeches for." Anderson sat down and "wrote a couple for him on occasion but the problem was they were not *his* speeches." (The relationship between these two men sounds fascinating, like an old married couple who, in some ways, drive each other crazy. On one occasion, Dion awoke his deputy at three in the morning—"Why should he sleep?"—to go over a file with him.[185] And Anderson didn't like the way Dion put his worms on the hook—"He was not always a gentleman"—when they went fishing at a club in the Gatineau Hills.)

Whenever he could, Dion spent hours on his speeches, laying out the facts and developing an argument for each speech, and he had an exhaustive mailing list for their distribution in his academic and political milieux. University of Toronto political scientist Peter Russell was on that list and would eventually find himself compelled to compile them into a book. "I found a marvellously focused combination of Dion's scholarly rigour and passionate appreciation of his country," Russell wrote in his preface. "In his day-to-day engagement with what for a generation has been the dominant preoccupation of Canadian politics, the so-called national unity issue, Stéphane was expounding an understanding of the genius of this country, Canada. It became increasingly clear to me that no one in Canadian public life today came close to articulating what Canadians have achieved together since the founding of their federation in 1867—and what they are capable of achieving in the future."[186]

Dion took writing seriously. Over the years, Janine Krieber would read his material, just as his mother, Denyse Dion, had been an integral part of his father's work. "For me, a sentence has a subject, an object, and a verb," Janine said once, explaining that she helped her husband clarify his writing style.[187] Dion may well have accepted insight and advice, but his speeches were at their core his own. "A speech has a music," he said over lunch in the Opposition Leader's Office in January 2007. He spent the next fifteen minutes delivering a writer's primer. His writing is clear in both languages. "I try to be Colombo instead of Agatha Christie," he said. "Most of the time in Colombo, you know the end at the beginning but you don't know how you are going to get to the end. In Agatha Christie, you need to read the novel until the last paragraph to understand everything. Then you have the punch. That's possible in a novel. But in my speeches, the topic as such is not so sexy. If you want to make it sexy, say something surprising at the beginning."[188]

Intergovernmental Affairs Minister Dion developed a rhythm in his life, too. Janine stayed in Montreal with their young daughter, Jeanne, dropping her off with friends in the morning before making the early fifty kilometre commute to the Saint-Jean-sur-Richelieu campus of the Royal Military College, south of Montreal. Stéphane spent weekends with his family and, during the week, stayed in Ottawa. The days were becoming longer and more hectic as the federal struggle with Quebec intensified. Dion would be in the Commons for Question Period and often have speaking engagements or meetings around town later, or would have to go to the airport. He would walk out of Centre Block to the limousines waiting for their ministers on Parliament Hill. François Goulet would be waiting for him, at the wheel of the Oldsmobile or Chrysler, or whatever he was driving at the time. His car was always grey because it was one of the few tones the colour-blind Dion could recognize ("see" as it were) and it made things a little easier for him.

IN QUEBEC CITY, the Guy Bertrand case moved forward in the courts. In August 1996, Justice Robert Pidgeon dismissed the Quebec government's motion to have the case dismissed and ruled that Bertrand's case should be heard. Federal lawyers had seen themselves as having "a duty to protect the integrity of the Constitution and to uphold the role of the courts as the primary guardians of the Constitution and the rule of law."[189] Stéphane Dion was on a golf course with his Uncle Marcel when he got the news. His reaction was that Ottawa should skip the Bertrand case entirely and go to the Supreme Court of Canada. "I argued very strongly and, again, everybody was against it except Allan Rock and the prime minister." Chrétien called his cabinet together and, after a very long meeting, they decided to go to the Supreme Court. "And with [senior department lawyer] Mary Dawson, I wrote the three questions for the court." They had to be exactly right. "I remember that maybe a couple of hours before we made the questions public, we kept changing them. It was very clear that for me there was a distinction between the Government of Quebec and the people of Quebec. I was protecting the population of Quebec against abuses by the Quebec government and I wanted to make that so clear. And I kept changing it right up until the end." The questions were announced September 26, 1996, and filed four days later with the highest court in the land:

1. Under the Constitution of Canada, can the National Assembly, legislature or Government of Quebec effect the secession of Quebec from Canada unilaterally?

2. Does international law give the National Assembly, legislature or government of Quebec the right to effect the secession of Quebec from Canada unilaterally? In this regard, is there a right to self-determination under international law that would give the National Assembly, legislature or Government of Quebec the right to effect the secession of Quebec from Canada unilaterally?

3. In the event of a conflict between domestic and international law on the right of the National Assembly, Legislature or Government of Quebec to effect the secession of Quebec from Canada unilaterally, which would take precedence in Canada?[190]

Government lawyers took until February 28, 1997, to file their written arguments with the Supreme Court. It was a team effort. The case would be argued in court by a legal team led by Yves Fortier under (by the time the ruling was announced) Anne McLellan in her role as attorney general of Canada, but Dion was closely involved in the process, as was his deputy, George Anderson. "I wanted to be sure there must not be an inch of Canadian nationalism in our argumentation. The nationalist argument is always written: 'We cannot break up a country as beautiful as Canada.' Drop that! You cannot break up a county ruled by the rule of law this way. You cannot break up a country that is democratic and respecting the rule of law this way. I wanted something that the separatists would agree with. It was not about the cause, it was not about the substance, it was not about why not secede—it was about *how to secede*. It's not the job of judges to say they are right to break up or stay united. The role of the judges is to tell us how we may do it."

The die had been cast. It had been a huge decision, and all Stéphane Dion, Allan Rock, Jean Chrétien, their lawyers, and their officials could do, once their arguments had been filed, was wait for the verdict of the Supreme Court of Canada. Lucien Bouchard's government refused to participate, saying flatly that Quebec's right to separate from Canada was a matter to be decided under international law: the Parti Québécois government did not recognize the authority of a Canadian court. On August 28, 1997, the Supreme Court appointed an *amicus curiae,* a friend of the court, to argue Quebec's position, choosing Quebec City separatist lawyer André Joli-Coeur. That decision was spurned by the Government of Quebec.

AT THE BEGINNING of 1997, relations between Stéphane Dion and Lucien Bouchard deteriorated to the breaking point, at least for the premier. Dion had accused Bouchard of playing by a double standard when he argued that Quebec could separate from Canada but that nobody could separate from Quebec as a result. Bouchard was withering in his response: "Mr. Dion is a firebrand. So I leave him to his firebrand activities. I don't respond to statements by Mr. Dion. He doesn't exist for me."[191]

That summer of 1997, Dion took a break. He and Janine rented a cottage near Sainte-Véronique in the northern Laurentians. It was on a lake halfway between Ottawa and Montreal by road, and the perfect location to forget about work. But of course Dion kept reading his newspapers and read that Bouchard had fired off an angry letter to New Brunswick premier Frank McKenna for writing to the Quebec Committee for Canada. "I not only give my unequivocal support, but I applaud your effort and your initiative in the formation and continuation of this group," McKenna had written on July 23, 1997.[192] The PQ government loathed the Montreal group of English-speaking Quebecers, which had formed a year earlier in 1996. It had begun a grassroots campaign urging municipal councils across Canada to adopt "unity" resolutions binding their municipalities to Canada in the event of Quebec separation. The committee's banner theme was "Staying Canadian," and forty municipalities in Quebec had pledged support. For the PQ, it was tantamount to supporting partition, although the committee didn't use the word. Thundered Bouchard in his letter to his fellow premier McKenna: "Your intervention in this file constitutes not only an unprecedented interference by a provincial premier in Quebec affairs, but comes in support of a fundamentally antidemocratic position that international law and the history of people have rejected many times."[193] McKenna maintained that he was merely supporting Canadian unity.

McKenna was host that year to the annual premiers conference. When Bouchard arrived at the St. Andrews-by-the-Sea resort where it was being held, he told reporters that "since the beginning of Quebec democracy, all premiers have defended the integrity of [Quebec's] territory. I will not be the first premier of Quebec to give in!"[194] McKenna was equally emotional, saying of the country's unity crisis, "I am not a Canadian who is prepared to put my hands over my eyes and sleepwalk through the whole situation and pretend it doesn't exist."[195]

Dion, supposedly on holiday, interpreted Bouchard's reference to an "undemocratic position" as an attack on the prime minister. "I thought when was the last time that the premier wrote that the prime minister of Canada was against democracy? We cannot let that go, we need to react." And react he did. On August 11, 1997, Dion wrote an open letter to Bouchard, telling him he'd read his letter "with great interest" and considered it "part of the public debate" about how Quebec might separate. He then proceeded to contradict the PQ's core arguments: that a unilateral declaration of independence was supported by international law; that a majority of fifty percent plus one was sufficient; and that international law rejected any changes to the border subsequent to separation. Dion noted that Canada's position was "highly unusual" in maintaining—as Canada had—that it would accept the clear desire of Quebecers to secede, contrasting the Canadian position with the "indestructible union" of the United States or the "indivisible" Republic of France. Dion cited international leaders who had supported the Canadian federation, including U.S. president Bill Clinton (without mentioning that Clinton had been lobbied aggressively by Ottawa to make a positive statement— "wonderful partner for the United States," etc., etc.—in the final days before the Quebec referendum).[196] And Dion quoted another speaker on Canada—"Canada is a land of promise and Canadians are people of hope ... a society in which all citizens and all groups can assert and

A well-dressed baby Stéphane Dion surveys the scene
in Quebec City in 1956.
Photo courtesy of Denyse Dion

Léon Dion with baby
Stéphane in his lap
and big brother, Patrice,
on the front steps of their
Quebec City home in 1956.
Photo courtesy of Denyse Dion

The Dion children, left to right, Stéphane (b. 1955), Patrice (1953), Francis (1959), Georges (1956), and, front, France (1961).
Photo courtesy of Denyse Dion

Stéphane Dion's French-born mother, Denyse, in an undated portrait taken in Quebec City.
Photo courtesy of Denyse Dion

Political scientist Léon Dion, right, is shown conferring with
Quebec premier Robert Bourassa in a photo circa 1990.
Photo courtesy of Denyse Dion

Denyse and Léon Dion relax in the downstairs family room
of their home in Sillery, Quebec, in the mid-1980s.
Photo courtesy of Denyse Dion

A young, bearded Stéphane Dion in Paris, the city he said "civilized" him, in the spring of 1981, while studying for his PhD.
Photo courtesy of Janine Krieber

Janine Krieber and Stéphane Dion are informal at one of the numerous parties in their Montmartre apartment in Paris in the early 1980s.
Photo courtesy of Janine Krieber

Stéphane Dion and Janine Krieber cut their wedding cake
at a reception in their Montreal apartment on April 2, 1987.
Photo courtesy of Janine Krieber

Stéphane Dion puts a protective arm around his newly adopted daughter,
one-year-old Jeanne, who clings to her father in Cusco, Peru, in 1987.
Photo courtesy of Janine Krieber

Stéphane Dion wades with
Jeanne, aged about four,
in a swimming pool in
Washington, D.C., during
his 1990–91 sabbatical
in the U.S. capital.
Photo courtesy of Janine Krieber

Janine Krieber, Stéphane Dion, and Jeanne, aged about five,
in their Montreal apartment in the early 1990s.
Photo courtesy of Janine Krieber

Stéphane Dion, the new minister of intergovernmental affairs, with his boss, Prime Minister Jean Chrétien, in Ottawa in 2003. The inscription reads *"Stéphane, an old professor who keeps an eye on a younger one, best wishes, Jean Chrétien."*
CP photo by Tom Hanson

Stéphane Dion and Janine Krieber with their daughter, Jeanne, eighteen, on a sunny afternoon in the Montreal Harbour in 2005.
Photo courtesy of Janine Krieber

Proud fisherman Stéphane
Dion shows off his catch to
fishing companions, from left,
Bill Deeks and Peter Russell
in Cognashene, Georgian Bay,
August 2002.
Photo courtesy of Susan Sewell Russell

Environment Minister
Stéphane Dion takes
time out to land a
Japanese blowfish from
the Indian Ocean, off the
coast of Perth, Australia,
October 2005.
Photo courtesy of Jamie Carroll

express themselves and realize their aspirations"—before revealing that it had been Lucien Bouchard himself speaking as federal secretary of state in 1988. A clear consensus on separation was necessary, wrote Dion. "It would be too dangerous to attempt such an operation in an atmosphere of division, on the basis of a narrow, 'soft' majority, as it is commonly called, which would evaporate in the face of difficulties." About territorial integrity, Dion wrote: "There is neither a paragraph nor a line in international law that protects Quebec's territory but not Canada's." He reminded Bouchard that Bloc Québécois leader Gilles Duceppe, who had taken over from Bouchard in Ottawa, had himself said that the position of Aboriginal peoples in Quebec might have to be referred to an international tribunal. "Neither you nor I nor anyone else can predict that the borders of an independent Quebec would be those now guaranteed by the Canadian Constitution." Furthermore, Dion pointed out the contradiction in the Quebec government's position: "In effect, you are saying simultaneously: 1) that the procedure leading up to secession is a purely political matter, in which case the established law is not relevant; and 2) that the established law demonstrates you are right and those who contest the procedure you intend to follow are wrong."[197] He didn't send the letter immediately. "The PMO was against it, my office was against it, and my civil servants were against it." So Dion sent it over to Jean Chrétien. He had phoned Chrétien to tell him that "nobody wants me to send the letter … I think it's very important that we react. I won't accept that my prime minister is called undemocratic…. He told me, 'Send it over.' Then he said, 'It's a very good letter. Send it!'"

Bouchard did not respond. How could he? Dion did not exist. However, on August 12, 1997, Bernard Landry, Bouchard's deputy premier, took pen to paper, figuratively speaking. Landry wrote that Dion's letter had merely confirmed the federal government's drift to an undemocratic position. The Quebec government, said Landry, was the only player with an orderly plan—certainly not Ottawa—because Quebec was proposing to negotiate with Canada after a pro-sovereignty vote. "I'm sure Bouchard would never have done that," said Dion of the Landry letter. He was pleased to get a response, however; his purpose after all had been to have a public debate. But Dion would not reply to Landry with his characteristic promptness. The letter wouldn't arrive on Dion's desk in Ottawa until the following Wednesday, August 20, when he would have other things on his mind.

STÉPHANE DION WAS BACK in Ottawa from his cottage the week of Monday, August 18, 1997; he was enjoying the public exchange of letters, caught up in the excitement of the intellectual tussle with his adversaries, particularly Lucien Bouchard. Dion was in his element. His father, Léon Dion, had been supportive of his son's venture into politics, as he had promised he would be during their walk in the snow in December 1995. They saw each other, spoke often by telephone, and, early in that August week, had chatted about the latest political developments. Stéphane valued his father's advice and kept Léon abreast of his plans. And then, on the morning of August 20, Stéphane received a telephone call in his Ottawa office telling him that Léon Dion was dead. The baseball man was gone.

His son quietly packed up his papers, tidied his desk, said his good-byes to staffers, and prepared to make his way home to Quebec and the home on Liégeois Boulevard in Sillery where he had grown up. He would comfort his mother, Denyse, and grieve the passing of the person who had most shaped the man he had become. It had been against Léon that Stéphane had measured his ideas, taken stock of himself, and learned the important life lesson that he must be prepared to stand alone against the current. Others had reinforced that message over the years. But it was the father who had most influenced his son. Stéphane Dion loved Janine and Jeanne, his mother and four siblings, and remained close to many in the Dion and Krieber families. After that morning, however, there would be a hole in his life that he would never be able to fill.

EARLIER THAT MORNING, Léon and Denyse Dion had been alone on Liégeois deciding how to spend the day. It was a glorious August morning, and Léon, as was his wont, thought he would go out and enjoy their backyard swimming pool. It was the centrepiece of the yard, with its patio area, lounge chairs, and long and happy tradition of family gatherings. Léon had aged well; in his seventy-sixth year he'd grown into his face, the deep furrows making it appear welcoming and kind. He didn't know how to swim but he adored splashing about and paddling as he bathed in the shallow end. When the kids were little, he'd tried to learn to swim but found that he was afraid of the water. He used buoys, didn't venture into the deep end, and made sure Denyse or somebody else was with him. That morning, however, as Léon prepared to go out, the phone rang and Denyse answered. She knew Léon would wait for her at the edge of the pool; he wouldn't go in by himself, so she chatted for a moment or two before putting the receiver back in its cradle. Instantly, the phone rang again. Denyse's next-door neighbour was on the line, asking Denyse if she had heard someone calling, "Help! Help!" Denyse hadn't, but looked outside and didn't see anything. The pool area appeared to be empty. Fear gripped her and she raced out into the backyard to check. She peered into the pool and there, at the bottom, lay the inert body of her husband.

Denyse was frantic. She managed somehow to pull Léon out of the pool and perform artificial respiration but it was too late. She called for an ambulance, and an emergency crew arrived very quickly and transported Léon Dion to hospital. But there was nothing to be done. Denyse would never know what happened. Léon had fallen into the pool at the place where he'd usually bent over to stick a hand in to check the temperature of the water. He had an old knee problem and Denyse thought that perhaps his leg had buckled and he'd lost his balance at the edge. There was speculation about a heart attack or a stroke, but it was just that: speculation. Léon's family would never know. But Denyse was wracked with guilt. More than nine years after the accidental drowning of her husband, Denyse stood at a window on Liégeois Boulevard and looked out at the pool. "If I had just left this window open that day, I might have heard him," she said. "I might have been able to do something."

The pool was as it had been on that August day, and the home was the same too. Little changed after Léon last walked in the door. It would give comfort to Denyse and the children to keep the house, and Stéphane Dion would talk almost ten years after his dad's death about the emotional stability in knowing the house was there with his old room and all the memories. It would take strength for Denyse to choose to live with memories, with the constant sight of that back-yard pool. In 2006, Léon's study was unchanged from 1997; his books and papers had been left as if he'd just gotten up to take a little break. The only thing Denyse had added to his study, because she didn't think he would mind, was her collection of blown glass objects on a low, round table. His easy chair was there, with the plank across it so he could spread out his papers and work. In another room, Denyse kept the many bound volumes of family photographs: her parents in France, Léon's family in Quebec, the young couple in Paris, the babies born in Quebec City, the growing children, the teenagers and adults, weddings and grandchildren, and all their pets over the years. Denyse meticulously noted the years and, occasionally, jotted cheery little asides in the margins. On one page, there was a photograph of Léon's empty chair, with the plank across its arms, just as it was in the study down the hall.

Prime Minister Jean Chrétien came to Léon Dion's funeral. So did Lucien Bouchard. That said a lot. John Meisel, Léon and Denyse's old friend, said the church was packed and he had never seen an event quite like it. It was a Catholic mass, of course; Léon Dion might have had rather liberal ideas about attendance at mass, but at the end of his life, there was a proper sendoff from the church of his ancestors. Denyse gave the eulogy. People thought it was quite amazing that she would have that kind of strength. Perhaps they didn't know Denyse very well. "Léon did not possess the truth; he was always seeking it, closing in on its slightest nuances, admitting sometimes, without indulging himself, that he'd been deceived," said Denyse. Léon had been demanding of his children, she continued. "He taught them what excellence was, always trying to bring out the best in them. He instilled in them rightness, courage, the desire to fight for their convictions and for a better society. He also taught them kindness and love for their fellow human beings." She spoke also of how he had demonstrated "a great generosity" towards the media. She had heard him give reporters "long telephone lectures on the subject of their next articles, without ever being impatient or asking to be cited. Never have I seen him vindictive after reading a critique or an article that misrepresented his thought. He was always ready to help them with his advice and his friendship," said Denyse Dion. Her remarks would be reprinted in *La Presse* after the funeral.[198] One mourner remembered Denyse having been critical in her eulogy of the eternal Quebec–Canada battle that seemed so futile and without end, but those comments were not included in the authorized version in *La Presse,* so perhaps they weren't said at all. Guy Lévesque, Stéphane's friend, remembered how Stéphane stood apart from the others, alone in his grief.

Denyse Dion thought her husband had been lain to rest, but in the years to come, she would discover that would not be the case. Denyse would be angered by articles in the Quebec press that she felt misrepresented her husband and her son, Stéphane, just as had occurred when Léon was alive. "There were people who said he drowned himself because his son went into politics," she said, in her home in 2007. "I am angry when I see idiotic articles like, *'Dion contre Dion,'* when I hear idiotic journalists talking about how Léon Dion committed suicide because his son went into politics ... It drives me—" and she threw up her hands. "It's totally false. It's really stupid." She shook her head angrily. In December 2006, just such an article was published, with the title *"Dion contre Dion,"* in *Le Devoir*. The story restated myths in order to debunk them (of course), calling the idea of killing one's father "one of the most overworked metaphors in contemporary literature."[199] The article raised the Freudian angle through which it said many people, especially separatists, saw Stéphane Dion through the prism of Léon Dion having died of shame after seeing his son stuck in federal politics. The article quoted Patrice Dion, the oldest son, on the beautiful relationship between Léon and Stéphane and how "there was no kind of conflict between them." Still, the paper felt the need to include a quote about how Stéphane likely wrote his MA article on the Parti Québécois to rile his father and another that Stéphane "on the whole wants to prevent Quebecers from becoming Léon Dion." Denyse Dion delivered a final pronouncement: *"Idiots!"*

In the house on Liégeois, Denyse had been saving something else, the letters she and Léon had exchanged for more than three years after World War II. "I burned them when he died," she said in 2006, sitting on a sofa on Liégeois Boulevard, with a binder of family photographs on her lap. Her son Francis was visiting from Ottawa that day. "What! You burned them! No!" he exclaimed when he heard her comment. The letters were private, she replied. Reason enough. When he heard about the letters having been burned, Stéphane Dion would also be dismayed because his mother had promised that she would leave them to him when she died. Denyse would continue to insist that she burned them. Maybe she did, maybe not. It was her secret to keep.

WORK HELPED SAVE Stéphane Dion in the late days of August 1997, as did Janine and Jeanne. He missed his father, and, years later during his campaign for the Liberal leadership, he would say the thing he missed most was being able to talk to his dad. But in that summer of 1997, he had meetings to attend and speeches to give and, sitting on his desk, the letter from Bernard Landry to answer. On August 26, 1997, Dion wrote to Landry that the international community, rather than recognizing and rallying behind an independent Quebec, would see the issue as an internal Canadian matter that would be best left to Canadians. His letter to Landry adopted a professorial tone in which he reproached the Parti Québécois deputy premier for "not having considered his arguments." Dion concluded: "Mr. Deputy Premier, you think that being a Canadian prevents you from fully being a Quebecer. I think that being both a Quebecer and a Canadian is one of the most fortunate things that life has given me."[200]

Landry held a press conference in Quebec City the next day, August 27, 1997. He said that Dion had been wrong to say in his letter that, since 1945, the United Nations hadn't recognized a single newly independent state without the approval of the original country. Landry cited Slovenia as just one of fifty examples he could give. Unfortunately, he was too busy for more letter writing with *Monsieur* Dion. "A desperado has more time to write than a man of action like myself."[201]

Dion responded with great enthusiasm, surely flexing his fingers before digging in at the keyboard one day later, on August 28. "A man of action such as yourself needs to have accurate information," began Dion. He then proceeded to painstakingly detail the process by which the independence of Slovenia from Yugoslavia had been achieved. He chattily concluded by assuring Landry (as he would any student): "I am at your disposal to talk about the forty-nine other cases of international recognition you had in mind."[202]

Dion summed up what happened next: "From that point on, Bouchard forbade any member of his government to debate with Dion!"[203] There would be no more love letters from Quebec, but Dion would continue writing to an ever-widening group of people as he made use of what he had come to consider one of his most valuable tools in getting his message out.

On February 6, 1998, Dion wrote a letter to Claude Ryan, publisher of *Le Devoir* and a federalist who nevertheless disagreed with aspects of Dion's strategy. In the letter, he gave a glimpse into behind-the-scenes cabinet discussions about Quebec. "If the PQ government were to pull off a referendum victory through trickery and by means of an ambiguous procedure and question, the Government of Canada believes that it would have a duty not to consent to it. It would continue to use peaceful means to discharge its responsibilities, and thus would enable Quebecers to enjoy fully their rights as Canadians, in spite of the unilateral attempt at secession." Even if secession could be handled legally, he wrote, "there would be huge problems."[204] Quebecers would be divided and the two governments would face the practical problems of dividing the debt, redistributing territory, and transferring taxes.

Bouchard hadn't called a snap election in May of 1996, and as each month went by without the announcement of another referendum, Ottawa federalists breathed a little bit easier. But Dion still believed the Chrétien government was living on borrowed time without a clear action plan and that the situation was becoming more, not less, dangerous. Meanwhile, there had been no word from the Supreme Court.

At last, the Supreme Court of Canada announced it would deliver its ruling on August 20, 1998 (which happened to be the first anniversary of the death of Léon Dion). Two years earlier, Dion and his team, notably Mary Dawson, had scrambled to come up with their three questions. Pages of legal documentation had been added to the file as justice department lawyers presented arguments. But in a way it all boiled down to how well Dion had done with the three basic questions for the court about what the Government of Quebec was empowered to do. The Supreme Court of Canada's answers were relatively brief:

To question one, asking if the Government of Quebec could effect the secession unilaterally, the court said: "Quebec could not, despite a clear referendum result, purport to invoke a right of self-determination to dictate the terms of a proposed secession to the other parties to the federation … Nor, however, can the reverse proposition be accepted: the continued existence and operation of the Canadian constitutional order could not be indifferent to a clear expression of a clear majority of Quebecers that they no longer wish to remain in Canada."[205]

The court left it to the parties themselves, i.e., the Government of Canada and the Government of Quebec, to determine what constituted "a clear majority on a clear question" in the circumstances under which a future referendum may be taken. In the event of majority support, the court also left it up to Canada and Quebec to determine "the content and process of negotiations.... To the extent issues addressed in the course of negotiation are political, the courts, appreciating their proper role in the constitutional scheme, would have no supervisory role."

To question two, which asked whether a right to unilateral secession existed under international law, the court said that some decisions in the affirmation were based on the "recognized right to self-determination that belongs to all 'peoples.'" However, the court said that while Quebec shared many characteristics of a people, it did not fit the criteria to be considered a people requiring the right to secession under the principles of self-determination. "Quebec does not meet the threshold of a colonized people or an oppressed people, nor can it be suggested that Quebecers have been denied meaningful access to governments to pursue their political, economic, cultural, and social development."[206] The court concluded that Quebec did not enjoy a right under international law to secede unilaterally.

To question three, on whether domestic or international law would take precedent in a conflict between the two, the court said the answers to one and two meant the third question did not apply.

Both sides lauded the ruling. "The court decision said exactly what I wanted the court to say, that you cannot secede unilaterally ... but you may be able to secede," Dion would say of one of the most satisfying days of his political career. "You cannot secede unilaterally inside the law. You may secede outside the law with all the consequences, but then you say to the people, 'It will be an anarchic gesture' ... The word 'clear' was everywhere in the judgement, *clear* authority, *clear* question, *clear* everything.' You need a clear majority on a clear question and that was what I had asked for."[207]

Meanwhile, Bouchard also claimed victory, arguing that the Supreme Court ruling gave the PQ exactly what it needed to reassure soft nationalists wary of a leap into the unknown with a Yes vote. Canada would be obliged to negotiate after a "clear majority" of Quebecers had voted to secede. "I found out during the last referendum campaign that one of our weaknesses in the sovereignist camp was that everything was based on negotiation with the rest of Canada, of a partnership on the conditions of the access to sovereignty," he said. "Of course it's like tango; you have to be two to dance it." Bouchard's remarks were candid. He admitted "the other side" had understood very well that Quebec stood alone on the dance floor and "so they said and repeated and shouted that they would never, never negotiate ... I must say that it was quite damaging."[208]

At the same time, Bouchard insisted that the Quebec government didn't recognize the authority of the Supreme Court, which is why his government had refused to participate in the proceedings. Nevertheless, Bouchard seemed surprised that the Supreme Court had left the hot political issues sitting in the politicians' laps. "I thought and I still think that it is the business of the court to deal with that," said Bouchard. "But Mr. Chrétien and Mr. Dion, the Einsteins of politics, decided this was the best thing in the world … so here we are, this is the product of their inventive minds."[209]

Bouchard said that the PQ government would hold another referendum. What the Quebec premier may not have realized was that his nemesis in Ottawa, Intergovernmental Affairs Minister Stéphane Dion, had shown only half of his hand. Dion, and his boss, Prime Minister Jean Chrétien, believed that Bouchard had already made serious errors in judgement and they were counting on being able to finesse him one last time. Dion was about to take the riskiest gamble of his political career as 1997 turned into 1998, and the winds blowing along Slater Street seemed to be coming straight from the Arctic Circle.

CHAPTER SEVEN

CLARITY

M ONDAY, DECEMBER 13, 1999, marked the beginning of the final battle in the war over unity between Lucien Bouchard and his nemesis, Stéphane Dion. It always seemed deeply personal between these two political warriors. At stake for them was whether Quebec would stay in Canada or become an independent country.

On that December day in the House of Commons, Intergovernmental Affairs Minister Dion staked out federal territory by tabling his proposed clarity act, which set out the government's terms for secession from Canada. Bouchard was still premier of Quebec, with Dion still in his sights, having won the provincial election in November 1998. But it hadn't been an easy win for his Parti Québécois (actually, the Liberals won the popular vote), and Bouchard told Quebecers he would wait until he felt conditions were more "winnable" to call another referendum on separation. The timing of the federal legislation was no accident. Support for another Quebec referendum had been waning during the autumn of 1999, which some analysts saw as the result of the growing realization among Quebecers that separation was not going to be the cakewalk promised by Lucien Bouchard and the Parti Québécois. Queen's University pollster Matthew Mendelsohn said that negotiating secession with Ottawa would be "the beginning of the quarrel to end all quarrels." Writing in *The Gazette* in Montreal, Don Macpherson, the

English-language newspaper's astute and very funny Quebec affairs columnist, cited Mendelsohn's analysis in a column that suggested Stéphane Dion was responsible for the shift in public opinion. "While Dion may look like a graduate student, with his glasses and backpack, he has the bite-to-the-finish instincts of Mike Tyson. He's the most prominent of those in the Quebec cabinet who think Ottawa should set the terms for recognizing a Yes vote in another Quebec referendum, against those who think it's time to let sleeping dogs lie."[210]

Technically, Bouchard's federal rival was Prime Minister Jean Chrétien. It was indisputable that, while Dion's influence was powerful, it was Chrétien who ultimately decided to go to the Supreme Court for a ruling on the secession of Quebec and, in the aftermath of that ruling, to enshrine a federal position into law with the Clarity Act. But it was Dion who got to Bouchard ("He doesn't exist for me"): Dion, with his needling remarks and air of superiority that was often picked up on by the Quebec press. Chrétien didn't have that effect on the Quebec premier. Dion would hear everywhere how much Bouchard despised him. Newfoundland premier Brian Tobin told Dion that Bouchard would ignite at the very mention of his name. "So I guess I was not the most popular person for him," Dion said, with a chortle years after the fact.[211]

The two men were polar opposites in appearance and public temperament, the almost translucent quality of the low-key Stéphane Dion contrasting with the solid intensity of Lucien Bouchard and his fiery, hair-in-his-eyes performances. Dion talked often about the need to counter the separatist argument, but not to belittle it or demean those making the argument. Political scientist Peter Russell had commented specifically about how Dion would never be disdainful of Quebec nationalism in the way Trudeau had been. "Quebecers should not be made to feel guilty for being nationalists," Dion had written in a political journal during the 1995 referendum year. He said that secessionism must be opposed "not out of anti-nationalism but out of anti-secessionism." And "secession is a bad idea because— among other reasons—it creates an uncertain, explosive situation that is likely to raise tensions among individuals and groups."[212]

But with Bouchard, Dion couldn't seem to help himself. His tone would change and his arguments would become personal. Maybe it galled him that the man who had worked out of the deluxe accommodations of the ambassador's offices on Avenue Montaigne in Paris ended up spurning Canada. Dion loved to get in little digs at the separatist hero. In a 1998 speech to the Chamber of Commerce in Sainte-Thérèse-de-Blainville about the economic record of Jean Chrétien's government, with Paul Martin as finance minister and Marcel Massé at Treasury Board, Dion said Bouchard had changed his tune on Canada.[213] Bouchard had attacked Martin for spending cuts and then, when he had to make them himself as premier, argued that it was a necessary step to sovereignty. "Mr. Bouchard really is the master of the U-turn," said Dion. That's run-of-the-mill political rhetoric. Dion went on, however, to impugn Bouchard's intellect. "But there's no logic to his reasoning," Dion said. Bouchard's arguments weren't "logically coherent."[214] What was implied? Well, these men had all been influenced by the Jesuits in Quebec, and if Bouchard couldn't come out of a good Jesuit education with the ability to frame a sophisticated argument, then how bright could he be?[215]

Dion and Bouchard were as far apart in style as they had been during their first skirmishes of the 1995 referendum campaign. Bouchard was more charismatic than Jacques Parizeau, yes, and he could also charm an audience in a way that Stéphane Dion couldn't. That was why Bouchard had been so dangerous to the federalist cause during the referendum campaign, and why he pushed the buttons that most reminded Quebecers of their resentment towards Canada. Federal politicians from Quebec were very aware of how close to the surface that resentment bubbled. "Quebec is a very special cultural environment where every child is bred in French-Canadian society with some sense of the injustices of the past. And a lot of injustices were real, there is no doubt about this," said Marcel Massé, who had moved to the Treasury Board in 1996 to accommodate Dion in Intergovernmental Affairs.[216] By the end of 2006, Massé had become principal secretary to new Liberal leader Stéphane Dion and was working out of the Opposition Leader's Office on the fourth floor of Centre Block. Massé had grown up in the heart of Old Montreal and, in an interview shortly after being named principal secretary to Dion, he reflected on his own youth and how difficult it had been when he decided to go to law school in English at McGill University to the chagrin of his relatives. He remembered his own resentments and told the familiar story of Canadian National Railway bigwig Donald Gordon saying it would take ten years to get French-Canadians into management at the Crown-owned company. "He would get killed for saying something like that today," said Massé. His recollection of that incident, which had occurred forty-five years earlier when he was twenty-something, indicated to Massé how profoundly it had affected him. Every incident like that contributed to the creation of historical resentments and, in turn, the making of myths.

However, Massé was of the school of opinion that, in the wake of the 1969 Official Languages Act and other legislation arising out of the Royal Commission on Bilingualism and Biculturalism, Canada had changed, as had Quebec's place in it. His was the heartbeat federalist view. Canada had grown "in a way that had been extremely favourable to the Francophone, both in the public service and in terms of the ability of Quebec to play an important, essential role in the evolution of the whole country," said Massé, whose own career was proof of the former. "And you have to put Stéphane in that series of historical changes for having the courage of his convictions, for debunking old myths, and for having the courage to set down in writing and orally, in public speeches, what he believed—notwithstanding that people he worked with in Quebec, in Montreal, and even here in Ottawa thought that he was going too far. On the Clarity Act, a lot of people thought he was going too far."

The Clarity Act was the Chrétien government's response to the ruling by the Supreme Court that Quebec could not separate unilaterally, but neither could the federal government ignore a "clear expression of a clear majority of Quebecers that they no longer wish to remain in Canada." After the ruling in August 1998, Dion remembered Chrétien telling him, "I want a law!" Chrétien wanted clarity in the critical areas the Supreme Court justices (no fools they) had left to the politicians. What constituted a clear expression of will? What about a clear majority? But in August 1998 Dion advised Chrétien to wait, telling him the ball was in Bouchard's court. Dion would give the same advice three months later when Bouchard won the provincial election in November and told Quebecers that another referendum was a couple of years away. And he would keep giving that advice as the months passed into 1999. At last, in May 1999, Chrétien invited Dion to 24 Sussex Drive, and they went down to look at the river. The prime minister again said he wanted a law, and Dion again advised him to wait and see what Bouchard would do. Dion would later recall Chrétien's reaction:

"No, I want a law! I'm prime minister and I want a law!"

"Okay, then I want a law, too," replied Dion. "'But a *law*, Prime Minister, nothing less. I don't want a declaration in the House.'"

They discussed the matter further, with Chrétien insisting that it had to be kept secret that his government was working on a law. Chrétien gave Dion the green light to get to work, but the prime minister, and only the prime minister, would make the decision on the timing of any announcement. By the end of their walk by the river, Dion was totally committed to enshrining the federal position in law and was the one pushing the prime minister. He feared Chrétien would soften his position in response to the resistance he was sure to get. "Why did I want a law? Well, I wanted to show I was not afraid of the constitutionality test. If you had only a declaration, they would say you were afraid to have a law ... So it was a law or nothing. If somebody pretended that what we were doing was not according to the law, I wanted to be able to say, 'Sue me.'"

IN JUNE 1999, Dion wrote an article for the Ideas section of *Le Devoir*, laying out his perspective on the secession of Quebec. He hadn't changed his view that a sense of nationalism among Quebecers wasn't in itself a bad thing and that the problem lay with the desire to secede from Canada. "Secession in a well-established democracy is born from an exclusive nationalism that demands we choose between those fellow citizens we want to keep and those we want to transform into foreigners," Dion wrote. He made a distinction between the nationalism of separatist leaders that demanded people make that choice and a nationalism that was open, in which people felt both Québécois and Canadian. "The ideology of exclusive nationalism presents our Canadian dimension as being foreign to ourselves, we the Québécois. Foreign, useless and even worse than that: harmful and threatening." Dion accused Lucien Bouchard of spreading discord among Quebecers by arguing that the collective national identity made it impossible to be both Québécois and Canadian. "Not because being Canadian is bad, but because being Canadian is not us," Dion said of Bouchard's position. In Dion's view, Bouchard was saying: "We are Québécois.... Being Québécois means ceasing to be Canadian in one's mind and in one's heart, while waiting to cease being Canadian in fact. That is the unspoken rule in the debate on identity." Dion went further in characterizing the underlying sovereignist message as he saw it: "If we feel Canadian, then somewhere deep down, we don't like Quebec."[217]

Dion's article offered real insight into what it was like being a Quebec federalist at that time and the price paid by federal politicians. "Those who become prime ministers and ministers in Ottawa are particularly tied to the stake," Dion wrote. He pointed out that "in his most incantatory speeches," Bouchard referred to Jean Chrétien as the "enemy" and the *"matraqueur"* (bully). But Chrétien wasn't just a bully. The word *matraqueur* bore the ugly connotation of totalitarian regimes. Dion's ability to present intellectual arguments in human terms had always been a quality of his writing. The former academic was described as dull but his prose showed verve in both languages. A muddled brain translates into muddled prose, and writers often try to mask a lack of understanding of a subject with overly complex phraseology. Dion didn't fall into that trap, and his writing had the muscular immediacy of anecdote. In his article for *Le Devoir,* Dion said that during a recent House of Commons debate, he'd heard Bloc Québécois leader Gilles Duceppe calling Chrétien a "collaborator" and a "French Canadian for hire," while his Bloc MPs were shouting *"vendu"* (sellout) at the prime minister. Outside the Commons, Duceppe had called Chrétien "Uncle Tom," Dion wrote. "These are slanderous remarks that try to convince the Québécois they cannot work for Canada without disowning themselves, without working against Quebec."[218]

In Dion's opinion, the problem that separatist leaders faced was that for more than thirty years, the vast majority of Quebecers had shown they didn't believe in exclusive nationalism. "They feel at once Québécois and Canadian and live these two identities beautifully hand in hand and not as a contradiction or by pulling teeth."[219] Dion argued that the Supreme Court of Canada ruling obligated separatist leaders to be clear. In Dion's opinion, they would no longer be able to confuse Quebecers into thinking that secession didn't mean a complete break from Canada.

CHRÉTIEN KNEW he would have a battle on his hands with a law on clarity, particularly with his own Quebec caucus and with the senior levels of the federal bureaucracy. The soft nationalist approach had been considered unsuccessful in the razor-thin results of the 1995 referendum, but it was still the preferred strategy of Quebec MPs who, at the end of the day, had to go home to their ridings and live with a *"vendu"* label pasted to their foreheads. According to Chrétien, "the bureaucracy was totally against it, but I said, 'Do it, do it.' ... It was a very unusual thing but when I made the decision to move on the Clarity Act, I asked [Dion] to take the file. It was a special mission."[220] His Quebec MPs were very nervous or, as Chrétien put it in his inimitable way, "Why awaken the sleeping dogs?" But he believed he had the advantage over sovereignist logic. "Which Quebec politician in their right mind could make the 'I don't want clarity, I want confusion' argument?" asked Chrétien. (How could one argue with the need for clarity? The bill ultimately would woo with its very name.) Deciding to go for a law was difficult, but, as Chrétien would reflect, "You are the leader and you have to trust your judgement. If your advisers give you bad advice, and you accept that advice, it's on you as the prime minister."

Dion and Chrétien haggled over timing. Eddie Goldenberg, who was privy to the behind-the-scenes action on the clarity bill, wrote that the problem for ministers and advisers, himself included, was not with the principle of the legislation, but rather that they "were concerned that Chrétien would create a dangerous backlash in Quebec. They thought it was better to let sleeping dogs lie. I was among those who worried the prime minister's confrontational approach might give Bouchard the 'winning conditions' he was seeking for the next referendum."[221]

But Chrétien got his way. And so did Dion. The Clarity Act would be considered Dion's greatest contribution to Canadian politics (and to Bouchard and the Parti Québécois his greatest blunder) and would remain so in 2006, the year he became leader of the Liberal party. By then, Dion would have achieved other things in Ottawa, but none requiring the personal sacrifice of the Clarity Act. Chrétien had trusted his judgement in bringing Professor Dion to Ottawa. "Stéphane was not very comfortable as a person in politics. It was one thing to teach politics and another thing to become a politician. But I knew his potential: he was very curious, he was very well read, and the one thing I had that he didn't was political experience," Chrétien said in an interview in 2007. Chrétien knew he could teach Dion, and, by May of 1999, he didn't hesitate to entrust him with his special mission. He saw Dion as "very competent, very intelligent, a very dedicated, very keen person—a great brain." Dion was impatient, Chrétien knew, but he could deal with it. It was the big brain he needed.

Work began on the law in the summer of 1999. Dion didn't operate alone, but Chrétien, worried about leaks, wanted a select inner circle. Dion was the point person, aided by Mary Dawson, the senior justice department lawyer with whom Dion had written the three initial questions for the Supreme Court referral on secession; George Anderson, his trusted deputy minister in Intergovernmental Affairs; and Morris Rosenberg, deputy minister of justice. From the Prime Minister's Office, Chrétien sent Jean Pelletier, his chief of staff, as well as senior policy advisers Patrick Parisot and Eddie Goldenberg. There were others, but that was the core group. "It was a big step and for me too. I was well aware of that," Dion would reflect. He was writing a law that would affect the future of Canada. "Just don't say it's a law yet," Chrétien kept reminding him over that summer of 1999 and into the fall. Dion saw Chrétien wavering on whether and when to proceed. "He wanted flexibility on timing, I guess," said Dion. He began to feel like an undercover agent. Chrétien insisted that all telephone calls about the clarity bill be made on landlines so there would be no security leaks. At one point, Dion was in his car between

Ottawa and Montreal when he got an urgent message to contact Prime Minister Chrétien. Dion's chauffeur François Goulet searched in a driving rain for a place to pull over. Dion called Chrétien from a phone booth, with a door that wouldn't shut against the wind and his coat blowing open. Dion said Chrétien told him that perhaps they shouldn't table a law at all but rather keep it in their back pockets for an emergency (or "under their elbows," in Dion's English lexicon).

Meanwhile, Dion's Quebec caucus colleagues were not happy. "They were all looking at me like, 'Tell us there's a law. You know there's a law and you won't tell us.'" Dion knew these MPs were afraid they would be hammered in the next federal election, losing seats to the Bloc Québécois. In fall 1999, Chrétien invited the Quebec caucus to 24 Sussex. "It went well. It was a good move, very good," said Dion. Chrétien had relieved the tension among his caucus members; the only problem was that MPs from outside Quebec got wind of the evening and felt they were being excluded. It was a balancing act until Chrétien was ready to advise his cabinet he intended to introduce legislation in response to the Supreme Court ruling on the Quebec secession question. George Anderson talked about the tension of those final weeks. "We had been working on the draft, and when it came time to take it to cabinet, there wasn't a consensus. Stéphane wanted to plow through but the prime minister kept saying, 'No, no, no, a little longer.' Stéphane was central, no question, but he would never have been able to operate without the strong support of the prime minister." The clarity legislation was an example of the practical value of Dion's special relationship with his boss. "[Chrétien] ran things like a chairman of the board [and] cabinet ministers did not have easy access to him," said Anderson, "but Stéphane had that kind of relationship where he could phone him on short notice and always say things others would never dare."[222]

On November 23, 1999, Chrétien held a two-hour cabinet meeting, which Goldenberg describes in his memoir. Chrétien told his ministers: "We are all in the same boat and we will all row together or I will find different rowers." Then it was Dion's turn, and he stressed that the Supreme Court had left it to the political actors to define clarity and, therefore, it was their responsibility to enact a law that was reasonable, respected the National Assembly of Quebec, and fell within the framework of the Supreme Court decision. Dion described the terms of the bill his team was preparing and stressed that it would require a communications plan. Most ministers responded positively but sought a delay. Goldenberg walked out with Dion, who he said dismissed the arguments of his colleagues over process. "So, bull-headed as only he could be," according to Goldenberg, Dion insisted that his cabinet colleagues had agreed on substance and Chrétien could deal with the politics. Dion calculated that the bill "should be introduced in the House of Commons the day after tomorrow."[223]

It would not be tabled quite that quickly—but almost. It took three weeks, record time for drafting a bill on Parliament Hill, and, on December 13, 1999, Stéphane Dion would rise in the House of Commons to table it.

HIS CLARITY BILL was entitled legislation to "give effect to the requirement for clarity as set out in the opinion of the Supreme Court of Canada in the Quebec Secession Reference." The bill had three main components (summarized and largely paraphrased):

1) The House of Commons would consider the referendum question within thirty days of its release in order to determine if it was clear in expressing that the province "would cease to be part of Canada and become an independent state." The House of Commons would not consider any question that did not make that point clear, or that "obscured" that main issue with questions about other possibilities, such as economic or political arrangements with Canada. In making its determination, the House of Commons would listen to

the views of all political parties in the legislative assembly of the province involved, statements from other provinces, the Senate, resolutions from groups representing Aboriginal groups, and "any other views it considers to be relevant."

2) The House of Commons would consider, in determining whether there had been "a clear expression of a will by a clear majority of the population," the size of the majority of votes cast, the percentage of eligible voters, and "other matters or circumstances it considers to be relevant." The House of Commons would take into consideration the same opinions it had promised to listen to in the bill's first clause, adding that same tag line of "any other views it considers to be relevant." The Government of Canada would not enter into negotiations with any province wishing to secede unless these conditions were met.

3) It was recognized that there was no right under the Constitution to effect the secession of a province from Canada unilaterally and that, therefore, an amendment to the Constitution would be required in order for a province to secede. That would require negotiations between the federal government and "at least" the governments of all ten provinces. No minister would propose a constitutional amendment on secession unless negotiations with Canada for the terms of secession included "the divisions of assets and liabilities, any changes to the borders of the province, the rights interests and territorial claims of the Aboriginal peoples of Canada, and the protection of minority rights."[224]

Well.

There was an outcry in Quebec, which would be best expressed officially by Quebec Intergovernmental Affairs Minister Joseph Facal when he testified during parliamentary hearings on the proposed clarity act, Bill C-20, in February 2000. Dion would come under even more withering criticism from the Quebec media. And he would require the protection of the Royal Canadian Mounted Police because of threats, the nature of which were not made public. The terms of the clarity bill, said its opponents, made it more than evident that Quebec, or any province, would have to jump through hoops, perhaps unreachable hoops, in order to secede legally from Canada. What is more, the secession of a province, which had already met everybody's requirements on its referendum question and had shown itself to represent the clear will of the majority, would have to be approved by constitutional amendment, and that was nigh impossible to achieve. The 1982 Constitution contained an amending formula that required passage by both the House of Commons and the Senate and at least two-thirds of provincial legislatures (a minimum of seven provinces), and those two-thirds had to represent at least fifty percent of Canada's population. Ontario and Quebec were the most populous provinces, and it was highly likely that Queen's Park could end up being the deciding vote on whether Quebec should be granted independence as a nation, or not. In 1999, it appeared even to strong federalists like former Quebec Liberal leader Claude Ryan that Dion (and he, rather than Chrétien, was seen as the law's originator) had gone too far. No province could ever meet such stringent requirements. The proposed clarity act seemed to make it impossible to do what it set out to do, which was to establish a set of terms under which a province *could* secede, should its population so desire.

However, Stéphane Dion rejected the argument that no province would be able to separate. In an interview in early 2007, he was insistent that the Clarity Act was meant to help a province secede if that was what its population really wanted to do. Speaking specifically about Quebec, Dion said he saw no way to secede legally *without* the Clarity Act. "If we start with the premise that to stay in Canada is against the will of the population, it will be done," Dion said. "[There is no argument] 'No, no, you don't separate.' I am not aware of any serious party arguing for keeping Quebecers in Canada against their will. To continue this logic, if they were to want to separate, what use would it serve, to what purpose, to try and keep them in Canada? Most people would be very sad but ready to accept a clear will by a clear majority of the population. It would be easier to accept separation because you had clearly expressed that will. And the only way to separate is with the Clarity Act. [Secession] would already be very difficult under the rule of law," Dion explained. "I would be sad, like everyone else. I would think it was a big mistake—a tragedy—but if people don't want to stay in Canada, it would be very difficult to make them do so."

Writing in 2007, Quebec journalist Benoît Aubin summarized what Dion had done: "Today, the idea that a Parti Québécois government, elected with, say, 38 percent of the population, could launch a referendum campaign, win it, and then separate unilaterally with everyone improvising along the way would be impossible, thanks to Dion's Clarity Act." Aubin went on to quote Laval University political scientist Guy Laforest, a sovereignist supporter, who said that Dion's work was "made easier by the fact that the PQ never did a serious in-depth post-mortem analysis after losing the referendum."[225]

That omission came on Lucien Bouchard's watch. He had led the referendum campaign in 1995 and marshalled Quebecers against the federal government, as he would in 1999 when Stéphane Dion tabled his Clarity Act in the House of Commons.

EVEN BEFORE THE HEARINGS BEGAN, Dion was a target in the Quebec press. Serge Chapleau at *La Presse,* who liked to draw him as a rat, added the cartoon character of psychiatric patient. "There's good news," the doctor tells him. "You're not paranoid, people really do hate you."[226] Humorist Jean-Simon Gagné wickedly satirized Dion in *Le Soleil.* Gagné wrote that Quebec's "constitutional nightmare took shape. We even gave it a name: Stéphane Dion." Dion couldn't get anything right. Gagné mocked the very way he talked about separatists, with "the indignant air of a granny who's found a dirty hair in her tisane."[227] By the eve of the clarity bill's debut in the House, Gagné had turned into Dion's nightmare, calling him "the deplorable minister of intergovernmental affairs." He imagined what else Dion could have done with his life, envisioning him as "a Mother Superior, cold chicken pâté, or as a great encyclopedia of the 20th century that is missing a volume. I'll stop here. What good does dreaming do anyway? To our great misfortune, Stéphane Dion chose politics."[228]

The drubbing in the media was tough on Dion, and on Janine Krieber. There was a period when she tried to avoid even looking at a newspaper. How bad was it for Dion in Quebec? Loïc Tassé, a sinologist by profession who worked for Dion in his Saint-Laurent-Cartierville riding for a couple of years, encapsulated it perfectly: "If it was raining too much in Quebec, it was the fault of Stéphane. Not enough? It was also the fault of Stéphane … Point the finger at him and blame him for everything."[229]

Taking lumps was part of the political game; Dion understood that. But in his case, as Stanley Hartt had observed during the C.D. Howe fiasco, there was an air of hysteria. Don Macpherson had been a political analyst for fifteen years by 1999 and hadn't seen that kind of attack on a Quebec politician before. "Chrétien wasn't despised and derided in the way that Dion was," Macpherson said. "In Dion's case, the feeling against him was more intense because he was seen not just as an ethnic traitor, but as a class traitor. He was not just a Francophone but a francophone intellectual."[230] In 1998, when Peter Russell suggested editing Dion's ministerial speeches for a book, Dion agreed, with the proviso that it be published in English and French. Russell had no problem finding a scholarly publisher in English, and McGill-Queen's University Press came out with *Straight Talk*. But there was no interest in Quebec, and, after the book had been turned down by several publishers in 1999, McGill-Queen's decided to publish *Le Pari de la franchise* itself. Russell said that he was told that some Quebec publishers were blunt about their disdain for Stéphane Dion and his politics.

On the political side, Dion was making waves in Quebec. "He didn't just wait for questions in a scrum. He was proactive in terms of challenging the assumptions of Quebec nationalists," said Macpherson.[231] Moreover, Quebecers continued to lose their taste for a referendum. When Dion had arrived in Ottawa in 1996, the polls showed that two-thirds of Quebecers wanted a referendum on separation; by 1999, the results had flipped, with two-thirds against holding another vote on separation. Dion appeared to be changing the architecture of the theatre (as Lenny Bruce once observed in his comic-at-the-Palladium number), and society had never taken easily to architecture-changers. Stéphane Dion had learned that lesson as a little boy questioning his faith to a stolid priest, and he was seeing it again with his clarity bill. The difference was that the adult Dion no longer kept his opinions to himself, and, as one of the most powerful ministers in Jean Chrétien's cabinet, he had the power to use them to change the law of the land.

Still, the price was high. Dion's friend François Goulet would remember when the RCMP security detail moved in. He couldn't talk about the specifics, but years later, his thin face pinched even tighter as he remembered what it had been like.[232] "There were a lot of threats on his family and we had a lot of security around us," Goulet said over coffee one afternoon in 2007, when he was no longer Dion's chauffeur. The protection lasted for a few months, during which time there were Mounties outside the Dion townhouse in Montreal and his Ottawa apartment, and there had been a routine they all had to go through. Dion was able, however, to find peace whenever he had a fishing rod in his hand. Fishing was his passion.

Dion and Goulet spent long hours together in the car, talking about fishing, and, whenever they could, maybe a couple of times a summer season, they would meet up with Goulet's brother, Norm, and sometimes Dion's friend Guy Lévesque from Quebec City and drive to a fishing camp in Témiscamingue in northern Quebec. Goulet would always organize the trip and they'd leave on a Friday after work. They'd spend the weekend, "just the boys," at a camp without electricity, cooking on a propane stove, and heading out every morning at 5:00 A.M. with the hope of catching dinner. "We had a real good time fishing," said Goulet. First-night tradition called for Goulet to prepare his special spaghetti with meat sauce. After that, though, they expected to be dining on trout—Quebec red and rainbow and brown, none very large but all scrumptious eating. A big fish was two pounds, maybe three max. "I can tell you one time we partnered up," began Goulet, lighting up at the telling of a fish story. He wasn't with Dion (whom he very properly called *Monsieur* Dion), and, at the end of the day, Goulet was sure he had the biggest fish. As Dion's boat put-putted back to the shore, Goulet waded out to meet him, yelling that he had won the day's bet for the biggest catch. "Are you sure?" asked Dion, with a grin, and Goulet's "face sure went red when he pulled out his fish. Everybody was laughing." Goulet said Dion was patient on the water. He'd flick his wrist and cast out his line, most often using a little silver spinner and a worm. The line holding the worm would descend from the lure anywhere from a couple of inches to three feet, depending on the time of year and how much fight the fish had in them. (Rainbows and browns put up the best fight, especially in the late spring.) Peter Russell, who thinks fishing style reveals character, called Dion a "brilliant" fisherman. "Stéphane's very patient," he had said. "He's got a very nice feel and if you don't have the right feel, you're going to pull too fast and not let him take [the hook]."[233]

In Témiscamingue, the guys would sit around the stove at night talking about sports, starting with hockey. Goulet's team was Boston; Dion loved Montreal. Dion always measured other players against his

favourite, Jean Béliveau, but they talked about everyone: Maurice
Richard, Bobby Orr, Wayne Gretzky, Mario Lemieux. (Dion would
say in 2007 that nobody could match Sidney Crosby.) Goulet and
Dion had both been wrestling fans as kids and they talked about their
memories of wild matches, about the Expos, and about how they
couldn't wait to get out and play ball hockey that winter in Ottawa.
They played on grounds near the Governor General's residence.
"He was untiring, a good runner," said Goulet. "When he was writing
the Clarity Act, we'd have ball hockey competitions at night, with
lights." It was a good break; Dion was working exceptionally long
hours, even for him. Goulet was driving for a Conservative minister
in 2007 and, after an hour of chatting, he had to leave. He summed
up Dion: "He's a very hard worker, easy to get along with, and he
loves fishing." Anything else? "No," he said and got up, turning back
to add, "He makes a good friend."

PARLIAMENTARY HEARINGS on Bill C-20 began in February 2000.
The legislative committee, chaired by Deputy Speaker Peter Milliken,
heard from thirty-nine witnesses and reported back to the House of
Commons on February 24, 2000. Testimony before the committee
revealed an opposition to the bill that ran deep in Quebec, one that
Dion would not be able to erase with his legislative success. The unity
issue would grow or fade, depending on public support for independence in Quebec.

Intergovernmental Affairs Minister Stéphane Dion testified first,
saying that in 1980 there had been no agreement between Prime
Minister Pierre Trudeau and Quebec premier René Lévesque on what
the repercussion of that year's referendum would be. Trudeau had
excluded the possibility of negotiation with the Parti Québécois
government in the event of a Yes victory. It was Dion's last opportunity to win his argument on the need for clarity and he stressed that
the Supreme Court of Canada had used the term "clear majority"

thirteen times in its ruling on the secession question. He criticized the Parti Québécois government for its central argument that fifty percent plus one constituted a majority while it had ignored the referendum by the Cree of northern Quebec, in which they had voted by ninety-five percent to remain Canadian in the event of a Yes win in the 1995 referendum. "So is the fifty percent plus one rule more universal for some people than for others?" asked Dion. He continued: "Mr. Bouchard is quite right not to want to hold a referendum until he is guaranteed to win it. I do not blame him for that position. However, he must also acknowledge that the wording of the question ought not to be part of his arsenal of winning conditions. He must not word a question which may give him a win. The wording of a question must ascertain what the people want: 'Do you want to leave Canada to live in an independent country, namely Quebec?' That is the question."[234]

Dion admonished the Quebec government that the timing of a referendum could not be dependent on tactical considerations. "It would be morally wrong for a democracy to seek a permanent decision to settle a temporary situation … The public interest lies in knowing that the evening a referendum is held, if unfortunately there is another one, a Yes vote would mean one thing only, which is that Quebec should be an independent country with its own seat at the United Nations, as independent countries are entitled to, distinct from Canada." The vote had to be solid; if support for the Yes victory broke down in negotiations for secession, "we would all find ourselves in a useless and dangerous impasse."[235]

And Dion made a final point, the issue that had caused such bitterness since he had raised it publicly during the 1995 referendum campaign in Quebec, the issue he'd written about in an essay for the storied political journal *Cité libre* and refused to back down from on his first day as minister: partition. The clarity bill said borders would be part of secession negotiations. To the committee, Dion talked about the border of the new state of Quebec, noting that the Supreme Court had said in its ruling: "Nobody seriously suggests that our national existence, seamless in so many aspects, could be effortlessly separated along what are now the provincial boundaries of Quebec." To that, he added, "What we know is that it is possible that borders may be redefined within the framework of a separation agreement. The Government of Quebec cannot hide its head in the sand; only last week, Aboriginal leaders reiterated that it would have to face up to that issue." Dion's appearance before the committee was the culmination of a political journey that had begun when he searched for an identity apart from his father as a young Péquiste. Now a fearless advocate in defence of Canada, Dion concluded his remarks by saying that his bill established clarity as much as was possible under the circumstances. "Secession remains a black hole full of uncertainty."[236]

Joseph Facal addressed the committee on behalf of Premier Bouchard and the Parti Québécois government of Quebec. "On October 30, 1995, 2,308,360 Quebecers voted Yes in answer to the question you now know so well," Facal began. "Today, the federal government would have you—the 301 elected members of the federal Parliament—wield the power to decree that these 2,308,360 people did not understand the aforementioned question and they must therefore be protected against themselves. 'Father, forgive them, for they do not know what they are doing.' That is the Bill C-20 message being sent to Quebecers. Thus it is believed this Canadian disorder may be swept from sight, while ignoring the fact that more Quebecers voted Yes than there are voters to be found in Saskatchewan, Manitoba, Newfoundland, Nova Scotia, and Prince Edward Island, all rolled into one."[237]

Facal told the hearings that federal government legislation would not sweep sovereignty away. And he went to the heart of the problem with the proposed clarity act for the Parti Québécois. The Quebec government derived its legitimacy from the National Assembly, which he characterized as the "sole depository of the Quebec people's right to choose their political status by themselves." Facal reminded the committee that the province had "exercised its right to freely choose its political status when it contributed to the formation of Canada in 1867. This must always be borne in mind.... By adhering to this federation, the people of Quebec neither renounced its right to choose another political status nor sought to subject its destiny for all time to a Parliament of which the majority of members originate from outside Quebec." And yet, he said, the clarity legislation allowed a majority of MPs from outside Quebec to determine whether the question was clear, whether it represented a majority, and whether it was adequate to allow negotiations on secession to proceed. Scoffed Facal: "Three clauses, three schemes for derailing a democratically expressed determination."[238]

The Quebec minister then moved on to the part of the clarity bill that conferred upon the legislature of any other province "an absolute veto on the future of the Quebec people through the amendment formula contained in a Canadian constitution of dubious legitimacy, since it was imposed on Quebec and never ratified by a Quebec government." René Lévesque hadn't signed the Constitution Act of 1982, nor had any subsequent Quebec premier. Facal said that Quebecers would be in the position of being told that their referendum, freely chosen, was not acceptable. "By the same token, it becomes more important to take into account the opinion of a Manitoba or Saskatchewan MP, who would know better than the Quebec electorate what is clear and what is not." Facal asked: "Members of the federal Parliament, do you realize what a ridiculous situation the authors of C-20 have created for you?"[239]

Moreover, he said, the Supreme Court had not given the federal Parliament the right to dictate the content of the referendum in this way. "The federal government played with fire when it made its reference to the Supreme Court. It got burned, because what it got was an acknowledgement of the fact that the territory of Canada can be divided based on provincial territories ... and an admission that, in the case of bad faith on the part of the federal government, international recognition of a sovereign Quebec would be facilitated." As for the clarity bill's assertion it would seek "any other views it considers to be relevant," Facal was caustic. "Whose views are we talking about?"[240]

The Quebec minister put the Parti Québécois perspective on the entire matter before the committee in his concluding remarks. "On the day Quebecers decide to form a new country, Bill C-20 will not stand in their way. You are deluding yourselves if you think otherwise," Facal said. "The Soviet Union tried this in 1991 and the rest is history. Not only is Bill C-20 unacceptable for Quebec, but it is also unacceptable for all parties represented in the National Assembly." He insisted, as did Lucien Bouchard and other Parti Québécois ministers, that the Quebec government did not require approval or legitimacy on the part of the federal government when it came to the issue of the right of Quebecers to decide for themselves what their future would be. "The National Assembly will adopt the question it wants to adopt," Facal said. "As in the past, the Quebec people alone will decide what constitutes clarity. The victorious option will be the one that wins 50% plus one of validly expressed votes. Who fears Quebecers' democratic determination?"[241]

When it was Claude Ryan's turn, the former publisher of *Le Devoir* (and old friend of Léon Dion) said that by enshrining the criteria that would guide Parliament in making a determination on a question's clarity, the federal government was interfering directly in the wording. "This is no longer true federalism, but a trusteeship system ... It might even push Quebec public opinion in a direction opposite to the one the federal government ... had intended." Ryan also saw the legislation as "unrealistic and dangerous for the federal government to have its hands tied by a resolution" by Parliament about a course of action. He said, however, he found it "quite appropriate" for the Parliament of Canada, by law if it so desired, to convene a meeting of members of Parliament, provincial and territorial partners, and Aboriginal leaders in the event of a Yes vote.[242]

Gordon Gibson, former Liberal leader in British Columbia and a senior fellow in Canadian Studies at the Fraser Institute in Vancouver, vociferously opposed the bill. He characterized the bill, which he said was unpopular across the country, as unnecessary and said it would be ineffective in the real world. "I ask you to imagine that this bill had been law at the time of the referendum in 1995," Gibson said. "Imagine that the referendum has passed by 50% plus 1 and you are Paul Martin telling a New York banker on the phone at midnight, when the votes are counted, that there is no problem, we have a *Clarity Act*. Imagine the politely stifled giggle at the other end and the cry of 'sell the loonie!' as the phone is hung up. In other words, 50% plus 1 is important, no matter what this bill says."[243]

THE HOUSE OF COMMONS passed Bill C-20 in record time—on March 15, 2000. Stéphane Dion was jogging when he got word on June 29 of that year that the Clarity Act had received royal assent. His reaction was mundane—"Phew, oy"—but he understood the importance of what he had achieved. The law set rules for secession; it did not, however, address what would happen if Quebec voted unilaterally to secede. And the stated position of Lucien Bouchard, both before and after the ruling of the Supreme Court of Canada, was that Quebec had that right, and that the new nation of Quebec would be recognized by international law. It was a premise that would remain untested when Stéphane Dion stepped down as intergovernmental affairs minister at the end of 2003.

The bitterness over the legislation would continue; it would become another chasm between the federalist and separatist sides. In early 2006, Jean-François Lisée, head of a Montreal research centre and a former adviser to Quebec premiers Jacques Parizeau and Lucien Bouchard, wrote an analysis for the Quebec magazine *L'actualité*. In the style of Émile Zola, he wrote: *"J'accuse Stéphane Dion."*[244] Lisée said that without Dion, the Clarity Act would not exist. "What does it clarify? Thanks to Dion's law, federal parliamentarians could accept or reject the Quebec referendum question before the referendum is even held." He criticized the involvement of federal MPs and their right to judge whether the question improperly talked about other post-referendum scenarios, including economic or political arrangements with Canada. "As a result," wrote Lisée, "if the law had been in effect since 1980, even if 65% of Quebecers had voted Yes in 1980 and 1995, the federal Parliament would have been legally forced to disregard the result." Furthermore, he argued that the Clarity Act betrayed the spirit and letter of the Supreme Court ruling by opening negotiations to other participants and putting borders on the table. "Dion's inexcusable attitude thus becomes irresponsible," wrote Lisée. "Before him, federal politicians have sometimes given speeches raising the spectre of 'Divisible Canada, therefore divisible Quebec.'" But nobody had done it—until Dion. In the rest of the world, he wrote, "Partition is accepted only with regret and *a posteriori,* after the bullies have talked of arms and making blood run like in Kosovo. It's true of everywhere, except in Canada, except in the Dion law."

But Lisée's arguments had been challenged before, many times, and the Supreme Court of Canada had indeed raised the issue of redrawing borders if Quebec separated. (In answer to a question during a 2007 interview, Dion said that the federal government had begun to explore post-referendum scenarios in 2000, including the complicated task of dividing up territory and deciding who owned what. "Some started, but I said, 'No, don't do that!'" he said. "I was sure it would be leaked." It was an intriguing revelation, but Dion declined to elaborate.)[245] Lisée's angry and eloquent manifesto spoke for one side of the debate over the Clarity Act that was, in its essence, the same struggle over independence that had been passed down by generations of Quebecers. *L'actualité* is the sister publication of *Maclean's* magazine. At the beginning of 2007, two journalists, Benoît Aubin, writing in English, and Lisée, writing in French, took opposing views on the legacy of Stéphane Dion, federal minister for unity. Their perspectives were a microcosm of the struggle itself. Aubin didn't argue on behalf of the Clarity Act (his was a straight-forward profile); however, he wrote matter-of-factly that, post-Dion, no Parti Québécois government would be able to separate unilaterally "with everyone improvising along the way." That was an assumption, albeit a very positive one, with which many Canadians agreed. From the other side, the passion of Lisée's position fairly leapt off the pages of *L'actualité*.

It was clear that Dion and federal lawyers had interpreted the Supreme Court ruling one way, and separatist lawyers for the Parti Québécois another. Politics was, as Jean Chrétien had said, an art, not a science. The issue of Quebec joining Confederation as a partner (the principle of two founding peoples) and then being outvoted by MPs from Westaskiwin or Nanaimo-Alberni was fundamentally wrong, from the separatist perspective. However, federalist Marcel Massé, the former intergovernmental affairs minister, had a very different take on that central issue. Massé argued that the "original agreement that was made was clearly made in circumstances that have changed. That's historically true." But Massé pointed out that the British North America Act, 1867, had given the National Assembly jurisdiction over certain areas (natural resources) and the federal government jurisdiction over others (national defence, foreign policy). "The National Assembly cannot say they are sovereign on all matters because the original agreement that was made split these powers," said Massé, referring to the original clauses on the separation of powers. "As soon as circumstances change, do you get a right to revise the initial contract? ... That cannot be done in any country in the world."[246]

Massé also rejected the argument that Quebec had rights but that Ottawa was not supposed to exercise its power. "I used to major in international law," he said. "You can look at the sovereignty of the federal government and ask, 'Why are these sovereignties not equal?' The people who are members of countries also have the sovereignty of a country. Why would they have nothing to say if a piece of their land, in this case Quebec, takes another piece? ... The notion of sovereignty, as it is viewed by the separatists, is a false notion because you have many groups who would then have that sovereignty."[247]

On the night of the Quebec referendum, October 30, 1995, Prime Minister Jean Chrétien had vowed the federal government would not be caught flat-footed again. He brought in Stéphane Dion because Dion was not afraid to stand up and fight for a united Canada, even if he made enemies. "The Clarity Act was Plan B," said Macpherson, in an interview in 2007. "It said separation was not going to be easy, it was going to be hard. It was intended to assert the idea that in any [negotiation for] secession, Canada has rights too, and was going to assert those rights. It's still a radical notion." He wasn't a fan of the Clarity Act. "What I don't like about it," he would say, "is that it's unilateral in the sense that a majority government would have a free hand in deciding whether to negotiate the terms of secession." But he enjoyed watching Ottawa stand up for itself. In that, Macpherson was a federalist—and a Quebecer.

Meanwhile, as the debates over the Clarity Act raged on in 2000, something very interesting was happening away from the intellectual spasms on the TV political shows, in magazines and on the op-ed pages of newspapers. Stéphane Dion—and his boss, Jean Chrétien—were winning in the court of public opinion. In the summer of 2000, Lucien Bouchard told Quebecers to prepare for another referendum, announcing a series of rallies leading up to a vote on a still unspecified date.

Shortly thereafter, on November 27, 2000, the Chrétien government won its third straight majority. In Quebec, the Liberals took six seats from the Bloc Québécois under Gilles Duceppe. Clearly, the reception to Dion's Clarity Act was positive, just as he had predicted it would be. "The separatists, to their dismay, could not garner any traction for their opposition to the legislation," wrote Goldenberg in his memoir.[248] He was pleased to point out that the European Union had cited the Clarity Act and the Supreme Court decision in settling minimum requirements for a vote on the separation of Montenegro from Serbia (fifty-five percent, which was achieved), and France had agreed to the Canadian precedent in a new standard set by the European Union that more than a simple majority of voters was required for separation.

Then came the shocker. On January 10, 2001, Lucien Bouchard announced he was stepping down as premier of Quebec and leader of the Parti Québécois. Early TV reports said Bouchard had already made plans to move to California with his American wife and two children, although in fact he remained in Quebec, working for a Montreal law firm.[249]

Péquistes reacted with stunned disbelief. "We are losing a great man, the best man for the cause," said Bernard Landry, the deputy premier who would take Bouchard's place. "He said his decision was irrevocable. There is a series of reasons, political and personal, and an accumulation of reasons, personal and political. That's life."[250] Bouchard had been buffeted by a scandal involving one of his deputies, as well as by internal party tensions. But he would lash out at Quebecers in his televised address announcing his departure. Bouchard said the people of Quebec had let him down by reacting with passivity to Stéphane Dion and his Clarity Act. "Astonishingly passive," was the term he used. "We have not been successful in increasing fervour for sovereignty," said Bouchard. "I assume the entire responsibility, which is mine for not having succeeded in rekindling the flame and making our fellow citizens aware of the gravity of the situation." Bouchard had been able to inspire during the 1995 referendum, bringing his fellow citizens to the "threshold of a new country." But he hadn't been able to go all the way. Perhaps in the same way the federalists had seen the abyss in their brush with death in the referendum vote, Quebecers had seen the abyss of an ever-lasting struggle to separate from Canada, their "beginning of a quarrel to end all quarrels."

The magic wasn't there for Bouchard in changing minds about the Clarity Act. His departure would ease, at least for the time being, the question of what to do if Quebec separated unilaterally, and, in two years, Liberal Jean Charest would be premier of Quebec. Bouchard had been left reeling from the federal election results two months earlier in November. It had felt to him like a rebuke. "In any case, if there is discontent [with the federal government], it's scarcely visible in the results of the last federal election."[251] Bouchard became emotional during his televised remarks the next day when he spoke of his wife, Audrey Best, a former flight attendant whom he'd met on an international flight, and his two young sons. Bouchard said that, at sixty-two, he wanted to seize the moment and live for his family. He had always been a mercurial man. He had stunned his friend Brian Mulroney when he abruptly left his side in federal politics. It was pointed out by the media that the day of Bouchard's televised announcement, January 11, was Jean Chrétien's sixty-seventh birthday. The prime minister was vacationing in Florida when he heard the news. There was no mention whether the day held any particular personal interest for Stéphane Dion, other than forever after marking the day his rival stepped down. In an interview with *La Presse,* Dion made the modest observation that the separation of Quebec appeared to be further away than ever, and that his prime minister should be proud for having followed his instincts on Quebec.[252] Bouchard's departure heralded a victory for Dion. Bouchard had more passion, eloquence, and charisma than Dion; what he didn't have was the staying power.

How odd it was then, after all they had been through, the skirmishes and putdowns, the sulks and the silences, that Dion would miss Bouchard when he was gone. In the same way that Bouchard put aside hard feelings to attend the funeral of Léon Dion, Stéphane Dion spoke highly of his former rival when asked about him in 2007. There were, after all, more important things in life than political disagreements, even one as fundamental as over the future of Quebec. They were two sons of Quebec. "It's a bit strange but there is a kind of solidarity between politicians. I understood that his decision was very personal. He was exhausted and I had some sympathy for that ... No, I cannot say I was so pleased that he was leaving," said Dion, almost wistfully. Did he take credit for having saved Canada? For having trounced Lucien Bouchard? "Oh please," he said quickly, "don't think I am bigger than what I am."

In assessing the Parti Québécois after Bouchard left, Dion offered, "My sense is that Bouchard was better than Bernard Landry, and Landry was better than [his successor] André Boisclair." Nobody, however, was as talented as Lucien Bouchard. Long after the questions had stopped, Dion kept praising his old adversary, who, by the late winter of 2007, was living as a private citizen in Quebec and practising law. "It was always very interesting with him. He had a very personal style; it was the old French style of politician. You would never say he was boring. He had an incredible charisma and everyone was a little bit afraid of him ... Oh no, not me!" and Dion laughed before adding a postscript: "He was very charming. Everybody wanted to be his friend."[253]

CHAPTER EIGHT

DEAD MAN WALKING

"**A**SK, STÉPHANE, just ask, *please*," friends of the ex-minister of intergovernmental affairs urged him in the early weeks of 2004. Stéphane Dion had turned into the uninvited guest at the Liberal party, the sweaty, awkward guy over by the door who just wouldn't go away. Jean Chrétien was out of office; Prime Minister Paul Martin was in and there were no more walks along the river at 24 Sussex Drive for Dion. Suddenly, he was *persona non grata* on Parliament Hill, and his closest friends and former staffers hated to see him humiliated. The word had been put out to Dion by "people around the prime minister" that he would receive offers of a posting abroad were he so inclined.[254] Things were done that way in power politics. Dion would get a gold watch for disappearing, a really nice one. Geoffroi Montpetit, a political staffer for Dion for almost eight years, was one of those who begged him to ask for an appointment. An ambassadorship, perhaps? The rumour was that a soft landing was being prepared for Dion at the Organisation for Economic Co-operation and Development in Paris. Mightn't he like that? "You are allowed to leave on your own terms, Stéphane," Montpetit told Dion. "You don't deserve to be shown the door."[255]

But Dion refused to ask for anything. There were phone calls to his closest aides, such as André Lamarre, asking, "How do we get rid of him?"[256] How much clearer could it get? Bye-bye. Stéphane Dion had not been invited to join Paul Martin's cabinet in December 2003, and it had become plain he wasn't wanted even as a Liberal member of Parliament for the Montreal suburban riding of Saint-Laurent-Cartierville. There was election buzz in the air, and the same people around Martin who'd whispered to Dion about a posting abroad had said they didn't think he could win his own nomination. *Win his own nomination?* That floored Dion. He had never had to fight for a nomination. Sitting MP Shirley Maheu had stepped aside as MP for Saint-Laurent-Cartierville in 1996 so that Dion could take her Commons seat in a by-election. The riding was considered a safe Liberal seat. How would you like to be a senator, Shirley? Chrétien had asked Maheu.[257] In 1996, Dion had been Chrétien's golden boy, coaxed into coming to Ottawa to help save the country. But that was then; things were different with Martin at the helm. The leader always has the option of declining to sign a candidate's nomination papers, even those of a sitting MP. If Martin didn't want to go that far—and apparently he didn't in 2004—memberships could be sold and a nomination meeting would be packed with instant Liberals who would vote against Dion. Patricia Bittar, Dion's former MA student who ran his riding office in Saint-Laurent-Cartierville, kept getting phone calls from concerned constituents: "Listen, I received a call yesterday and they told me Mr. Dion was a dead man. Why are you going to support a dead man?"[258]

Stéphane Dion had fallen very far, very fast. "A week before, I was one of the most powerful politicians in Canada," he said of being dropped from the cabinet. "A week after, I was with three or four people in my riding office wondering how we would survive and what it was that we needed to do."

THE RIVALRY BETWEEN Jean Chrétien and Paul Martin had simmered for years. Chrétien defeated Martin for the Liberal leadership in June 1990 at the convention in Calgary and went on to win three consecutive majorities, in 1993, 1997, and 2000. For a time, Chrétien worked successfully with Martin, who became one of Canada's most successful finance ministers. His budget of 1995 tackled the deficit with massive spending cuts, a strategy that led to large government surpluses within a few years (although Martin would be criticized for cuts to the provinces that resulted in ensuing cuts to social programs). Chrétien and Martin were a good team, and Martin was the heir apparent. Martin was an appealing personality, a handsome, bilingual businessman who had turned good connections at Montreal's Power Corporation into the ownership of an international shipping company, Canada Steamship Lines. He was Canadian political royalty and, like Stéphane Dion, had lived with the "son of" tag throughout his life. His father, Liberal cabinet minister Paul Martin Senior, had run unsuccessfully three times for the party leadership. Martin was a devout Catholic and would remark during the 2004 election campaign that he felt his father was watching over him.

Martin's people, who had kept their network alive after the 1990 leadership race, assumed Chrétien would retire after two terms and leave the field open for their guy. But when Chrétien sought and won a third term in November 2000, it was too much for them. Many argued that Chrétien had won only because Liberal voters intrinsically understood that he would soon step down in favour of Paul Martin. When Chrétien began to muse about staying to fight another election, Martin loyalists began to organize openly. Not surprisingly, Chrétien was furious. At a cabinet meeting, he warned that he demanded loyalty and would not tolerate politicking for his job. Relations between Chrétien and Martin deteriorated until, in one of the most spectacular weekends in Canadian politics, they blew apart in full public view. One Sunday afternoon, June 2, 2002, Martin heard on CBC's *Cross Country Checkup* on his car radio that Chrétien had shuffled his cabinet and replaced him with John Manley. Martin had been fired, but he wouldn't be out for long. Chrétien announced in August 2002 that he planned to retire and, after what seemed like an interminable wait for the Martinites, the party held a leadership convention the following year, in November 2003. It was no contest; Martin defeated his only opponent, Sheila Copps, with more than ninety-three percent of the vote to become party leader and was to be sworn in as prime minister on December 13. There was a great sense of optimism among Liberals, who were confident that Martin would sail to victory in the next election with an even bigger majority than Jean Chrétien.

Stéphane Dion's year of 2003 had begun with a scolding. In February, Alberta premier Ralph Klein said in his throne speech that his province's ability to be a partner in Confederation was being compromised because federal Liberals weren't listening to the people of Alberta. Klein's remarks were seen as a warning about rising separatism in Alberta. Dion, as intergovernmental affairs minister, took the matter seriously and fired off a letter to Klein. "I know you are a committed Canadian and how much Albertans love their country," wrote Dion. "I am sure you will agree that nothing justifies secession—or the threat of secession—in Canada. Nothing justifies such a threat, whether in Alberta, in Quebec, or anywhere else in our great democracy."[259]

Klein didn't respond to Dion. Instead, he wrote his boss, Prime Minister Jean Chrétien. "I seek to know whether you think it is productive for your minister to send such an inappropriate letter to a premier ... I also ask you to instruct him that further correspondence from him should be sent to his Alberta counterpart, the Honourable Halvar Johnson, as long-established precedent and protocol requires."[260]

It was an uncomfortable episode. Otherwise, things were relatively calm for Dion. His file on Quebec had been productive and he was proud of what he'd accomplished with the Clarity Act. "I served my country well and my fellow citizens, especially from Quebec," Dion would observe.[261] Overall, he'd enjoyed being a minister, the eight years in Intergovernmental Affairs had flown by, and he hoped to continue to serve in the cabinet. And Dion was feeling good about his relationship with Martin; he saw no reason why his achievements in a frontline ministry wouldn't carry the day. Moreover, he'd stayed out of the leadership struggle between Chrétien and Martin, or at least thought he had.

True, at the height of the feud, Dion had given Chrétien an assessment of his chances of survival, and he'd essentially warned his mentor that he was finished. "I knew that he had lost control of his party," said Dion. "I remember that months before [Chrétien announced he would retire] he invited me to his offices, and he said: 'I have learned that you have difficulties in your riding over me,'" Dion recounted. "My own executive was not supporting Chrétien … It was, 'Well, Chrétien is now over, it's Martin that we like.' And I said to the prime minister: 'If I am unable to give you the support of my own association, how many of my colleagues can give it to you? This party is Martin, Martin, Martin.' But other colleagues were still telling him, 'If we organize well, we will still be able to control the party.'" Dion knew Chrétien wasn't ready yet to accept such bleak advice. "He was still thinking that he knows more about politics and would be able to stay."[262]

But for all his closeness with Chrétien, Dion continued to assume everything would be fine with Martin. He saw Martin through the prism of his relationship with the only leader he knew well: Jean Chrétien, a man who took advice, or didn't, depending on his own instincts. As a result, Dion appeared to completely miss what he most needed to understand, and that was the importance of the role of Martin's people in the decisions that were being made, especially in those early days of transition from power struggle to power.

In a telephone conversation after Martin won the leadership, Dion asked him outright about his cabinet prospects. Recalled Dion:

"[Martin] told me that it was unlikely that he would keep me in the cabinet. I thought that 'unlikely' doesn't mean certain. So I expected another phone call would come when he would tell me, 'You're not in the cabinet.' But that was a big mistake. Another phone call did not come."

"Why?" he said he asked Martin. Why was it unlikely he wouldn't remain at the cabinet table? (*"Pourquoi, pourquoi, pourquoi?"* Denyse Dion had said about her second son. Why, why, why?)

"Because of the need for renewal," Dion remembered being told by the prime-minister-to-be. "The need for renewal is too great."

"But renewal of what?" asked Dion. "If it's the renewal of ideas, I have a lot that Mr. Chrétien was not interested in, as was his right. But maybe you are interested?"

Then Dion made a little joke. "But if it's renewal of my face you want, well, it's painful, it's too costly, and my wife wouldn't like it."

There was no confusion in Dion's mind about what Martin had said: *unlikely.* Perhaps another politician, smoother in the art of social interaction, would have recognized that Martin appeared to be trying to be the nice guy. (*The Economist* would famously dub him "Mr. Dithers.") And with hindsight, it would appear obvious he was speaking in code. Who wouldn't get that? It looked as though Martin didn't want to have to make it final. From his end, the conversation must have been horribly awkward. The incident perfectly encapsulated Dion as a person. He could be rather dense about picking up on social nuances. The trait made him likeable in a weird, antipolitician kind of way when he was running for the leadership in 2006. It was part of his low-key charm. Stéphane Dion had to grow on a person; he wasn't about boatloads of charisma.

Dion's leadership campaign manager Mark Marissen thought that was a good thing. In Marissen's eyes, Dion was the prototype neopolitician. "There's been a fundamental shift in human attitudes, at least in Canada," Marissen said in his Vancouver living room, shortly before his position as Liberal campaign director was announced in 2007. Modern culture had enough speed, sparkle, and gloss without looking for more in politics. "And so when you find something meaningful and sort of quirky, it's something that you can trust. If somebody's too glib or too charismatic, people don't trust them. They want to be able to sense what someone is about," he said. Marissen pointed to a trend of anticharisma success stories in Canadian politics: Dalton McGuinty, Stephen Harper, Sam Sullivan, Gordon Campbell, and Stéphane Dion.[263] Marissen thought Dion's lack of edge gave him an edge.[264]

In their telephone call in the late autumn of 2003, Dion took Martin literally. If their roles had been reversed, he would have called Martin back. And that explained the poignant situation in which Dion and his aides found themselves a few weeks later on December 12, 2003, awaiting a telephone call that would not come the night before Martin's new team was sworn in at Rideau Hall.

Dion got off the phone with another impression. He thought that Martin was seriously interested in his ideas. In the next few days, the offices of the intergovernmental affairs minister would be a beehive of activity, as Dion's staff helped him produce a twelve-page memo on Senate reform here, a fifteen-page memo on equalization payments there, and stacks of material on every other topic imaginable for Paul Martin. "You name it, he wrote it," said Geoffroi Montpetit, who'd gone from political rookie to senior policy adviser to friend with Dion. Montpetit recalled the sense of urgency as Dion worked. He also remembered a similar urgency emanating from the other side as Martin's people prepared to assume power. Montpetit said he dealt with Martin's executive assistant, Tim Murphy, as well as other staffers, in shipping Dion's work through the pipeline. "They started calling us wanting ideas," said Montpetit. Martin had a meeting with the premiers in Toronto scheduled for January 2004 and he needed to be brought up to speed on outstanding issues.

According to Montpetit, "Martin's office called and asked, 'What should he say?' … Stéphane wanted to show good faith so he wrote more memos. They were not files, they were strategic memos." There was a lot of interaction with Martin's office, and Dion worked even harder; his staffers even sent material out to Martin when he was at the Grey Cup game in Regina that November, and Montpetit remembered overnight hours during which Dion went beyond the call of duty. But Dion would not hear back from the leader.

Montpetit was still bitter more than three years later, in early 2007. "The bugger named his cabinet and he couldn't even pick up the phone and say to Stéphane, 'These are my reasons [for not including you]. It was nice working with you,'" said Montpetit. "Of course he was hurt. I had never seen Stéphane depressed or saddened in eight years of working with him, but that night I saw the man hurt. It broke my heart … I will never, ever forgive Paul Martin for not calling Stéphane Dion. That was a really crass thing."

Others on Dion's staff had similar emotions, feeling that Martin had let Dion down. But Dion himself would say later he understood what had happened. "I didn't feel anger against Mr. Martin. I think it is part of politics," said Dion in 2007, from his desk in the fourth-floor offices of the Opposition leader in Centre Block. "These kinds of things happen. My concern was to avoid a clash publicly for the sake of the party … I had no hard feelings against the prime minister. Never! In fact, I did my best to help Mr. Martin to stay prime minister, to be a good prime minister."

As for Martin's rationale for wanting a senior minister dropped from cabinet? Well, his people had spent years in hand-to-hand combat against the forces of Jean Chrétien.[265] It was no shocker. And who was more closely allied with Chrétien than Stéphane Dion, his protégé and architect of his Quebec policy? Dion described himself as "too Chrétien … [Martin] thought that a cut with the Chrétien years was necessary." Besides, Dion understood that "it's not a right to be a member of the cabinet. It's a privilege. If the prime minister decides, for whatever reason, it's not your turn, you need to accept it."

Still, it was the same-old, same-old in Martin's attitude towards Quebec: the Martin government was reverting to the strategy to appeal to soft nationalists that, in the view of Chrétien and Dion, had almost lost the 1995 referendum. It was the "little lamb" approach to Quebec. Dion had always opposed that way of thinking. "No, in my view, the people that are called 'soft' nationalists are undecided people," he said. "And they will not vote for you because you are undecided as well. They will vote for you if you show them conviction that you have a better option for the future." Dion pushed the idea of being a strong Canadian and a strong Quebecer. Just as it was not easy sometimes selling Canada in Quebec, it was not always easy selling Quebec to the rest of Canada. "But I'm proud to be a Quebecer. And Quebec is more than an address for me. It certainly has been my society."

Prime Minister Martin, however, quickly brought in a Quebec lieutenant who would promote a more conciliatory approach to Quebec. No more tough love from the Chrétien-Dion team. Jean Lapierre, a junior cabinet minister under Liberal John Turner, had stood out on Parliament Hill in the late 1980s for his bushy moustache and Question Period chippiness towards Brian Mulroney's Progressive Conservative government. He'd supported Martin in the 1990 leadership and had organized demonstrators who wore black armbands and shouted *"Vendu!"* at Chrétien over his opposition to Meech Lake. Lapierre quit the party over the failure of the constitutional agreement and, with Lucien Bouchard, was a founder of the Bloc Québécois. He sat briefly as a Bloc MP but would leave politics for broadcasting in 1993 and say he'd never really been a separatist. Lapierre would develop a great deal of influence with the media in Quebec, both French and English, as the years passed. The inability among many journalists at the 2006 leadership convention to grasp that Dion actually could win it was largely attributable to the influence of Lapierre.

Just as Chrétien had brought in his guy, Dion, Martin wooed Lapierre to Ottawa in 2003 and would appoint him to cabinet the following summer. Lapierre hated the Clarity Act. In early 2004, he called it "useless" in an interview with veteran Ottawa reporter Joan Bryden of the Canadian Press. If there were a clear will to separate in Quebec, argued Lapierre, "they would not be able to stop a will like that by trying to have tricks." Martin didn't leap to defend the Clarity Act; far from it. He said he wouldn't repeal the law but stressed there wouldn't be a referendum while he was prime minister because "we're going to have the kind of country where Quebecers will want to build a stronger Canada." Manitoba premier Gary Doer, a New Democrat, denounced Martin's position, seeing it as soft on separatism. "I think the musings on the Clarity [Act] will hurt him in the West," Doer told Bryden. "Any kind of retreat on the principles of the Clarity [Act], either through the nomination [challenge] of Stéphane Dion or the musings of the new Quebec ... Messiah [Lapierre], I think is sending the wrong message to the rest of the country."[266]

Ultimately, Lapierre wouldn't be able to deliver the big gains he'd promised Martin in Quebec. In the June 2004 election, Martin's Liberals lost fifteen seats in Quebec, taking only twenty-one compared to the Bloc's fifty-four. By then, a scandal had erupted over the Chrétien government's spending to boost federalism in Quebec. Martin had barely moved into 24 Sussex Drive when Auditor General Sheila Fraser reported that over $100 million had been misspent by the Chrétien government in trying to sell federalism in Quebec. Martin quickly appointed a commission headed by Justice John Gomery of Quebec to handle the sponsorship scandal, a move that would backfire for Martin. The Chrétien strategy for Quebec, including pumping money to advertising firms, had been approved in principle at the Vancouver cabinet meetings in 1996, where Stéphane Dion had been a rookie minister. Although "Sponsorgate" would strip Martin of his majority in 2004—and would be compared by Lapierre to being hit by a Mack truck—it would take another eighteen months for its full-blown effects to cost the Liberals the government. There would be few light notes in the process, but one of them would occur when Stéphane Dion would take the witness chair before Mr. Justice Gomery. That comedy, however, lay in the future in 2003, when Dion was not so much flying as plummeting.

Dion would look back on his time with Martin, after their rocky start in 2003, with affection. He remembered Martin's kindness when he first entered politics and thought he was in the doghouse over a newspaper headline. "Well, Paul, like me, is not a one-dimensional person," he said. "We had a very good relationship." Dion's history with Paul Martin didn't end after an unplaced telephone call over a cabinet position in 2003, but, for his staff, the pain of that rocky time was deeply wounding.

ANDRÉ LAMARRE, who had been Dion's director of communications at Intergovernmental Affairs, would recall December 12, their last day in the minister's eighth-floor offices at 66 Slater Street. The winds still blew cold from Parliament Hill, and everybody would remember that year as a particularly brutal winter. Dion's staff had already thrown a little going-away party for him and had had a presentation. Montpetit had gathered all of Dion's speeches together and had them bound in leather binders, one for English texts and one for French. "There," said Montpetit, pointing to the binders. "That's what eight years of work looks like."

Dion took time to go through the binders and remember events with his staff. "When you think of it," said Montpetit, "the achievements of the man were right there. His job was never about cutting ribbons. It was about defending ideas."

Everybody had chipped in for another gift—all of them, the directors, director generals, program analysts, policy advisers, media relations people—and picked out the most magnificent fly fishing set they could find. It came complete with a basket, rods and reels, boots—the works. They wanted to show Dion they cared. "This was the best minister I could hope for. He's a great guy," said Montpetit. "He doesn't suffer fools gladly and he has little patience for people who can't defend their arguments, and he's very demanding. But he brings out the best in you. You think differently and you work better."

Montpetit had been impressed in November when Dion, who didn't know whether he'd keep his cabinet job, hadn't changed his ministerial agenda. Dion had been invited by officials in Spain (where people lived with bombings by the Basque separatist group ETA) to talk about the Canadian experience with Quebec. "You really ought to stay here. You want to keep your job and there are certain things you can do here," Montpetit advised Dion. "I can't," Dion replied. "They want to talk about unity and I have a responsibility to go."

On the last day on Slater Street, his staff packed up boxes for the National Archives. Dion's material included documents leading to the decision to refer the Quebec secession question to the Supreme Court of Canada; his work on the arguments for the Court; his papers on the Clarity Act; his correspondence, including letters to Lucien Bouchard, Ralph Klein, and other politicians and their deputies; his speeches and his briefing notes. They were all there, all the players in the cross-Canada drama over unity. They packed up Canadian history and boxed it for posterity.

Dion was still signing Christmas cards that would go out from the minister's office under his name. Rumours were flying that both Jean Lapierre and Pablo Rodriguez wanted Dion's Saint-Laurent-Cartierville riding.[267] Montpetit would remember Dion poised to sign his name on a card to Quebec Liberal supporter

Rodriguez, and then stopping. "Come on," said Dion. "I'm a nice guy but this is too much!" .

They were all convinced the phone was going to ring with a call from Martin. Pierre Pettigrew would get a call to tell him he was being named minister of foreign affairs. It had been Dion who had asked Jean Chrétien to bring Pettigrew into cabinet, and they had come to Ottawa together, the "two doves" from Quebec. Dion was worried about the fates of his political staffers who, unlike public servants, would not keep positions in the bureaucracy; he ensured that the final deals of their severance packages had been put in place. There was a lot to do until, at last, Montpetit said the hardest thing he'd ever told Dion: "It's our time to go."

"You're right," said Dion, and they walked out together; Dion, Lamarre, Montpetit, and François Goulet. It was late, and they took Dion for burgers at Le Twist in Hull. They tried to be cheerful, to have a few laughs, before Lamarre on his way home dropped off Dion in the Watergate apartments on Wurtemberg Street and called it a night. Montpetit and Lamarre agreed: "It was the end of an era."

Martin was sworn in the next day. Dion ran into him a week later at a Christmas party. "Hey, I'm not part of the cabinet and it's your choice, but I've got an idea," Dion told Martin. He explained that he'd like to be principal of what he called "a university for Liberal candidates." It would help everyone to understand the Liberal platform, get ideas for winning their debates, that sort of thing. Dion thought such a training ground was lacking in politics. "You know, people go into politics and nobody is there to take their hand." Dion told Martin he would be pleased to do that. Martin wasn't interested. Dion could see it in his eyes.

The end of 2003 was the beginning of Dion's problem in his riding. He always took the glass half-full approach to life. So he had decided to throw himself into being the best member of Parliament he could be, telling Montpetit that being an MP was important, and, besides, he could go back to teaching part-time at the University of Montreal. "If I'm not in cabinet, I am still a member of Parliament," Dion said. But would he be an MP for much longer?

The campaign to oust him was in full swing, or as full a swing as something that existed in the shadows could be. "It was difficult to build a team, not only to find people who are willing to support you, but willing to work hard to help you survive," said Dion. "And you don't know what you're fighting against. Come on, who are these people who are not supporting Dion in Saint-Laurent-Cartierville? It's not like an election when you know who you are fighting and for what. I did not enjoy this fight because it was quite a shock. But I know it helped me become a better politician."

Dion would say he became a street fighter, which was hard to visualize. His leadership website showed a photograph of the candidate Trudeau-style, with his thumbs through his belt-loops and a quasi-cocky air. The pose was jarring; it wasn't him. But it was true that, after eight years in politics, Dion had learned what it was to be a politician in the trenches. There had been a skirmish with his riding association in 2002 over Paul Martin, but Dion hadn't seen it as a revolt against him. In 2004, he was fighting for his survival. He met in early January with a few staffers—Shirley Maheu's husband, René; Francesco Miele; Bittar—in his riding headquarters on Marcel Laurin Boulevard in Saint-Laurent. They assessed a grim situation. "At first, it was a shock for everyone. We couldn't believe what had happened because we thought he did a great job," said Bittar. They knew memberships were being sold in volume by unknown opponents; that they were being challenged publicly by one candidate; that the riding was probably intended for somebody else; that attempts were being made to create divisions within the riding association; and that the idea was to have Dion bow out rather than be put through the wringer. "The party was trying to put Mr. Dion aside. They wanted him to resign," said Bittar. She describes a down-and-dirty struggle in which everybody started saying Dion couldn't win. "At first, some people thought he would go," said Bittar. "But I think the more he saw the machine against him, the more he became a fighter … We knew he would win but we knew we had to fight and he knew he had to fight."

Dion got encouragement from key people in his life, starting with his wife, Janine Krieber. "We are fighters, especially Stéphane. He is more of a fighter than me," she would say. "I always knew he was a street fighter … It was really difficult to see it was coming from your own party." She remembered Aline Chrétien's advice to "hang in there" when things got tough in politics.[268] And Dion talked to Jean Chrétien. "He came to me to consult. He was discouraged," said Chrétien. The former prime minister had found it "amazing" that Dion had not made cabinet after what he had achieved as minister. Said Chrétien: "I told him, 'Don't let them push you around.' He stood his ground and they backed down."[269]

Dion, the intellectual from Quebec City, was out every morning at dawn at bus stops, trying to sign up Liberals himself. He scrambled to find membership lists, which turned out to be out of date and usually wrong. He was on the telephone nonstop, making fifty calls for every one supporter he found. "Who are you?" people would ask. Dion would introduce himself and say, "I've been your member of Parliament for the past eight years." His biggest problem at first was trying to convince people who did know him that he had big problems in the riding. "Oh, Mr. Dion, you're not in trouble," he was told. "There was an incredible gap between the warm reception I had everywhere—I was meeting elderly ladies at their tea parties where everybody was for me—and the little support I was able to have for this fight that was so mysterious." People kept telling him: "Oh, don't worry, we love you."

The date for the nomination meeting was set for March 8, 2004. Dion made the rounds of synagogues and was received warmly.

"Don't worry, we'll support you," people in the Jewish community told him.

"So come out and vote for me," said Dion.

"Oh, sorry, but you know at that time of year, we're going to be in Florida," some said.

Dion won his nomination. There was literally no contest. Opposition evaporated as mysteriously as it had begun. Undoubtedly, Sheila Copps played an unwitting role in Dion's victory. It had been wrenching for many longtime Liberals to watch party stalwart Copps lose the nomination to Minister of Transport Tony Valeri in the post-redistribution riding of Hamilton East–Stony Creek. Copps had appealed to Martin and accused him of forcing her out of politics. "We didn't do that on purpose," Martin would later say. "I really felt badly about the whole thing, I really do … I think we all regret it. I wish it hadn't happened."[270]

On March 8, 2004, 450 people turned out to cheer for Dion, even though he was the only candidate. "It was just extraordinary, a good souvenir," said Bittar, who would soon move into city politics as a councillor for the same area. "He had no bad feelings. I remember I had bad feelings, even today, but I don't have the same quality that Mr. Dion has to forget and say, 'Okay, now we work together.' He has that very strongly in him."

The gang from the riding association would stay loyal to Dion right through two elections, in 2004 and 2006, and into the Liberal leadership race of 2006. Bittar would be at the convention at the Palais des Congrès in Montreal with René Maheu, who was getting up in years and using a walker. They joked that they gave Dion the votes he needed on the first ballot to place a crucial two votes ahead of former Ontario cabinet minister Gerard Kennedy. It was a psychological victory for the Dion campaign. Maheu was with his sons, Richard and Rénard, but his wife had passed away earlier in the year.

Stéphane Dion spoke at the funeral of the Honourable Senator Shirley Maheu in February 2006. "He made people laugh by imitating the way she spoke," remembered Bittar. "She had a special way of speaking in French that was very charming and he imitated her very well." Dion had gone with René Maheu to see her at the hospital a few days before she died of brain cancer. In his remarks, Dion imitated what she had said to him at the hospital, too. Bittar couldn't remember what it was, just that everybody had laughed a lot. Dion had made her come to life.

CHAPTER NINE

PROJECT GREEN

S OMETHING BIG was going on at the Palais des Congrès, no
doubt about it. The Montreal convention centre was crawling
with security and rumour had it that Bill Clinton would be the afternoon's surprise guest speaker. Around noon on Friday, December 9,
2005 conference chair Stéphane Dion had gavelled the plenary to
a close and some eight thousand people (jammed into a room built
for six thousand) trundled out into the hallways to make way for
an RCMP security detail with sniffer dogs. Nobody knew what was
going on; the program said only there would be a "side event" at
1:00 P.M. in the Saint-Laurent room.

Things had not gone well at the United Nations Conference on
Climate Change, either for weary international delegates or for the
host, Canadian minister of the environment Dion. It was the last day
and hope was fading for saving the much-heralded Kyoto Protocol
on combating the effects of global warming. What was needed in
Montreal didn't look all that earth shattering: the right choice of verb
in a particular clause; an agreement to review the record; the establishment of an ad hoc committee. But in diplomatic terms, it was like
climbing a mountain. Failure in Montreal could break Kyoto, and
Dion had put tremendous effort into organizing the event. He had
pushed for Canada to be host country and logged thousands of kilometres in air travel to make the kind of personal contacts he knew he

would need on the floor. On one trip alone, the minister had visited Beijing, Shanghai, Sydney, Adelaide, Perth, Singapore, and Delhi.

Dion, in fact, had worked nonstop in his new portfolio since Prime Minister Paul Martin had restored him to cabinet in July 2004, after the June election that put the Liberals in a minority position. Senator David Smith, the legendary eight-hundred-pound gorilla of Liberal party politics, wouldn't claim responsibility for Dion's return to grace but acknowledged that he might have had something to do with it. Smith kept his ear to the ground; it was part of his value to the party, along with skills that had made Ontario a solid wall of Liberal red since 1993. Smith eschewed a computer, wrote notes in longhand, and wasn't into text messaging. But nobody in Canadian politics turned down a phone call from the senator. Smith had been watching backbencher Dion during the first half of 2004. He knew the former cabinet minister was respected on Parliament Hill and that people listened to his opinions. "Look, Paul," Smith told Martin. "Every time he speaks, people are going to be thinking, 'There's a mistake that [Martin] hasn't fixed yet.'" Later, Smith would say: "I've never asked Paul about it, and maybe he had heard it from other people, too. But I saw something click—you know how you can see that in a person—and Dion got back in."[271]

Global diplomacy on climate change was definitely at a crossroads at the Palais des Congrès. On the eve of the conference, Peter Gorrie, veteran environmental reporter for the *Toronto Star*, summed it up: "Will [the] talks, and the campaign to curb climate change, continue under the United Nations? Or will that scheme collapse and individual nations or blocs go their own way?"[272] Certainly the portents hadn't augured well. The day it opened, Monday, November 28, workers at the Palais had gone on a twenty-four-hour strike. Oh, and there was another snag. On that day, too, the Liberal government had fallen on a non-confidence vote in Ottawa, and, by December 9, the country was almost two weeks into an election campaign.

"What's happening to Canada?" delegates from around the world kept asking environmental activist Elizabeth May, who was executive director of the Sierra Club of Canada at the time. "Don't worry, don't worry," she reassured people. Meanwhile, Stéphane Dion kept reassuring her. He told May that he wouldn't think of abandoning his duties as conference chair in order to campaign. "I am not a politician [again] until December 9," he promised.[273] He would be there until the end of the conference, which, at that point, everyone expected would be 6:00 P.M. on its last scheduled day.

That was a big commitment: it wasn't as if the Liberals were on top of the world about their chances in the vote set for January 23, 2006. The fall of the Paul Martin government couldn't have come at a worse time for the Canadian delegation in Montreal: Stéphane Dion, who, as chair, was acting on behalf of the United Nations rather than Canada; Foreign Affairs Minister Pierre Pettigrew, who headed the Canadian delegation; and teams of federal bureaucrats who had been assigned to the climate change file.

The conference would end with a dramatic push to the finish, the likes of which left even seasoned veterans of global diplomacy reeling. It would turn out to be an exercise in sleep deprivation. Victory would go to the fittest, and Stéphane Dion was an all-nighter from way back. It would be touch and go until Dion's final gavel at 6:17 in the morning on Saturday, December 10. The story of the overnight drama would be, in the main, overshadowed by the exigencies of the federal election. The Canadian media would focus on the campaign, which would soon build towards its own finale with the defeat of the Martin Liberals and the election of Stephen Harper and a Conservative minority. Dion's success as indefatigable chair would become lore among environmentalists and chronicled in cyberspace on scores of blogs. Dion didn't do it alone, far from it. Others played critical roles, among them: Pierre Pettigrew, Paul Martin, Russian foreign minister Sergei Lavrov, U.K. environment minister Margaret

Beckett, Ottawa public servant David Drake, Montreal mayor Gérard Tremblay, Elizabeth May, and Bill Clinton.

But it was the quiet presence of Dion that kept it going. All of his strengths came into play—endurance, tenacity, patience, and the ability to think on his feet—during the last dramatic hours. Looking back from the vantage of 2007 when she was leader of the Green Party of Canada, May would be full of praise: "What Stéphane did at a personal level—well, there wasn't a single environmental group there that wasn't deeply indebted to Stéphane Dion. He got the strongest possible conclusion ... He was magnificent."[274] John Bennett, a senior policy adviser with the Sierra Club, had been dealing with Dion since his appointment and commented: "I personally buy into this guy. I think he is really committed."[275]

The consensus was that Dion got everything he could get. Gorrie, who captured the drama in his report for the *Star* ("Environment Minister Stéphane Dion appeared positively giddy when ...") would agree with that assessment.[276] Gorrie's account was clear-eyed in describing the banality of international negotiations. "Anyone who had watched the previous days of proceedings could be excused for doubting delegates' sincerity as they squabbled over weighty issues such as whether some document should be 'welcomed' or merely 'received with appreciation.' At almost every turn, national self-interest appeared to trump determination to cut emissions of greenhouse gases that are warming the atmosphere, even as fresh scientific evidence poured in of the likely calamitous consequences."[277] There was disagreement about what had been achieved. Many thought that the United States had blinked. But as John Stone, a Canadian climate scientist, told Gorrie: "These negotiators seem to operate in their own world. There doesn't seem to be any understanding that time is running out."[278]

Dion had had to keep the conference going through difficult days, exacerbated by such factors as a speech and scrum by Paul Martin and the arrival of a former American president whose administration had taken a different position on Kyoto than the current president, George W. Bush. William Jefferson Clinton, the forty-second president of the United States, couldn't just waltz in and address the conference. That's because there were actually two overlapping conferences in Montreal that day, both chaired by Dion. Washington was a party to one, the larger United Nations framework agreement on climate change, but an opponent of the other, a meeting on the Kyoto Protocol. There were diplomatic niceties to observe, wheels within wheels, and even then it would be a rough go.

The first process, with the United States onboard, was entitled the "United Nations Framework Convention on Climate Change." Participants numbered their conventions and, in shorthand, Montreal was COP-11, or the eleventh time nations had met since the signing of the legally binding U.N. regime for climate change at the Rio Earth Summit in 1992. Canada and the U.S. had ratified the agreement along with 155 other countries. By the 1990s, scientists were warning about the heavy buildup of carbon dioxide and other gases that trapped the sun's heat in the atmosphere and caused the "greenhouse effect" of global warming. Many of these experts pointed to human activity, from big-industry emissions caused by burning fossil fuels in the developed world to the reliance on charcoal fires in developing countries, as the cause of climatic shifts. By the early part of the next century, scientific opinion had solidified and millions of people had become aware of the effects of carbon-based energy on the environment. Al Gore would lose his run for the presidency to Bush in 2000 but go on to be nominated for the Nobel Peace Prize for his crusade on climate change. Gore's documentary, *An Inconvenient Truth,* showing the planet's receding ice caps, rising waters, and bizarre weather patterns, would become popular weekend fare at movie theatres everywhere.

Environmental diplomacy hadn't stopped with the United Nations framework agreement. Indeed, U.N. talks to achieve concrete targets for reducing greenhouse gases pushed on, and, in 1997 at COP-3 in Japan, the Kyoto Protocol was born. Clinton had been president in 1997 and his State Department negotiating team had helped frame the protocol, with its reduction targets for member countries set to begin in 2008 and run through 2012. Nations set their own targets, with an average 5.2 percent reduction over the five-year timeframe. When the Canadian Parliament ratified Kyoto in February 2005, for instance, it accepted a reduction target of six percent between 2008 and 2012. However, Kyoto couldn't go into force until fifty-five countries representing fifty-five percent of the world's total production of greenhouse gas emissions had ratified it. Therefore, it was considered a huge setback in 2001 when Bush pulled the United States out of the process. It looked as though Kyoto was dead, and Washington faced criticism from the highly organized green lobby as well as backroom pressure from Kyoto nations.

"There is a widespread impression that the United States is not taking climate change seriously and has been acting 'unilaterally' in its approach because of its rejection of the Kyoto Protocol," Harlan L. Watson, senior U.S. climate negotiator, would say in 2004.[279] "This is not the case, and I welcome the opportunity to set the record straight.... The U.S. climate change policy, as articulated by President Bush, reaffirms the U.S. commitment to the United Nations Framework Convention on Climate Change and its ultimate objective—to stabilize atmospheric greenhouse gas (GHG) concentrations at a level that will prevent dangerous human interference with the climate." Watson detailed a series of measures accepted by Washington that revolved around a single concept—"voluntary." Furthermore, Watson, like his president, questioned the scientists. "One of the greatest barriers to advancing climate change science is the lack of necessary environmental data—especially in developing countries—required to understand the Earth system."

But months of dogged talks to save Kyoto paid off when Russia ratified the agreement in 2005. Kyoto participants also numbered their meetings, and Montreal was called MOP-1, or the first Meeting of the Parties of the Kyoto Protocol (making the official unofficial full title of the Montreal meeting COP-11/MOP-1). Never dreaming that it would take eight years to get Kyoto ratified, its framers had scheduled crucial business for the first meeting after ratification, notably setting terms for review and finding a way to have new reduction targets kick in so there would be no gap when the first commitment period ended in 2012. Understandably, the chair of the first meeting faced a challenge. Adding to the overall stress for Stéphane Dion and others in Montreal in 2005, Bush was in his second term in the White House, which meant Washington remained opposed to Kyoto and was unhappy about the prospect of having to listen to a speech by Clinton, whose government had negotiated the Kyoto Protocol in the first place. Dion had to be alert at all times. A wrong knock of the gavel, and it could be the end of Kyoto, in spirit anyway. His skills would be much in evidence, as May would recount: "He'd gavel us in and say, 'I'm calling to order the Conference of the Parties,' and he'd get through some business. Knocks. 'Adjourning Conference of the Parties.' Knocks. 'I now call to order the Meeting of the Parties.'"[280]

There were efforts in Montreal to commit the overall U.N. convention on climate change to its own negotiations to reduce emission levels, quite apart from Kyoto. But the word "negotiations" had to be avoided because the United States didn't like it. At one point, a motion was on the table saying, "all parties would agree to an ongoing dialogue not to lead to negotiations." May recalled Watson's reaction: "That's unacceptable, that says 'negotiation.'"

May recalled: "And Dion said, 'No, it says ...' and Dion's trying to finesse this and [Watson] finally said, 'If it walks like a duck, it quacks like a duck, it's a duck,' and he walked out of the room, leaving

Stéphane Dion, minister of
the environment, visits the
Great Rift Valley in Kenya
in October 2005, during
a working visit.
Photo courtesy of Jamie Carroll

To prepare for the United Nations Conference on Climate Change
in Montreal, Environment Minister Stéphane Dion confers
with officials in Beijing in 2005.
Photo courtesy of Jamie Carroll

In January 2005,
the environment minister
gets a bird's eye view
from a helicopter over
Nain, Labrador.
Photo courtesy of Jamie Carroll

Environment Minister
Stéphane Dion gets set to
try the fare at Carnivore
restaurant in Nairobi,
Kenya, in 2005.
Photo courtesy of Jamie Carroll

After the Liberal election defeat in January 2006, Member of Parliament Stéphane Dion and his new pup, Kyoto, at his cottage in Quebec's Laurentians.
Photo courtesy of Marta Wale

During the Liberal leadership race in August 2006, candidate Stéphane Dion carries his own bags to the airport parking lot in Quebec City.
Toronto Star *photo by Richard Lautens*

Liberal leadership candidate Stéphane Dion works alone
in his hotel room in Quebec City in August 2006.
Toronto Star *photo by Richard Lautens*

Stéphane Dion gives a speech while on the endless barbecue circuit
of the leadership race in 2006. Shown seated from left are candidates
Hedy Fry, Scott Brison, Ken Dryden, and Carolyn Bennett.
Photo courtesy of Jamie Carroll

Liberal leadership candidate Gerard Kennedy, left, makes a point
at an October 2006 Canadian Club event in Toronto,
while Stéphane Dion and Bob Rae look on.
Toronto Star *photo by Tony Bock*

Gerard Kennedy throws his support to Stéphane Dion after
the second ballot in Montreal, December 2, 2006, and celebrates
with Martha Hall Findlay, who had come to Dion that morning.
Photo courtesy of Barb Swanson (Martha Hall Findlay campaign)

Winner Stéphane Dion embraces a defeated Michael Ignatieff after the fourth and final ballot in Montreal, December 2, 2006.
Toronto Star *photo by Richard Lautens*

A victorious Stéphane Dion is flanked by, from left, Jean Chrétien and Bill Graham and, on right, Paul Martin and John Turner at the Liberal leadership convention on December 2, 2006.
Toronto Star *photo by Richard Lautens*

The new Liberal leader Stéphane Dion makes his first comments
in the House of Commons, December 4, 2006. On Dion's right
is Ralph Goodale, while Michael Ignatieff sits to his left.
Photo courtesy of the Opposition Leader's Office

Stéphane Dion
at his desk in the
Opposition Leader's
Office on Parliament
Hill, with his trade-
mark leather knapsack,
January 2007.
Photo by Linda Diebel

Stéphane Dion celebrates his first Christmas as Liberal leader
with a friend, Nicole Gaudet, at a party near his cottage
in the Laurentians, December 2006.
Photo courtesy of Janine Krieber

Stéphane Dion poses
with Kyoto in the home
of friends Norman and
Marta Wale in the
Laurentians during
the Christmas holidays
in 2006.
Photo by Linda Diebel

people from all around the world saying, 'What's a duck?' Chinese delegates, Brazilian delegates, everyone, 'What's a duck?'" The next day, activists from the Climate Action Network showed up with little rubber duckies to distribute to delegates.[281]

Clinton's upcoming appearance presented a real problem. The U.S. delegation got the word Thursday, December 8, that he had accepted an invitation to speak. "So on Thursday, we discovered that the U.S. delegation had told Stéphane Dion and the U.N. group, 'If you let Clinton in the building, we walk.' So, okay, that's pretty nasty," said May. She offered to "uninvite" Clinton, since she'd been the one who'd pulled his trip together (in rather unusual circumstances), but she said officials from the U.N. Secretariat told her it had never asked a nongovernmental group to do something like that and would not start with the Sierra Club of Canada. "I don't think the U.S. delegation went so far as to threaten to leave," Dion would say later. "But they were not pleased."[282]

Clinton did appear and thanked the City of Montreal (whose newly re-elected mayor was Gérard Tremblay), the Sierra Club of Canada, and his "old friend" May in his introductory remarks. Clinton and May had met in 1972, when he was twenty-six and a student at Yale Law School and she was a seventeen-year-old at Miss Porter's, *the* Connecticut finishing school for girls. Her family had deep roots in the history and politics of the United States. Through her grandfather, Thomas Middleton, a tenth-generation South Carolinian from Charleston, May had three ancestors who had signed the Declaration of Independence. "And here I am, happily back in the Commonwealth," she said in 2007, when she was leader of the Green Party of Canada and a Canadian citizen of thirty years. In 1972, Clinton was campaigning for Democratic presidential candidate George McGovern (who would lose to Richard Nixon) and came to May's home in Hartford. Clinton was hoping to enlist the support of her mother, Stephanie Middleton May, who had been a successful fundraiser for the 1968 Eugene McCarthy campaign (though not successful enough). "We stayed friends," said May.[283]

She was a powerhouse on the environmental scene in Canada, a law school graduate and activist who was known for her humour as well as her smarts. In the buildup to Montreal, May had tried to coax Clinton to make an appearance, along with big U.S. names such as California governor Arnold Schwarzenegger (whose environmental record had been praised) and Jon Stewart from *The Daily Show*. The importance of Montreal was that it was so easily accessible for American journalists, who would be able to see for themselves that international support for Kyoto had not died with the Bush decision to pull out. And Clinton was arguably the most charismatic speaker in the world. "Honestly, I never thought Bill would say yes," said May. "I have asked him to events in Canada in the past and gotten nice notes back eventually, but getting him to Montreal was a very long shot…. Then, suddenly, after the meeting was underway, it appeared he would come." May thought a Friday appearance would be too late to make a difference but "it turned out to be crucial. So I had a crazy week trying to raise the money for the private planes we needed (U.S. security rules do not let [past presidents] fly commercial) and it was totally nuts. I actually phoned one of my favourite friends who had been a generous donor to the Sierra Club of Canada and got him to agree to put $10,000 on his Visa card to hold the plane," said May. "Dion was not involved in the invite but did have to sort out stuff in his role as president of COP due to the U.S. administration's hostility to their former president coming."[284] (May would be disappointed by the number of media queries that focused on how well Clinton knew Liberal MP Belinda Stronach rather than on the Kyoto process.)

The United States was unhappy, yes, but organizers could deal with that. What they couldn't allow was an actual diplomatic flap over some silly oversight. For that reason, while the RCMP sniffer dogs searched for explosives early Friday afternoon in Montreal, workers were busy turning all the chairs around to face the opposite direction in the room where the plenary had just wrapped up and Clinton would speak. It would become the "Saint-Laurent room." Clinton would stand in front of a hastily hung blue curtain and his audience would face away from the United Nations logo and convention symbols that had been the backdrop to Dion at the chair's table. As the program said, it was a "side event," and everybody pretended it had nothing to do with the conference. (Relations between the Martin government and the Bush White House were strained at the time and Clinton's appearance in Montreal didn't help. The decision by Jean Chrétien not to commit Canadian ground troops to Iraq in March 2003 had been the biggest factor in the deteriorating relationship after September 11, 2001. But the United States was not pleased with slights, perceived or otherwise, by Chrétien's successor, Paul Martin.)

Clinton told the crowd that negotiations for the Kyoto Protocol had gotten Al Gore involved in the climate change file.[285] The former president also said he knew the main criticisms of Kyoto were that the economies of developed nations would be hurt by "chaining them to greenhouse gas reductions that were not achievable" and that developing nations, already large greenhouse gas emitters, would become the worst unbridled offenders over the next decade. Clinton urged negotiators to find common ground "before it is too late to have meetings like this ... We'll have a meeting like this in forty years on a raft somewhere if we come to Canada to meet—unless we do something."[286]

Afterwards, Clinton and Prime Minister Martin held a joint press conference. Their appearance together further inflamed the U.S. team. American officials had complained to reporters privately about Martin's speech earlier in the week. On Wednesday, December 7, Martin had officially opened the plenary session, as was customary for the leader of the host nation, telling delegates, "The time is past to debate the impact of climate change. We no longer need to ask people to imagine its effects, for now we can see them.... There will be an economic toll. There will be a human toll."[287] That was message enough, but it was Martin's comment in the scrum that followed his December 7 speech that had most incensed the Americans. "To the reticent nations, including the United States, I say there is such a thing as a global conscience and now is the time to listen to it," said Martin.[288] It was a stinging remark, and one in which Martin appeared to be claiming moral superiority for Canada. Martin was exuberantly praised, with Bill Hare, director of Greenpeace International, calling his address "historic." John Bennett described it as "a barnburner" and Elizabeth May said it was "the best speech he ever gave and the best by a leader ever" to a climate change conference. But Washington found Martin's stance hard to stomach because, at least on the surface, the U.S. record on reducing greenhouse gas emissions appeared to be better than Canada's. In an interview with the Canadian Press, U.S. Ambassador to Canada David Wilkins lauded his country's record and noted: "It appears that oftentimes, some officials, in order to build Canada up, attempt to tear the United States down."[289]

On Friday afternoon, following Clinton's speech, another stumbling block arose. Russia suddenly opposed the language in the Kyoto provision on setting post-2012 targets. As the clock ticked past the official close of 6:00 P.M., Dion kept the meeting going, searching for a solution. But there seemed to be none. Shortly after six in the evening, he called for a break, adjourning the session. That break would last for more than twelve hours, while exhausted delegates continued to talk in closed committee meetings.

STÉPHANE DION was facing a difficult time as environment minister with the U.N. conference in Montreal, but he continued to relish his time back in cabinet after his political exile as a backbencher. The telephone call Dion had been awaiting from Prime Minister Paul Martin in December 2003 did arrive, after a fashion. More than six months later, in July 2004, Martin called Dion to invite him to accept a cabinet position. "He had a lot of phone calls to make and I didn't want to be too long," said Dion. "I told him, 'Thank you so much.'"[290]

Dion had loved nature since his childhood, had served on the environment committee (as well as justice) as a backbencher, and felt himself well positioned for the environment ministry. He would talk to Martin about how he wanted to bring the ministry to the core of the Ottawa decision-making process. In an interview in late 2006, he talked about rejoining the cabinet and what he had wanted to achieve. "I had seen how much the minister of the environment was alone. The classic way to see it was that the environment was a social policy, among others, and you can't do too much because you will hurt the economy. What I wanted to do was to change the paradigm: to put it at the core of the decision-making process and at the core of industrial strategy of the country."[291]

Dion focused on his central point, making the environment and economy work together, in his first public speech as environment minister to the Calgary Chamber of Commerce in September 2004. He would claim victory in getting a section on the environment included in the government's throne speech that fall. But not long after his appointment, Dion had seen how far he would have to go to have a real impact as minister. "One day at the cabinet table, I realized that there had been work done by colleagues of mine on a new industrial strategy for Canada. And I had not been invited to be part of this work, and neither had my department. But the minister of natural resources, industry, finance, and trade had been," said Dion. They had put together a report, and Dion told Martin he was "disappointed" not to have been included. "The prime minister reacted angrily. Mr. Martin wasn't happy. He told me, 'If you are not part of this, you need to involve yourself in working with your colleagues,' and so on. 'But Prime Minister,' I said, 'I never heard about this. Nobody came to me and told me.'"

He saw his work was cut out for him. "The prime minister wanted this new paradigm to be true, but he had difficulty in stopping to think about the old paradigm. The environment was a social policy, not at the core of the economic development of the country," said Dion. "[Martin] was angry but it was normal that he was angry from time to time, so I didn't take it personally. But very clearly, there was difficulty in shifting [thinking]. It is not because something is in the throne speech that it is in the genes of the decision-makers in Ottawa ... it was not the reflex of the machine and the PMO."

Dion recalled that he advised Martin: "If you want the environment to be noticed by the people, don't ask the minister of the environment to deliver a speech on it. I will always have the support of the [environmental] network. But if you want to reach out to the nation, ask the minister of finance or the minister of industry to deliver a speech ... So you see the paradigm I was trying to break? It was a fight, not because the prime minister was not willing to accept it in theory, but it was a fight to put it into practice."

It was during his period as environment minister over eighteen months, beginning in July 2004 and ending with the government's defeat in January 2006, that Dion began to develop a strategy for linking the economy and the environment and how he would implement the strategy. "If I were to succeed in being prime minister, I would send very clear signals: 'If you want to succeed in your career as a minister or a deputy minister, accept this change and show me that you understand it and you want to make it happen.'" Everybody would be involved, he said, citing agriculture, fisheries, trade, natural resources "obviously," everybody. "I will not necessarily put my 'greenest' minister at the department of the environment. Maybe it will be in public works, I don't know, but a department where I need a shift in bringing the environment to the core of the decision-

making process—to be sure that energy efficiency, resource production, recycling, habits of conservation will be at the core of what we
need to do," said Dion. Although he would further define his ideas,
he already had the basis of a philosophy that he would take into
the Liberal leadership campaign in 2006 and, after that, into the
Opposition Leader's Office.

Dion's deputy minister was Sammy Watson (the PM had thought
it a good idea to link a senior public servant from Western Canada
with a Quebec minister), and he told Dion he liked the plan to link
the economy and the environment. "What you are telling me is music
to my ears," Dion said Watson told him. Dion also found an important ally in Brian Guest, deputy principal secretary in the Prime
Minister's Office, who would go on to join his leadership campaign
team and follow him into Opposition. "Brian thought exactly like
me ... and he knew the network of experts in Canada and abroad,"
said Dion of the adviser who would help him prepare his climate
change document "Project Green." "Brian thought that it was possible to come up with something, while my bureaucracy in the
department of the environment was ready to give up. They thought
that they would not be able to get the government to have a climate
change plan that would be full of muscle," said Dion. "And when
Brian said 'No, no, it's possible,' then, with the [support] of the
others, we did something that was very strong."

Dion's briefing meetings in the ministry had quickly turned into
marathon sessions, catered affairs because no one could get in and
out before Question Period without a meal. "Getting material to his
satisfaction never stopped being a problem in the department," said
Jamie Carroll, who signed on with Dion as director of parliamentary
affairs in July 2004. "Departments just weren't geared to satisfy an
insatiable minister."

Stéphane Dion's tenure as environment minister was marked by
controversy and criticisms, although nothing that compared with the

turbulent days of the Clarity Act. He battled to gain influence at the cabinet table. Not unexpectedly, there were tensions between Minister of Natural Resources John Efford and Dion over how to handle negotiations with automakers to reduce greenhouse gas emissions. Unlike Efford, Dion wanted to legislate and was soon threatening publicly to do so. Eventually Dion and Efford reached a compromise. In a memorandum-of-understanding signed with the federal government on April 6, 2005, automakers agreed to voluntarily reduce emissions in all new vehicles. As environmentalists pointed out, however, it was not legally binding. There was another nonbinding agreement in March of that year among the federal government, the Ontario government, and the Canadian Steel Producers Association on greenhouse gas emissions. And, on April 13, 2005, Dion unveiled his much-touted $10 billion Kyoto plan. It included a $1 billion climate fund that could be increased to $5 billion over five years. The Martin government had been criticized for not having revealed its emission reduction plan as promised when Parliament had been asked to ratify the Kyoto Protocol in February of 2005. Dion promised the targets would be part of his green plan. Critics suggested squabbling among Dion, Efford, and Minister of Industry David Emerson caused the delay. On the same day, February 17, Martin announced that Montreal would host the December summit on climate change.[292]

Dion's green plan set Canada's Kyoto target at an annual reduction of 270 megatonnes of greenhouse gases from 2008 to 2012. He was criticized for not going far enough and for going too far. *Financial Post* columnist Terence Corcoran disagreed in principle on Kyoto.[293] Of Dion's plan, Corcoran wrote: "What we couldn't appreciate, until it was all assembled in a single monster document, is the mind-blowing madness behind Kyoto. Only by looking at the whole plan, half-baked though it is, does this mass exercise in collective insanity become clear." Corcoran argued that carbon dioxide was released in general by animal respiration and taken in by plants during photosynthesis. Was Dion proposing, he asked, that the exhalation of carbon dioxide become illegal? Moreover, Corcoran argued that federal measures would shut down one-third of the economy.

The Martin government, and particularly Stéphane Dion as environment minister, would be mocked by the anti-Kyoto club for the hypocrisy of its position on climate change. It would soon become clear that Canada had not only failed to meet its six percent Kyoto reduction target, but that greenhouse gas emissions had risen by 24.9 percent over the base year of 1990. That anomaly was the context for Washington's scathing reaction to being lectured by Martin about a "global conscience" in Montreal. And that attack on Dion's record would be a recurring theme, both during the leadership race (the "You didn't get it done" taunt of Dion's rival Michael Ignatieff) and later by the Conservative party's attack ads against the new Liberal leader that relied heavily on the Ignatieff clip from a leadership debate.

But Elizabeth May, among other environmentalists, flatly rejected the criticism. "One big fat piece of misinformation is that somehow the Bush administration has done better at reducing emissions than Canada. The U.S. has not done better," she said in a Winnipeg speech in 2005. "The U.S. has not reduced emissions at all. [Emissions] have risen by more than one billion tonnes since 1990." May said it had to be taken into consideration that Canada accounts for three percent of global emissions, far below the twenty-five percent of the United States. "So our 24.9 percent increase, while deplorable, pales in comparison to the U.S., which has increased its emissions by 16 percent above 1990 levels." And May blamed the rise in Canadian emissions on the boom in oil production from the mammoth tar sands project near Fort McMurray in northern Alberta. "The tar sands are the reason—not one reason, they are *the* reason—that on a percentage basis, our emissions have gone up much more than those in the U.S."[294]

Moreover, May argued that Chrétien didn't help efforts by Martin's government to lessen the burning of fossil fuels and the resulting impact on the environment. In 1996, Chrétien had flown to Edmonton to announce federal investment in the tar sands and promise that his government would not bring in a carbon tax. That year Chrétien also agreed to a series of measures to benefit the oil and gas industry, such as being able to write off one hundred percent of equipment costs against the year's income. There was another concession, a large one, which Chrétien outlined in a 1996 letter to the Canadian Association of Petroleum Producers. Oil companies were required to reduce greenhouse gases as a ratio to the number of barrels of oil they produce. After 1996, Chrétien's plan ensured that if the cost to the producer of reducing emissions exceeded fifteen dollars per tonne, the federal government paid the difference. May also stressed that oil from the tar sands, which rose in production from half a million barrels a day in 1995 to 1.3 million barrels in 2006, goes to meet the huge demand in the United States. "Canada now sells more oil and gas to the United States than does Saudi Arabia," said May.[295] Added John Bennett: "The tar sands are supplying the Americans with energy … George Bush stood there and watched Canada [get criticized]. Not fair. What political party could stem the tide of that?"[296] However, Bennett cited another reason for the rise in Canadian greenhouse gas emissions: Nuclear power plants in Ontario had broken down during the 1990s and coal-fired energy suppliers were running around the clock.

Bennett was unabashed in his praise for Dion's record in the environment. "He pushed cabinet as far as it would go. He was stopped by policies that were in place and were not of his doing." Bennett had observed the outward signs that Dion had fought hard for power at the cabinet table. "He won the internal cabinet debate. At issue was the absolute aspect of the natural resources ministry's authority over the issues. [Dion] got the gist and he hit the ground running. What he did very cleverly was to move more authority on climate change over to environment and he took control of issues in a public sense," said Bennett. He would miss Dion. "He was the best environment minister we've ever had. When he took it on, he really took it on."

During the 2006 leadership campaign, Bennett would spot Dion at an airport, but didn't want to disturb him. Bennett was standing in line for his ticket when he felt a tap on his shoulder. It was Dion wanting to talk about climate change, about how things were going, and about what had happened since he'd left the ministry. Bennett would watch on television when Dion won the leadership on December 2, 2006. "I can't tell you what an emotional rush it was to hear the new leader of the Liberal party say in his first breath that he wanted sustainable development!"

MEANWHILE, at the Palais des Congrès on December 9, 2005, the hours crept by. The plenary session was set to resume at eight o'clock and then at midnight, and then at 2:00 A.M. Youth activists were curled up on chairs or sleeping on the floor. Finally, at 2:44 in the morning, Stéphane Dion gavelled the plenary back in session. According to May, the word was that "he was going to try and bluff the Russians." Their delegation was still opposing language in the section on a post-2012 protocol (Article 3.9). Each country had a little nameplate that delegates would flip up when they wanted to speak. The Russians flipped up their nameplate and objected. "It was quite an extraordinary moment," said May. "[They said] 'We never saw this language before, it is new to us ... We object on behalf of the Russian Federation.'"[297]

According to May, Dion replied: "As you are now blocking important progress for the fate of the world, I suggest you explain your reasons to the entire world." She thought, "At 2:44 A.M., that's pretty good." And then, British environment minister Beckett interjected: "I appeal to our dear friends from Russia, you who more than anyone else have given so much to bring this agreement to life."[298]

Still, there was no progress. Dion again adjourned the session. Delegates formed a "contact group" and crammed into a small room to discuss the unresolved language. At one point, David Drake made an important intervention. May would call Drake "a Canadian diplomat whose name you will not know but for whom you should name your children because thank God for him." Drake was contact group cochair and he kept the meeting going against moans of fatigue from people, quite reasonable people, who wanted to retire to their beds. "I have not slept for thirty-six hours. I would like to," said a Brazilian delegate. Replied a Russian: "You think you have not slept! You can well imagine that I have not slept for longer." So, as May remembered, "everybody was getting depressed."[299]

It was getting so serious that Ottawa brought in its secret weapon: the PMO switchboard. Operators were burning up the lines trying to reach Russian president Vladimir Putin. Martin had been awakened to take the call if operators got through. André Lamarre, Dion's press secretary, recalled that he had searched the internet for contact numbers at the Kremlin and that Ottawa was talking to fourth and fifth assistants. Allan Rock, Canada's ambassador to the United Nations, had been awakened in New York and was trying to contact his Russian counterpart. The Canadians believed the Russians in Montreal had reacted to pressure from the U.S. delegation and were not under instructions from Moscow. Why would they suddenly change their minds and block the clause? Russia had ratified the Kyoto Protocol. The suspense grew; people's nerves were frayed. At last, Pettigrew got Russian foreign minister Lavrov on the line.[300]

Lavrov told Pettigrew his instructions had been different and asked to speak to his delegation. Pettigrew raced back into the hall waving the cell phone and looking for the Russians. Behind him sprinted Lamarre. Successful, Pettigrew held up the phone to the Russian representative but the man refused to take the call.

"Your boss is on the line," Pettigrew told him, according to Lamarre. Lavrov could probably hear them in Russia. With great reluctance, one of the Russian delegates finally took the phone from Pettigrew, spoke to his foreign minister, and, as Lamarre would remember, "did not look too proud."[301]

At 5:30 A.M., David Drake rushed out of his meeting room, then hurried back in to tell everyone: "Something's happening. Let's get back to Plenary." By that time, the conference hall was like a movie set that had been struck. Carpets had been rolled up, the furniture was being moved, and the United Nations logo was gone from behind the chair's table. A lot of delegates had left.[302]

At last, at 5:50 A.M., Dion gavelled the conference back in session. "You could see everything in his face," said Lamarre. "It had been accomplished." They would go on to an election campaign in which Lamarre would remember Dion scratching his head and telling reporters that he couldn't believe they weren't more interested in what had been achieved in the last exciting hours of the COP-11/MOP-1 conference that Saturday morning in Montreal. They had pushed the Kyoto Protocol forward and kept the concept of another target period alive after 2012. That was something.

With the end in sight, Dion wanted to move the session along. There was another round of his banging gavel. As May described it: "Okay, agreement on the Conference of the Parties, do I hear objections? No (knocks). I now close the Meeting of the Conference of the Parties (knocks). Now I move (knocks) we open the Meeting of the Parties. Accepting language of Article 9 (knocks). Carried. Accepting language of Article 3.9 (knocks). Carried. Accepting CDM [Clean Development Mechanism] (knocks). Carried. Accepting the Marrakech agreements (knocks). Carried." May was exultant that "every single thing" carried.[303]

By 6:14 in the morning, Dion was almost finished. He kept having to admonish May and other activists at the back of the room: "Quiet, please! I don't want to lose the translators. We must finish this business." Actually, the translators' shifts had been over for quite some time. But they had remained, watching the proceedings from their glass booth. "I have prepared some closing comments … I wonder if anyone might stay and translate it?" Dion asked them.[304] They applauded him before translating his last few comments to the exhausted crowd. At 6:17 A.M., on Saturday, December 10, 2005, Dion banged his gavel one final time and the conference was over.

CHAPTER TEN

POLITICS IS AN ART

S TÉPHANE DION LEARNED WELL from Jean Chrétien. By the
time he ran for the Liberal leadership in 2006, he was even
talking like his mentor. That was in evidence at the Liberal leadership
convention in Montreal, where, late at night on Friday, December 1,
Dion was sequestered with Gerard Kennedy in Kennedy's third-floor
campaign office at the Palais des Congrès. The two rivals were struggling at the last minute to agree to a deal for one to throw support to
the other the next day. As they were meeting (at the same site where
Dion had achieved his U.N. success the year before), some five thousand Liberal delegates awaited the results of the first ballot. Nobody
expected a winner on that first vote, but the field of eight candidates
would begin to be winnowed down as the last-place finisher dropped
off each successive ballot. Moreover, there could be other dropouts.
Montreal hummed that night with the sounds of deal-making.

Timing was critical for Kennedy and Dion; they both understood
that. They'd been talking for weeks about a deal and now they were
down to the crunch. Kennedy kept pushing Dion to agree to specifics,
and they were going over the same ground. "We need to make sure
that one of us will win," Dion said Kennedy told him. "He was
concerned that I would go to him too late," said Dion, and if that
happened, Kennedy was certain that front-runner Michael Ignatieff
would win. "But Gerard wanted some kind of mathematical rule,"

recalled Dion, and he couldn't accept that. They were only five years apart in age: Dion was fifty-one and Kennedy forty-six. And they'd both made their political debuts in the same year, 1996. But that night, Dion admonished Kennedy as if he were a much less experienced man: "Politics is not a science, Gerard ... I cannot tell you when I will conclude that I need to pull out."[305]

Outside the closed door, officials from both camps stood impatiently in the hallway or sweated it out in Dion's campaign office nearby. The two campaigns had been talking since so-called Super Weekend, the mad blitz at the end of September in which Liberals in ridings across Canada met to select their delegates for the upcoming convention. Super Weekend was nirvana for political junkies, who could tap into the Liberal party's website as often as they wanted for up-to-the-minute results. The original idea for some sort of merger between these two camps came from Raymond Chan, the Richmond MP who was a Kennedy organizer in British Columbia. Talks occurred at all levels of their respective campaigns: Kennedy's top political people, Katie Telford and David MacNaughton, met with Dion's Herb Metcalfe and Andrew Bevan; their respective policy teams worked together—Brian Guest for Dion and Rob Silver for Kennedy; and Dion's campaign manager Mark Marissen and deputy Jamie Carroll talked to everybody on the Kennedy side, including MPs Mark Holland from Ajax-Pickering and Navdeep Bains from Mississauga-Brampton South. They'd met in restaurants in Toronto, Ottawa, and Vancouver, had drinks across the country, and rendezvoused in countless coffee shops. Bevan once flew down for a meeting at the Toronto Island airport terminal, then turned around and flew back to Ottawa. Their thumb pads were worn down from using their BlackBerries. And, of course, Dion and Kennedy kept talking.

After Wednesday's opening ceremonies, Dion and Kennedy had talked over a beer in the lounge of the Place d'Armes Hotel in Old

Montreal. The Dion delegation had rented the entire hotel, and it was packed with Dionistas with their red paraphernalia. On Wednesday, Dion and Kennedy had realized that the plan for a full merger wasn't going to fly. Their respective teams had hoped to put out a joint policy statement on Thursday, with an accompanying op-ed piece for English and French newspapers. "The idea was to let it bounce around the convention for a couple of days that we were basically a joint campaign—you know, let it circulate among people as they were voting," said Kennedy.[306] They couldn't pull it off. Kennedy saw that "it wasn't essentially [Dion's] natural position ... and I was never that comfortable with it either." And on Thursday, Dion and Kennedy met again, leaving the convention site after the gala tribute to Paul Martin to drive over to Dion's Montreal townhouse. That meeting was late, too, because the gala had run so long.

And so, there they were late on Friday night, down to the wire and without a deal. They faced two strong opponents with more support than either of them. Ignatieff, an urbane academic and author from Toronto, had been out in front from the beginning; his entry onto the Canadian political scene after three decades abroad had been skillfully stage-managed on the advice of, among others, his canny Toronto agent, Michael Levine. And then there was Bob Rae. His huge advantage was the political acumen of his brother and backroom adviser, John Rae, of Power Corporation. John Rae was like Senator David Smith; people took his phone calls.

Super Weekend results had put Ignatieff in the lead with about thirty percent of delegates, Rae was second with twenty percent, Kennedy third with seventeen percent, and Dion next with sixteen percent, followed by the bottom group of four, Ken Dryden, Scott Brison, Joe Volpe, and Martha Hall Findlay, all with five percent or less.[307] But in the run-up to Montreal, delegate polls were showing that Rae, who had been New Democratic Party premier of Ontario, had the momentum. Ignatieff and Rae had a disadvantage though:

polls also showed a polarized reaction among delegates, many of whom said they would never vote for either man. Working together, Dion and Kennedy thought they could make use of that disadvantage to propel one or the other to victory. Each was convinced that person would be himself.

The recollections of both men suggest that Kennedy did more talking than Dion that night. They also suggest that Dion was not totally forthcoming with Kennedy or, more precisely, was only as forthcoming as Kennedy demanded him to be, which was not very. They had just delivered their speeches to the convention and Kennedy was in an upbeat mood. He thought he'd done better than Dion, who'd been cut off at the mike, but he was tactful. "If you've had a good speech and the other guy's had problems, you don't raise it, right?" Kennedy took one last stab at trying to "coach" Dion into accepting rules for Saturday, including an agreed-upon "trigger" for pulling out of the race. Dion continued to balk. Their meeting, which had begun after 10:00 P.M., lasted about ninety minutes. As Kennedy remembered it, the "business end" took only two or three minutes once they got down to it:

"Okay, Stéphane, well, I guess what it comes down to is who is your second choice?" Kennedy asked Dion.

"It's you," replied Dion.

"And you're mine," said Kennedy. "Okay, that's good. Why don't we leave it at that?"

They shook on it. After weeks of talking, that was the only deal Stéphane Dion and Gerard Kennedy would make, and they did it less than an hour before Liberal party officials announced first-ballot results. "Ultimately," said Kennedy, "we just looked each other in the eye and I said, 'We're going to have to trust each other on this ... I mean, what it comes down to is it's just you and I. You'll make your judgement and I'll make my judgement on whatever we think is the best time and, hopefully, we'll stay in touch on the floor.'"

It was that loose. Still, their organizers were ecstatic. For the first time, Andrew Bevan, the cagey Welsh-born analyst who was Dion's communications and policy director, knew there was a deal and was relieved. There was no quid pro quo. On that, Kennedy was adamant. "No, zero, zero," he said. "He didn't ask for anything; I didn't ask for anything." Kennedy elaborated: "It was only about trying to win. I was not looking for a safe landing and there was no inevitability that we would have to have somebody [withdraw]." Dion said that "deal" was not a good word; they had more of an "understanding." He had found Kennedy in general to be "motivated, full of ideas, more experienced than me on those kinds of things. He was leading the conversation more than me; I was listening. He was telling me it was win-win." Kennedy's campaign focused on renewal, said Dion. "He was [about] renewal of processes and I was [about] renewal of ideas and he liked that."

Kennedy was confident he could deliver his delegates to Dion, whereas Dion's people "seemed to be a little less committed to him, let alone to his choice ... the polls had shown that I had the highest loyalty component." Kennedy was right about that. There was an almost cult-like devotion among his supporters. Bruce Young, a lawyer and Kennedy supporter, who is a tall man built like a line-backer, got teary-eyed talking about his candidate over pizza one Saturday night in Vancouver. He quoted from the warrior speech in *Henry V*—"We few, we happy few, we band of brothers"—and talked about how Kennedy was saving the world when he was twenty-two, having dropped out of his last year of university to work at a food bank, while Young, like most frat boys, was more interested in girls and parties.[308] Kennedy had spent thirteen years at Edmonton's Food Bank and the Daily Bread Food Bank in Toronto, mostly as executive director.

Comparing their two organizations, Kennedy had concluded: "They seemed to be a campaign with loose wheels and not that organizational sort of strength, and we had a lot of very effective people." Kennedy believed that his most serious mistake before the convention had been handling the issue of how well he spoke French. "We didn't manage that ourselves and I didn't perform in some of the situations the way I thought I was capable," said Kennedy. "Which added up, for a lot of people there, to the simple equation: 'We need Dion because we need the comfort of Quebec.'"

Kennedy and Dion had gotten off to a rocky start at their first meeting in a Montreal restaurant around June 2006. The Kennedy campaign had a rule. "Our team had said, 'Don't knock anybody down. This is not a candidacy against the Conservatives; this is different. At the end of the day, everybody's got to be on your side.'" Kennedy was careful with his leadership rivals. He remembered Dion had been needling him in one debate and Kennedy let his prepared rebuttal—"Well, you've never really gotten anything done on Kyoto!"—go by. "I bit my tongue," said Kennedy. Not so Dion. "It was seen that he had been very aggressive and that I had been less so," said Kennedy, preferring the passive voice to criticize. "And it could be seen by some that he was pretty rude, and that's no way to make friends."

"I was not always being so nice with him during debates," admitted Dion. When they met in Montreal, Kennedy said that Dion was "true to his bad reputation of being distant ... and it seemed to me he was prepared to argue with me about the menu."

They tried again and pulled it off at a breakfast meeting later in June. They talked about their respective records as federal and provincial ministers (Kennedy had been Ontario education minister), cleared up misunderstandings on shared files, and came away liking each other. Kennedy recognized the outsider in Dion. "I guess I'm putting myself in that category, whether I achieve that in anyone's perspective or not. That's how I perceive myself." Kennedy had identified an important aspect of the Dion persona: he always seemed to go against the current of conventional wisdom. Kennedy and Dion were kindred spirits, which was why they were able to come to an understanding Friday night in Montreal.

It was Dion's status as outsider that, above all other traits, allowed him to offer himself as a leadership candidate in the first place. He had managed to get through 2005—and the two-part final report by Justice John Gomery of Quebec—without being smeared by the sponsorship scandal that helped put the Liberals in opposition in 2006 and, after so much effort, took away Paul Martin's shot at being a lasting prime minister. Kennedy wasn't the first to describe Stéphane Dion as an outsider. He had held on to that image during a decade of privileged access to Prime Minister Jean Chrétien and cabinet positions under both Chrétien and Martin. The sponsorship scandal could have stripped him of that advantage, and, for that reason, it is worth a detour from Stéphane Dion's moment of understanding with Gerard Kennedy in Montreal.

THE GENESIS OF "SPONSORGATE" lay in the summer of 2000 when *Globe and Mail* reporter Daniel Leblanc began looking into federal advertising in Quebec. In the aftermath of the 1995 referendum, the Chrétien government had created a $90 million public relations fund called the Sponsorship Program to boost Canada's image in Quebec, under the discretion of Minister of Public Works Alfonso Gagliano. It was supposed to sponsor events with the maple leaf and federal logos prominently displayed. Leblanc began to suspect mismanagement and teamed up with colleague Campbell Clark to follow the money. Story by story, the pair slowly broke what eventually became one of the biggest scandals in recent Canadian history.

The scandal blew wide open in February 2004—two months into Martin's tenure as prime minister—when Auditor General Sheila Fraser released a report showing that Ottawa had paid more than $100 million to Quebec advertising firms for little or no work. "I think this is such a blatant misuse of public funds that it is shocking," Fraser told reporters. "I'm actually appalled by what we've found."[309] Martin immediately fired Gagliano, who was then ambassador to Denmark, and announced that Justice Gomery would head the Commission of Inquiry into the Sponsorship Program and Advertising Activities. After extensive televised hearings, which saw Radio-Canada's ratings skyrocket among Quebec viewers and Liberal fortunes plummet, Gomery released his findings in two reports, the first blaming the Liberals for creating such a loosely defined and poorly regulated program, and the second proposing solutions. There were criminal charges arising from separate proceedings against two advertising executives and one federal bureaucrat.[310]

Dion had been called before the Gomery Commission, and that testimony, delivered at Old City Hall in Ottawa on January 25, 2005, helped illustrate why he hadn't become entangled in the scandal. He appeared to relish his afternoon on the stand. Dion was blunt, funny, at times the professor, at times the indignant moralist, and he repeatedly criticized the idea of using slogans and logos to win the unity battle in Quebec. He had faced higher stakes with the Clarity Act. Commission lawyer Guy Cournoyer asked Dion about the 1996 cabinet meetings in Vancouver where a committee report on Quebec had been tabled and accepted by ministers. The cabinet had recommended "the Liberal Party of Canada in Quebec be substantially strengthened" by, among other measures, hiring organizers and targeting ridings. Cournoyer asked Dion if he had found it "surprising" that cabinet ministers appeared to have been promoting partisan measures that benefited the Liberal party more than Canadians. "Yes, it's surprising," Dion replied. "I can tell you that I've never seen anything like it in my nine years in politics. That was probably the first document I read from the government. Perhaps it didn't strike me as odd at the time, but now, looking back, I'm astonished that public servants would engage in these types of reflections, which pertain to partisan politics."[311]

Dion testified that he didn't know exactly when he became aware of the existence of the Sponsorship Program or whether it had been mentioned in cabinet. But he didn't like the idea. Indeed, Dion had told reporters in May 2002 that he had never seen anyone change their mind about Canadian unity because of a sponsorship event, telling the Gomery Commission that his comment had been used to embarrass Chrétien. Cournoyer questioned Dion about his closeness to Chrétien, inquiring how he could have failed to know how funds were being used for sponsorship events when they fell under the auspices of the Ministry of Intergovernmental Affairs. "The Department of Intergovernmental Affairs is in the Privy Council," Dion said, as if addressing his public administration class. "The Minister of Intergovernmental Affairs reports directly to the Prime Minister and cannot function efficiently unless he has a close relationship with the Prime Minister."[312] Dion himself emphasized the uniqueness of his bond with Chrétien, whom he admired, stressing that he could pick up the phone and get him on the line anytime. They hadn't discussed the sponsorship issue, said Dion, and a particular unity fund in question had been handled by Chrétien. "I obviously had full confidence in Chrétien," he said, "or I wouldn't have gotten into politics."[313] Dion testified that he hadn't known the fund was supposed to be secret and would have told reporters about it if asked. He continued to underscore his skepticism about its supposed ability to strengthen Canadian unity.

His testimony over, Dion returned to his job at the Environment Ministry, tabled his Project Green in the spring of 2005, worked towards the United Nations conference at year's end, and, when he started to ask friends and colleagues what they thought of a leadership bid in early 2006, the sponsorship scandal did not appear to be a stumbling block. When the grassroots of the Liberal party complained in 2006 about old-style politics, about sinking morale, about the effects of the debilitating feud between Martin and Chrétien, and

about the legacy of a sponsorship scandal in which people had testified about briefcases full of cash, they did not include Stéphane Dion
in their criticisms. He had been attacked in Quebec and, indeed, had
paid a heavy price, but it was for the Clarity Act, not the sponsorship
scandal. His outsider status had served to win him the grudging respect
of his foes for his steely integrity and actions that, while perhaps
unpalatable, appeared to be honest. His supporters lauded that
integrity. Adam Campbell, party president in Alberta, compared
support for Dion going into Montreal to "a people's movement. It
wasn't a revolt by any means, but there were a lot of people saying, 'We
are Liberals and Stéphane Dion represents what we want in the Liberal
party'... I've known that right from the get go. I've known that was
what we were ready for ... People were actually tired of glib politics.
We didn't want that again. Stéphane represents that sense of the
collective—approachable, reasonable, and resonating with people."[314]

By 2006, there had been a mellowing in the Quebec media, especially after the United Nations conference. Quebecers had noticed
that the world had come to their city. Serge Chapleau had begun to
draw Dion as a mouse instead of a rat. And, under the headline "The
rehabilitation of Stéphane Dion," André Pratte, respected editorial
page editor of La Presse, wrote positively when Dion announced his
candidacy on April 7, 2006. Pratte argued that Dion deserved a
second chance in Quebec and that the Clarity Act wasn't so bad.
Polls continued to show that Quebecers had come to accept its logic,
and if Quebec did want to separate at some future date, the last thing
anybody needed was ambiguity in the referendum results. Pratte
made arguments long advocated by Dion. He had chosen the Palais
des Congrès for his launch. "Where else?" he asked. Wrote Pratte in
La Presse: "Although he dedicated the majority of his speech to
sustainable development, the first question from journalists was
about ... the Clarity Act. It was proof that 'Plan B'—of which he is
the proud founder—will be glued eternally to his hip ... Maybe it's

time Quebecers altered their perception of this distinct politician. One can find that Dion doesn't have an endearing personality. One can be opposed to 'Plan B' and note that the strategy does not fix the Quebec question. But it must also be said that Stéphane Dion is not at all the monster that his adversaries have taken an unhealthy pleasure in making of him."[315]

One couldn't point to a specific date and say that was when Dion made a transformation that allowed him to illuminate the art of politics for Gerard Kennedy in Montreal. But Peter Donolo, the sharp-eyed political consultant who had been Chrétien's director of communications, observed the change in March 2006 when they appeared together on a political science panel at Concordia University in Montreal. "I gave my presentation and I was more academic than Stéphane. It was clear in my eyes that he'd made the transition from academic to politician," said Donolo. When Dion talked about the possibility of running for the Liberal leadership, Donolo saw that "this was not the Stéphane Dion of 1995 saying this to me." While Donolo didn't think Dion had much of a chance, he was an advocate of the theory that nobody wins the lottery without buying a ticket. Besides, Donolo, who had been impressed by Dion in Ottawa, believed he "would raise the level of debate."[316]

Many reacted with skepticism to a Dion candidacy. On Parliament Hill, former environment ministry staffer Carroll explained to Dion, in stark terms, how difficult the task of winning the Liberal leadership—of even mounting a credible campaign—would be for him. His opponents laughed outright. So did his friends. Graciela Ducatenzeiler invited some of Dion's old university crowd, maybe ten people, to dinner on a Friday night. "I'm thinking of jumping into the race," said Dion. "No!" they all cried. "No way! No, Stéphane, no. You don't need this!" Denis Saint-Martin chortled when he remembered what he had told his friend that night: "You're going to waste all the nice political capital that you've been gaining in the past year with the Kyoto thing." Saint-Martin advised Dion to be smart and use his political capital to make himself indispensable to a new leader—who would not be him. "So that," said Saint-Martin, "was my advice—and of course he didn't take it."[317]

On the other side there were fewer, but more significant, voices. Senator Shirley Maheu had believed in Stéphane Dion. She was a firecracker of a woman who had been around municipal and federal politics for more than a quarter of a century. At seventy-five her health was fragile, but on election night, January 23, 2006, she nevertheless made it down to his campaign headquarters in Saint-Laurent-Cartierville. People were milling about shortly after the polls closed at eight, waiting for results. Maheu got up on stage and told the crowd that Dion would be prime minister one day. "She was sure, she was one hundred and ten percent sure," said Loïc Tassé, a young academic who had gotten to know Maheu while working for Dion. "She was very sick at the time and it was a tremendous effort for her to get there and make the speech. She had cancer in her brain, you know, and she was in pain. But she was there for that reason: because she believed. It was very touching when you think about it, going back … She was a really good person."[318]

As soon as Dion's own re-election was assured that night he headed over to Martin's riding in nearby LaSalle-Émard to wait out the defeat of the government and Martin's announcement that he would retire from politics. Dion travelled in a van with his wife, Janine, their eighteen-year-old daughter, Jeanne, political aide Gianluca Cairo, and, at the wheel, André Lamarre. Afterwards, on the drive back to the Dion-Krieber townhouse off Côte-des-Neiges Road in downtown Montreal, they talked about who should replace Martin, and that was when Janine had commented that it should be her husband. During the weeks to come, others would concur with her. Some would offer advice and encouragement. But none would match the emotional impact of Shirley Maheu revealing the depth of her faith in Dion in her last public appearance, nine days before her death. Time is never more precious than when one knows it's running out. By giving her time to Dion, Maheu had anointed him somehow.

Moreover, he had Janine. "I don't think he's going to listen to you," Janine had told Saint-Martin and the others at Graciela's.[319] What she meant was *she* wasn't going to listen. "Life is short," she always told Stéphane. "Don't do what you think you should do, do what you want to do." She knew he wanted to run; she agreed he should run. Her opinion counted. She had never been loud in her views and in social groups was most often the quiet one taking the photographs. But theirs was most definitely a partnership. Stéphane Dion and Janine Krieber couldn't be compared, say, to the two-for-one Bill and Hillary Clinton model of the early 1990s. Janine herself described their dynamic: "I don't advise him, we discuss."[320] But she offered Dion first-hand experience in areas where he lacked expertise, from an understanding of the international system of criminal justice to the study of terrorism. Her own list of published works was prodigious and, by 2006, she had long been a recognized international expert on security issues, had travelled to Afghanistan, had worked with the Canadian Security Intelligence Service (CSIS) on confidential matters, had done research for the federal Department of National Defence, and was involved in other intelligence issues.[321] Krieber was an artist, and several of her paintings of Afghan women were hanging in their Montreal townhouse. She could be fearless in expressing an opinion. When asked by *Gazette* reporter Jeff Heinrich in December 2006 if she had brought back a burka as a souvenir from Afghanistan, she shot back that she didn't collect "instruments of torture." She took breaks from the Montreal convention to smoke outside with her friend Marta Wale, a Dion delegate, and rolled her eyes when Dion won at the prospect of media stories about her wicked smoking habit. Said Wale, laughing: "If anyone expects Janine to be a politically correct wife, that's not going to happen."[322]

Janine told her husband she was "confident that if he ran, he could win," she said. She said he attracted many young, dynamic organizers because "they felt they could make a difference in this organization. It was not a question of backroom boys deciding everything. There was no hidden organization … There was no organization at all."

How right she was. Eventually, Dion was able to attract prominent people to his candidacy, although never in the numbers of Ignatieff, Rae, or Kennedy. Dion telephoned former Liberal minister Don Boudria, another exile from cabinet in 2003, about whom he would say, "If Don had told me, 'No, I don't think it makes sense,' I don't think I would have run. But he asked me for twenty-four hours and he phoned me back to say, 'Not only do I think you should run, I will help you do anything.'" Boudria became a senior adviser. Jamie Carroll never joined officially, but Dion knew he had him on the hook. "The man's like water on a rock," said Norman Wale, of Dion's incremental approach to coaxing people. He persuaded them to work for just a little while, and they ended up staying. Carroll brought in his girl-friend, Megan Meltzer, who became Dion's director of fund-raising, and she began tapping her extensive contacts across the country.[323]

Meltzer helped land the savvy Marissen. On April 26, 2006, Dion was on a low-budget swing to Vancouver, ostensibly for a Liberal meeting but in reality to meet Marissen. On that Friday morning, he gave a lacklustre speech to B.C. Liberals. That night, in the home Marissen shared in Vancouver with his wife, Christy Clark, former Liberal deputy premier of B.C., and their three-year-old son, Hamish, Dion gave the speech of his life. He stood in the stairwell and spoke to about a hundred people. It was a turning point in his campaign. Carroll had told him to wear jeans and speak from the heart. No notes with scribbles in the margins. "He talked about the country, about ensuring that we don't want to become foreigners to each other," said Marissen. "It was the sentiment, it was class on display. He confirmed to me that he was a good guy and people liked him." Marissen had planned to host all the candidates in his home and Dion's was the second event, after Nova Scotia MP Scott Brison's a few weeks earlier. But the next morning at a breakfast meeting in downtown Vancouver, Marissen told Dion, Carroll, and Cairo that he would join the campaign; within a day or so he had accepted the position of campaign manager. Marissen called the breakfast the "most absurd political interview of my life." He coined a new word that soon became hackneyed: "Dionesque." Carroll and Cairo were over the moon at having snagged Marissen; Dion seemed oblivious, trying to write a personal cheque to Marissen for $400 to cover expenses from the night before. It would be the first campaign expense, Marissen kept telling him.

Dion was a study in contradictions in the leadership campaign, as in his life. He could be both smart, as in the "politics is not a science" approach to Kennedy, and gutsy, as when he stood up for Chrétien's record. Other leadership candidates wanted to pretend the Liberal legacy had jumped from Pierre Trudeau in 1968 to the present day without mentioning anything in between. Jean Chrétien quietly smouldered over having his record treated like a smelly fish. On leadership night in Montreal, he beamed from the stage with former prime ministers Paul Martin and John Turner. But, in an interview, he denounced all the "hypocrisy going on" about his achievements. (He also referred to efforts to kick Dion out of his riding in 2004 as "a damned stupid move.") About the sponsorship scandal, Chrétien insisted: "Three guys were found guilty … and none of them was a Liberal … Not one single person [in his government] was accused of a crime … I'm not saying that errors weren't made." He couldn't wait to get out the memoirs he was still writing.[324]

Dion's good instincts were often evident. "I don't think he's naive," said friend Norman Wale. "I think he has street smarts … remember, an academic career is full of intrigue, jealousy, and competition. It makes federal politics look like child's play."[325] Still, Dion could appear to be politically obtuse. Carroll gave an example. In early 2006, people suspected Dion was about to make a run for the leadership when he showed suspicious behaviour by actually working the room at an event for Sheila Copps. Dion didn't like small talk and usually avoided such events. Soon after, Carroll was in a car with Dion, listening to him talk on the phone with Canadian Press reporter Joan Bryden. It was off the record clearly, but Carroll could hear Dion saying he was thinking about running but he didn't know what to do because his people wanted him to buy votes. "And I practically hit him over the head. 'No! For the love of God, don't be telling Joan you're trying to buy votes!'" Carroll shouted from the backseat. Dion was referring to having been told that his campaign workers would have to start signing up new members—as would all the leadership campaigners—in order to meet a July deadline. In the car that day, Carroll practically had a heart attack.

Another example was the dustup between Carroll and Dion over Super Weekend in the summer of 2006. By then, the campaign was whizzing along, relatively speaking. They'd brought Bevan in, as well as Brian Guest, who organized the website and tackled membership files. Marissen had signed up Denise Brunsdon, a Young Liberal whiz who was studying economics at McGill, and she started the all-important blog campaign. Other candidates had wooed Brunsdon, including goalie great Ken Dryden, who had taken her to see the Canadiens in the playoffs in Montreal. Veteran strategist Herb Metcalfe took on the self-described role as "father" to a younger campaign team, Geoffroi Montpetit was working on policy, and Lamarre was media director. Money was tight, but they made the decision to keep Dion working over the summer, travelling when he could. "We kept him accessible," said Bevan. "We knew the bookends of the summer were the more formal debates but [Liberals] were not going to sleep for the summer. So if there's a vacuum, we wanted to make sure we were the ones to fill it. Our plan was, 'Don't go quiet.'"

In the midst of all this activity, Carroll and Dion were in their campaign van one day when Dion asked, innocently enough: "Okay, how are we going to do this?" He was talking about strategy for Super Weekend. Carroll explained that they wanted to come out with somewhere between sixteen and nineteen percent of the vote, and then figure out where to place resources during the last two months leading up to the convention. Third place would be nice, in Carroll's opinion, and they could live with fourth. "Dion lost it," said Carroll. "*Only sixteen percent?* Why are you shooting that low? We should be aiming to win!"

Dion didn't seem to get Carroll's explanation that, with eight people in the race, etc., etc. "He was angry for the longest time," said Carroll. Even after their Super Weekend plan proved successful (not that they wouldn't have liked more delegates), Dion didn't apologize for his outburst. "There was no surrender as far as Dion was concerned," Carroll summed up. Carroll, roughly half Dion's age, clearly had a special relationship with his boss, not dissimilar to that of Dion with Chrétien. "There is no one who relates to Stéphane the way Jamie does," said Meltzer in 2007, after she had left the Liberal party to work for the Canadian Jewish Political Affairs Committee. "Jamie truly has his best interests at heart and can tell him when he has done something wrong or silly. And Stéphane knows this … Jamie was the only person who told Stéphane the truth one hundred percent of the time." Carroll was the campaign's "go-to guy," said Meltzer.[326]

The low point in the Dion campaign was the September Saturday at a Montreal CEGEP when Dion was booed for chiding the audience about having earlier booed Bob Rae. About a dozen people were involved, all with other campaigns, but on TV, it looked like he'd lost the room. Dion had voted against a resolution at the Quebec wing of the party recognizing Quebec as a nation. Dion said his years in politics had taught him how fractious the issue could be. Ignatieff had supported it; there was a rumour that Krieber had done so as well (she hadn't), and the issue enveloped the candidates in debate. It would be put to rest by Prime Minister Stephen Harper, who introduced a motion in the House recognizing Quebec as a "nation within Canada." But Dion's planned comments on national unity were lost in his scolding of the audience, which on TV looked like hectoring. Carroll was incensed. "What the fuck was that?" he had demanded of Dion, as Paul Wells reported in *Maclean's*.[327] There was more. Bevan and Carroll had hastily planned damage control by phone. At least they wouldn't let him scrum, they'd agreed, not right away. Bevan looked up at the television screen in his Ottawa room to see Dion scrumming in Montreal. He put his head in his hands. Things had to get better, he thought.

THEY WOULD. At the leadership convention at the Palais des Congrès on December 2, the results of the first ballot were announced shortly after midnight. They were almost a carbon copy of Super Weekend:

Michael Ignatieff: 29.3 percent (1,412 delegates)
Bob Rae: 20.3 percent (977)
Stéphane Dion: 17.8 percent (856)
Gerard Kennedy: 17.7 percent (854)

Dion was two votes ahead of Kennedy. The Canadian Press reported that some Kennedy ex officio delegates had decided to throw their support to Martha Hall Findlay as a gesture of solidarity with the only woman on the ballot. "I heard that there were four and then that there were six," said a disappointed Kennedy. Katie Telford had sent him the results by BlackBerry and he would never question his delegates about it. He figured they felt badly enough. "They persuaded themselves they could afford to vote for Martha in the first go-around. We had whips everywhere and they did a good job," said Kennedy, still shaking his head six weeks after the fact. Not enough.

Behind the leaders came MPs Dryden (Toronto Centre), Brison (Kings-Hants), Joe Volpe (Eglinton-Lawrence), and Toronto lawyer Hall Findlay, all with less than five percent of the delegate vote. Hall Findlay was off the ballot automatically and Volpe announced he had jumped to Rae, who said he was "delighted."

Dion supporters were ecstatic. Two votes—but third place. It was a psychological boost. "That really sealed it up for me in a serious way," said Brunsdon. For Bevan the evening was a double bonus: the Kennedy–Dion understanding and the results. Kennedy didn't stop working, heading to a Dryden bash at the InterContinental hotel, visiting suites, and "collecting on what seemed to be a big speech dividend."

Dion pushed too that night. Janine Krieber called Marta and Norman Wales's room at the Place d'Armes around 12:30 A.M. "We're having a drink. Come on down," she said. They had just gotten settled when news came that Rae and Ignatieff were working delegates at the Dryden party. Stéphane and Norman left for the event, while Janine and Marta talked until 5:30 A.M. Nobody got much sleep.

SATURDAY MORNING, Martha Hall Findlay went to Dion and Scott Brison threw his support to Rae. Hall Findlay didn't have much delegate power but she was well liked. She picked Dion up at his hotel in her red campaign bus and gave him a symbolic ride around the block to the Palais des Congrès. It had been Rae, Rae, Rae, said Denise Brunsdon, and someone was finally coming to Dion.[328] There was something else that morning. On the advice of former Progressive Conservative organizer Susan Walsh, the Dion team had added green as a campaign colour and delegates loved it. The plan had been kept top secret. Marissen had put out the word that nobody was to mention it on a cell phone.

Dion arrived to a sea of green. Marta Wale was with the crowd that welcomed him. "When they came in, it was like an honour guard waiting for them. Stéphane was in shock. Maybe you need to know him, but I could see it in his eyes. I am sure Stéphane doesn't even remember, but he was absolutely stunned," she said. "You know, Stéphane doesn't have a very big ego. He's a strange sort of politician."

Voting on the second ballot had begun at 9:00 A.M., and results were expected around noon. Around 11:40 A.M., Janine had a scare when Ignatieff and Rae conferred on the floor of the convention hall. Dion and Kennedy had briefly met earlier—"just stretching our legs," Kennedy had said about an impromptu conga line—but Ignatieff and Rae appeared to be serious. Janine had been upset the night before listening to media commentators who thought Dion wouldn't win and now she feared the front-runners had a deal. Norman Wale concluded the opposite. "When I saw Rae talking to Ignatieff, I knew at that moment there was no deal," he said. "The body language was not good." He told Marta and she called Janine. "She was on the floor with Stéphane and she was so stressed," said Marta. "I told her, 'Norman has figured out the strategy. Don't worry, it's in the bag.'" Marissen thought it was a bad move for Rae and Ignatieff. "Yeah, I thought, 'People are really going to want to vote for us now, because if those guys are colluding, they have a problem.' Like there's something weird going on in the Liberal party. This is the old Liberal party and there is the new Liberal party over there [with Dion]." At 11:55 A.M., the second ballot results were announced:

Ignatieff: 31.6 percent (1,481 delegates)
Rae: 24.1 percent (1,132)
Dion: 20.8 percent (974)
Kennedy: 18.8 percent (884)
Dryden: 4.7 percent (219)

At that moment, the longest twenty minutes in Kennedy's life began. "I'm a numbers guy, you know, I've always been able to read numbers and I like to think my approach has always been to be practically idealistic," he said. The numbers guy didn't like the numbers. Ignatieff had stalled, Rae appeared to have the momentum, and Kennedy was in the dreaded fourth spot behind Dion, just as he'd been on the first ballot, but this time trailing by ninety votes instead of two. It was decision time, and not the decision he'd expected to be making the night before. His own words echoed back to him: Don't wait too long to make a move because it could be too late. The TV cameras were on Kennedy when the vote was announced, and "I have these numbers in my head and this is a lower number, you know, and you smile for the cameras but you know something is not quite right."

Candidates had fifteen minutes after results were announced to notify the convention returning officer that they wished to have their name removed before the next ballot was printed. Tick-tick-tick.

Kennedy began consulting fast, first with his brother, Edward, and his father, Jack, then with the rest of his team. Dryden "was clearly going off the paddle," as he put it. "Mr. Rae was shaping up to be the safest choice and somehow my impression of Mr. Dryden was that that's where he would go." Kennedy was right. Dryden had gone off the ticket with 219 votes and Kennedy knew he needed more than half of them. It didn't look good. His problem was that his speech hadn't paid the "dividends" he expected. Kennedy felt the votes were there for him at the convention, but not necessarily on the next ballot when he needed them. Tick-tick.

Key campaign strategist Navdeep Baines had been doing a CBC radio interview in a booth on the other side of the hall. "Get Nav!" somebody shouted. They huddled: Kennedy, Katie Telford, Rob Silver, press secretary Amanda Alvaro, David MacNaughton, and MPs Holland, Chan, and Bains, who arrived on the run. "We knew the second ballot was everything," said Silver. "But Gerard hadn't fully appreciated how quickly the decision would have to be taken ... In his mind, he envisioned being in a boardroom with a scotch weighing the pros and cons, not in a football huddle."[329]

"I just had one question, you know, stay or go," said Kennedy. He wanted everyone's advice. "To those who said stay, I said, 'Do you know where those thirty delegates are coming from? Ten? Fifteen? I mean, *do you know?* Because this not an exercise for me.' And some people were shocked" at the idea he would pull out. For all the talk of a deal, they hadn't seen it coming. It was white-heat pressure. Thought Kennedy, like a mantra, "Your time's running out. Your time's running out."

Kennedy had his people on the phones. "What have you got?" he wanted to know. "What have you got?" It was a crush. "And then Katie looked up and she was really just crouched down on the floor, and she's small enough as it is ... and she looked at me and I pretty much knew ..."

Tick-tock. Kennedy decided he would go; he didn't have the numbers. Somebody had a scrap of paper for Kennedy to sign and rush it up to Liberal officials to get his name off the ballot. Some had already been printed with his name.

Silver sent a BlackBerry message to Jamie Carroll. "We're walking," he said. Carroll shot back: "What do you mean, 'We're walking?'" He thought Kennedy was walking *away* from a deal.

The candidates' booths were in a horizontal line in front of the stage. Between Kennedy and Dion lay Brison (now with Rae), Rae, Ignatieff, and Hall Findlay. Carroll and Silver had discussed box positions and pushed for the greatest distance to allow for maximum drama if one crossed to the other. They regretted it. The walk was pure torture, said Kennedy. He called that walk "Leadership Survivor." He looked ashen as he began to push his way through the crowd, with journalists thronging in, and his wife, Jeanette Arsenault-Kennedy, behind him, clinging to his hand. Her forehead was pushed against his shoulder and tears were running down her face. Journalists knew Kennedy was crossing the floor when they saw her tears. "A woman reporter with blond hair was trying to reach out a recorder and hit my wife on the head twice … Like twice. Once could be an accident but this was Bang! Bang! The behaviour was primordial." Kennedy tried to protect his wife. As he passed the other camps, Rae's, Ignatieff's, he saw the looks on people's faces. Briefly, hope. Then it was gone.

Dion had been about to take a break. "Keep him there," Kennedy said, and Dion's people pulled him back. At last, they met. "I'm here," said Kennedy. "Thank you very much," replied Dion. Janine and Jeanette embraced. "Stéphane himself was pretty cool," said Kennedy. "But there was a bit of a startled look on his face." They felt that Ignatieff and Rae had tried something themselves, but it was too late; nobody could build what Kennedy and Dion had in a few minutes on the convention floor.

Suddenly, Kennedy delegates wanted something green. Denise Brunsdon stood outside the voting station pleading with Dion delegates to donate something to a former Kennedy supporter. People were trying to avoid her. Her point was: "You've got the hat, you've got the scarf, you've got the T-shirt—don't tell me you can't hand me one of those pieces." Voting went smoothly and, at 2:45, the third ballot results were announced:

Dion: 37 percent (1,782)
Ignatieff: 34.5 percent (1,660)
Rae: 28.5 percent (1,375)

Rae was off the ballot. Kennedy had delivered his delegates just as he had promised. Between the second and third ballots, Dion had vaulted into first place, with his support going from 974 to 1,782, a stunning jump of 808 delegates. Kennedy had the support of 884 delegates when he dropped out. There was no way to know for sure, but it was a safe bet that all but a very few of Kennedy's delegates had moved over to Dion. It was clear who had the momentum now. Ignatieff eked up only 179 votes. Rae moved up by 243, but it was a moot point.

The fourth ballot was anti-climactic, marked only by its predictability and the agonizingly long five-minute wait for the results with the cameras panning in on Ignatieff's face. It had to be a profile in courage. The other camera shot was of Dion, looking confident, Janine beside him, Jeanne, Martha Hall Findlay, Kennedy, Jeanette: the new team. The results were announced just after six: Dion: 54.7 percent (2,521) and Ignatieff 45.3 (2,084). The Liberal party had a new leader, Stéphane Dion.

For Kennedy, the convention results showed that Liberals cared about Dion's issue of the environment—his three pillars of economic development, social justice, and environmental sustainability—and that they were tired of internecine feuding. "But it was about more than that, it was about winning in a way that people could be proud of." Kennedy had been concentrating on what had been wrong with the Dion organization. But he had to admit: "Obviously, they had the superior campaign because they won in the end." But his move was remarkable in that he made it in time to help Dion. It had not been easy. More than six weeks after the vote, Kennedy remained bewildered by the surprise that greeted the Dion–Kennedy move. "Why didn't people think this was a likely vote? Together we had more delegates than the other guys," Kennedy said. "So why would anyone be surprised?"

THERE WAS ONE last question left unanswered: what would Stéphane Dion have done had their roles been reversed? Dion had pledged that Kennedy was his second choice. At their last meeting Friday night, he had said enough to appease Kennedy. But would he have pulled out? Dion responded in a roundabout way when asked, without answering at all. "I knew the Kennedy people were overwhelmingly Dion in their second choice … When I was travelling the country, it was very clear to me. Most of the Rae people were Dion, I knew that, and almost all of the Kennedy people were," he began, in an interview at his Laurentian cottage a month after the vote. Of his own delegates, Dion said: "I think I would have been able to convince many of them to follow me to Gerard, but not most of them. Because there were many Francophones from Quebec and going to Gerard was a long shot for them. They would have gone to Bob or Michael. So I don't think—I honestly don't think—that Gerard would have won."

Asked if he would have voted for Kennedy, Dion replied: "Very likely." But he didn't say yes. He didn't think Kennedy could win. Dion was by profession a political scientist, a man who knew how to read polls and analyze data, and he understood very well how much strength he had on the convention floor. Faced with the option of seeing Rae or Ignatieff win, it's unlikely he would have pulled out. Nobody close to him thinks he would have. Dion even discounted the value of the two votes that put him ahead on the first ballot when some Kennedy delegates voted for Hall Findlay. "You need to assume that no Dion people did the same," he said. "The key point to ask was would the gap between Kennedy and Dion decrease or increase?" His opinion? It would have increased significantly. "Those two votes helped, definitely, but it was not everything."

Stéphane Dion couldn't satisfy Kennedy's quest for a deal carved in stone because he understands that politics is an art. He, too, would later scoff at the idea that his win was a surprise. "Everyone was saying it was a surprise, a surprise," Dion said. "To me … it was foreseeable that I would be third before Gerard, maybe not after the first ballot or the second, but I would grow more than him. It was foreseeable that he would come to me because together we would be stronger than Bob. And it was foreseeable that most of the Bob people would come to me. Then I would be stronger than Michael." Dion foresaw all that as he shook Gerard Kennedy's hand on Friday night.

CHAPTER ELEVEN

LET'S HAVE LUNCH

O N THE DAY he won the Liberal leadership, Stéphane Dion had an excellent idea to restore harmony after so many fractious months of hand-to-hand combat among the contenders. He instructed his staff to invite his former rivals to have lunch with him the next day, Sunday, December 3, at the charming, European-style hotel in Old Montreal where he was staying. "It was the first step in the healing process,"[330] said Herb Metcalfe. "We're a team; we're going forward." Dion's advisers didn't want him to make other people's blunders. Metcalfe had been around politics for a long time and pointed out, "Paul [Martin] didn't include his rivals in his administration and he ended up not being successful." Moreover, Dion prided himself on understanding the importance of working as a team. A leader, he liked to say, had to possess "strong views and team spirit."[331] The lunch was going to be fabulous. What Stéphane Dion didn't understand, however, was the depth of the hard feelings around the table. How was he to know that some members of his sparkling new team likely felt like gouging each other's eyes out with their salad forks?

Every detail had been well thought out. The table was beautifully prepared, with crisp linens and a name card at each place setting. Martha Hall Findlay sat at Dion's right and Gerard Kennedy at his left. Michael Ignatieff had been placed directly across from the leader and Bob Rae sat a little down from Ignatieff. The candidates were allowed to bring two guests and most were accompanied by their spouses and a senior aide. Rae appeared to be in a rather chippy mood. The morning before, he had received some very unpleasant news from Martha Hall Findlay and he wasn't smiling at her across the table.

Hall Findlay had called Rae on Saturday at 7:30 A.M. She had just given her good news to Dion a few moments earlier.

"Bob," said Hall Findlay, "I'm going to Stéphane."

"Oh, no!" said Rae. Pause. "Well, you learn a lot of lessons in politics." And he hung up the phone.[332]

Hall Findlay was "very upset" by the telephone call. "I had conversations with a few people after that, people who were Bob supporters, and I said, 'I'm sick. I feel really bad.' I did not feel I had made a commitment to Bob. I knew I was leaning towards him, but my view all along was that I was reserving my decision until the convention."

"Not true," said Rae. "That's not what she said. I had a clear sense from her that she was coming to me and so it was Saturday morning when she said that she wasn't." Rae explained that Scott Brison, who did come to him, had been careful not to make any commitment in advance, whereas he said Hall Findlay had promised her support after the first ballot. "It's one thing when somebody's saying, 'You know, I've decided to go to X,' and you say, 'Fine, I understand.' Ah, but it's different when somebody says one thing one day and another thing another day and it becomes a little harder to take."

He re-emphasized his point: "Let me be very clear, I know what our conversation was. I know what she told me, so if she's saying something now that's not what she said, then I'm sorry [but] that just tells me something else ... because I have a very clear sense of that conversation."

Rae made his comments in an interview six weeks after the convention, sitting in his cluttered office at Goodmans LLP, the Toronto law firm where he earned a living. He was still seething about Hall Findlay and repeated several times, "That's not what she said."

Dion's "healing" lunch lasted more than three hours, during which time Rae ignored Hall Findlay. And he would continue to ignore her attempts to make peace in coming days. "For whatever reason— maybe it's a case of you hear what you want to hear—Bob seemed to think I was going to support him," said Hall Findlay. She agonized over it. "I have just so much respect for Bob. I mean, he's a guy who started out idealistic, right? … Anybody trying to govern Ontario at that time [1990 to 1995] would have had a really hard time. And so there's been a lot of criticism, but I'm happy to stand up and say, 'The guy tried. And he tried for the right reasons.'"

Hall Findlay understood that losing the leadership had been rough on Rae. "I mean, I feel bad that he feels bad." It may be that Rae was still in shock the day after the vote. He had waited for the fatal third ballot results on the convention floor with his wife, Arlene Perly Rae. "It's a big deal in the sense that five or six thousand people have these cameras on you all the time. I said to my kids and I said to Arlene, 'We're going to have to act our way through this because whatever happens we're going to have to put on a brave face' … and we just did that," said Rae. "It's been tough in the sense that you go from highs to lows, from thinking you are going to win to realizing you've come in third and that you're not going to be on the final ballot and you're not going to win now that the momentum has gone to somebody else."

And there it was: that was the dynamic between two of the invited guests to Dion's little get-together that Sunday. And there were other tensions. It was also awkward between Rae and Kennedy. Rae thought he probably would have won if it hadn't been for Kennedy. "The deal affected everything. It must also have affected Martha Hall Findlay," Rae said. He found the whole thing implausible because he didn't believe that Dion would have gone to Kennedy. "I continue to be surprised by it, and you know, again, what was the deal? No one has ever told me what the deal was," said Rae. Of Kennedy he added, "What did he get in return?"

Rae apparently was unimpressed by the assertions of Stéphane Dion and Gerard Kennedy that there had been no hidden agenda. Kennedy, in fact, said he had talked to both Rae and Ignatieff about striking some kind of deal with one of them but that talks had never progressed past the preliminaries. "Neither Rae nor Ignatieff should be upset," said Kennedy in an interview in January. "There was some backwash afterwards from Bob's campaign. They used heavy duty words like 'betrayal,' and so on, and I find that highly regrettable."[333]

THE SUNDAY LUNCH at the Place d'Armes Hotel was buffet-style, and everybody waited for Dion and Janine Krieber to serve themselves. Once seated, Dion said they should get down to work and asked for input from everyone, urging frankness. Gerard Kennedy, who had played kingmaker the day before, went first, talking about the need for the Liberals to have a two-track approach in which the party was ready for an election in the short term while developing long-term plans for renewal. At his turn, Rae was blunt: "Stéphane, you're going to need an awful lot of good advice, and don't assume that the ones who brought you here are the ones who are best to give you that advice."

People looked askance, wondering if Rae was talking about anyone in particular. "Again, that was a product of my experience," Rae said later. "It's the easiest thing in the world when you are elected to think that the people that got you there are necessarily the best to run the show afterwards and my experience—again, my experience—is that you have to expand the team … And so I was pretty direct about that."

But Dion had already begun to announce his team that very morning, and he had gone to his supporters. Marcel Massé and

Ottawa businessman Rod Bryden headed the transition team. When Dion had reached Massé that morning at 9:00 A.M. he had been reluctant to accept. "I really need you," Dion had coaxed until Massé gave in. "Okay, for three weeks, maybe a month," he said, to the sound of Dion shouting to Krieber, "He said yes!" (By the end of December, Massé would be named principal secretary in the Opposition Leader's Office.)

The rest of the lunch was uneventful, and it ended around 3:20 P.M. Scott Brison had provided some comic relief; that and the wine eased the tension. But it took about three minutes post-lunch for one of Rae's aides to complain to *Maclean's* that the two "upstarts" had been given priority seating.[334] Yes indeed, they were off to a fine start.

STÉPHANE DION WAS EXCITED about the challenges ahead as he moved into his new suite in 407-S in Centre Block. The Opposition leader's private office had been designed by Ottawa architect John A. Pearson after the fire that ravaged the Parliament Buildings in 1916. Pearson had added beautiful oak panelling, a planked wooden floor, and a marble fireplace. There were wall frescoes, a secret passageway, and murals with scenes of knights and angels (one with the face of William Lyon Mackenzie King's "dear mother"). Emblazoned on the murals were inspirational words: "Integrity ... Fidelity ... Fortitude ... Fearlessness ... Wisdom."[335] Dion would need them all. It was an office whose occupants had included King in 1920 and moved through Lester Bowles Pearson and John George Diefenbaker to Martin Brian Mulroney and Stéphane Maurice Bernard Dion. It was a place to accomplish important tasks, and Dion set his beat-up leather knapsack on his desk and got to work. The knapsack had been a gift a decade earlier.[336]

With Massé already settled in down the hall from Dion, Andrew Bevan about to be named chief of staff, and André Lamarre set up in communications, the next order of business was to make use of the talent among the leadership contenders. Everyone knew there was a lot of sniping going on: the residue of almost a year of fighting. Of one candidate, it was whispered, "talking to him was like having amnesia"; of another, "he looked old. Did you notice?" It was nasty stuff, but the Dion team took the gossip in stride; they thought they could rise above it and bring everyone together, as they had at the lunch. "He will never get personal," Metcalfe said of Dion. First on Dion's to-do list was Michael Ignatieff, who had received 2,084 votes, or 45.3 percent of the Liberal delegates, to place second. Dion saw that as a significant consideration.

Dion thought about the role he wanted for Ignatieff and decided on platform chair. It made perfect sense for Ignatieff to write the policy book. "Michael is the best writer we have—after me," said Dion.[337] He knew that Martin had taken that assignment for Jean Chrétien, producing the Liberal Red Book of 1993. Even more importantly, as Dion explained, he would have done that for the new leader had he lost and been asked. It would have been an honour.

Dion invited Ignatieff to dinner at Le Tartuffe, a French restaurant across the river in Gatineau. They met on Wednesday evening, December 6, just four days after the convention; Dion wanted to get cracking. Over dinner, Dion told Ignatieff that he would "be pleased" if Ignatieff would write the Liberal policy platform. They chatted and Dion left thinking that Ignatieff had accepted. Ignatieff hadn't signed off on it officially, but Dion interpreted his comments favourably. Dion would later tell his advisers that he was sure it was mission accomplished.

Also on the agenda was Bob Rae, the third-place finisher. Dion wanted Rae in a top position but hadn't finalized his thinking. On December 5, the night before he met with Ignatieff, Dion had dined with Rae at Ottawa's tony Rideau Club. "We did not talk about any particular job for me, or indeed for any other candidates," said Rae. "We talked generally. It was a very good conversation. He made it clear he wanted me to be part of the team." Of course, the new leader couldn't offer Rae the post of policy chair—the plum in Dion's view—because he planned to offer it to Ignatieff the next night.

But Rae was comfortable with the evening. "I think Stéphane has been very thoughtful and very straightforward, *very straightforward*, as he always was," he would say later. "I've never had any difficulty in my relationship with him." Rae told Dion he was prepared to work with him. In Rae's mind, it was time for everyone to put "their personal ambitions to one side. The convention had met and the convention had chosen the leader and we all have to recognize that life moves on."

One week later, on Wednesday, December 13, Dion again met with Ignatieff, this time in the OLO (Opposition Leader's Office). Instead of the confirmation that Dion expected, Ignatieff said he didn't want to be platform chair. Ignatieff wanted to be deputy leader. Dion said that Ignatieff told him that platform chair was "too narrow" a position for him. Ignatieff argued that Dion already knew what he wanted in terms of policy and there would be little room for him to grow. Dion said he felt Ignatieff made a good point and that he couldn't really disagree. But he was disappointed.

The Dion transition team hadn't seen deputy leader as being a particularly big role. They saw it as more of a Herb Gray type job, an able parliamentarian who could share the business of the House of Commons but wouldn't necessarily be a shining star. However, according to Dion, Ignatieff said he wanted to serve over a broad range, and, as a result, Stéphane Dion agreed to appoint Michael Ignatieff as his deputy leader. It was all about unity; Dion understood that word better than anyone.

Mark Marissen, Dion's leadership campaign manager, had drinks with Ignatieff soon afterwards at the Four Seasons Hotel in Toronto. "I asked him," said Marissen, "'Why don't you want to do policy?

Why do you want to be deputy leader?' And he goes, 'Oh, you know, I want to be part of the team and being deputy leader we can work together more.' I said, 'Oh, okay.'"[338]

Dion's office made plans for him to announce his "dream team" on Tuesday, December 19, in Toronto. Ignatieff's move had forced different moves from Dion. A day or so after his second meeting with Ignatieff, Herb Metcalfe telephoned Bob Rae to ask if he would like to become policy chair. "I said that would be a job that interested me, and I talked to Scott Brison," said Rae. Brison would be policy cochair with Rae.

There had been a bit of a bump, fine, but everybody thought it was past. "He cut a deal, then danced the night away," blared the front-page headline over Jane Taber's story in *The Globe and Mail* on December 19.[339] Taber reported that Ignatieff had met with Dion to discuss his future the previous Wednesday. "Mr. Ignatieff was receptive to the offer of the position of deputy leader right away," wrote Taber. A senior Liberal confided, "There was no 'I want to think about it.'" The article said the meeting with Dion had been a prelude to a Christmas party thrown for Ignatieff by his supporters, to which Dion was not invited, and quoted the source as speculating that it would be "interesting to see how much further he goes." Ignatieff would soon embark on speaking tours, "get his face known" to the public, and so on. There was no mention of any offer to Ignatieff of becoming policy chair.

No one was amused in the OLO. It was not the spin they had been expecting, given how events had unfolded behind the scenes. *Receptive to the idea?* How was that for chutzpah? Moreover, Dion had to meet with Ignatieff separately in Quebec City on December 19, rather than at the press conference scheduled for later in the day in Toronto. According to a Dion staffer, Ignatieff was leaving that day on his Christmas break. Dion announced his "dream team" in stages—a novel approach to the concept of team.

That night in Toronto, Dion announced the rest of the appointments: Gerard Kennedy as special adviser on election readiness; Hall Findlay in charge of policy "outreach" (and expected to work closely with her buddy Bob Rae), and Rae heading the policy team that would write a new Red Book. Media analysts overlooked the fact that the policy chair differed with the leader's emphasis on his linchpin "three pillars" of economic growth, social justice, and environmental sustainability. Dion had built his leadership campaign on these much-touted three pillars. Rae added a fourth: addressing Canada's role in the world. "The three pillars is a very useful way of looking at the need for balance in public policy, which is a lot of what I've been talking about over my whole political life," Rae said later. "Looking at sustainability, economic growth, and social justice, recognizing that they all have to come together, is pretty basic."

Rae also didn't see the need to write a policy book. "I see it more as a face-book … something where we're connecting with people and putting our ideas out and getting a response." It was a completely different take on something Dion had seen as so vital after his victory in Montreal.

No, Tuesday, December 19, was not the new leader's best day. And it would take another zigzag downwards. After the press conference, well-connected Toronto senator Jerry Grafstein held a fund-raiser downstairs at the University Club. Grafstein shepherded Dion around to meet the Liberal elites of Canada's biggest city. For many, it was their first opportunity. Grafstein introduced Dion to Peter C. Newman, who'd been a friend of his father, Léon Dion. Stéphane Dion didn't know who Newman was, even though, as Toronto consultant Ray Heard observed, the author wore his trademark fisherman's cap. An hour later, Grafstein brought Dion upstairs to a private Christmas party where he again introduced him to Newman. Dion didn't recall having met him although, presumably, Newman was still wearing his cap.

Heard, who had been John Turner's communications director, didn't think Dion was having a big impact on Toronto Liberals. "I am also told that Dion recently attended a private session with bank CEOs and did not have a clue who they were," he wrote in an email in early January.[340] Heard followed up with another note in March, saying: "The inter-party rifts that supposedly ended with the election of Dion are NOT over. Behind the façade of unity, there is intense politicking between the Rae and Iggy factions because they sense that, like Turner in 1984 and after, Dion may be toast." Dion was not reaching out to party elders, most of whom (to the more Toronto-centric) lived in Toronto. Wrote Heard: "Massé is a throwback to the bad old days of Chrétien and the guy from Vancouver has no profile here." That "guy" was Mark Marissen, who, with Quebecer Nancy Girard, had been appointed Liberal national campaign cochair.

PRESSURE MOUNTED ON DION as the weeks passed in 2007. There was grumbling in his caucus over his leadership. Despite the growing unease, Dion continued to stress unity. "In Stéphane's mind, he sees everyone as a member of the team until such time as a person proves differently," said Metcalfe. By late winter, larger organizational and fund-raising problems within the Liberal party itself had become apparent to Dion's inner circle. In the heady days of the post-convention bounce in the polls, Liberals talked enthusiastically about taking on the Conservative government in an election campaign. But now that Liberal fortunes had sagged and the party had revealed itself to be in poor shape, there was less enthusiasm, albeit privately. In mid-February Jamie Carroll left his position as Dion's deputy chief of staff to become national director of the Liberal Party of Canada. Carroll was the "mechanic" who was expected to figure out why the Conservatives were raising three times more money than the Liberals and reverse it. Carroll also wanted to know why fund-raising appeared to be limited to a few donors, with no appeals going out to the grassroots. The

Conservative wealth was evident in the attack ads against Dion that ran constantly in early February (in both English and French) and had a negative impact on Dion's standing in the polls. Columnist Chantal Hébert identified the problem for the *Toronto Star* under the headline, "How soon will PM move in for kill on Dion?" Hébert wrote that Dion had failed to make an impression on Canadians. "It did not take a degree in physics to know that the Conservatives would take a hand in filling in the many blanks of Dion's political personality."[341]

Dion's own mood darkened, as he increasingly blamed himself for failing to live up to expectations. Just after New Year's, he and Janine had moved into Stornoway, the stately Rockcliffe Park home of the Opposition leader, while Jeanne remained in Montreal. In a telephone interview from Stornoway's Laurier Room (so named for its portrait of Sir Wilfrid Laurier), Dion sounded full of confidence in early February. A week later, as the Conservative attack ads began to take their toll, there was fatigue in his voice. However, he said that a short tribute to his hockey hero Jean Béliveau he was writing for an anthology had reminded him "nobody has it easy."[342] He joked and sounded in good spirits. By the first days of March, as Liberals continued to sink, Dion sounded tense in a phone interview. "I'm not surprised by the polls. They're not as good as they used to be," he said. "I know I need to improve."[343]

That same evening, Carroll sighed on the line from Ottawa. "It's becoming a real problem," he said.[344] Carroll was frustrated when Dion blamed himself. Nobody worked harder than Stéphane Dion, and the pressure he was putting on himself was not helpful. For example, his English deteriorated when he was under stress, and he was losing the huge improvements he had made over the months of the leadership. Dion still managed to squeeze in two or three classes with Mary Houle into his schedule every week. Her title was "speech and language pathologist," and she had been working with Dion to improve his English since May 2006. A young mother of a toddler and a newborn,

Houle was full of enthusiasm for the classes. She respected his ability in English; he had always written well and had an expansive vocabulary. (In fact, Dion's advisers didn't mind the lowered expectations that he couldn't complete a sentence in English. "People will be pleasantly surprised," said one aide.) According to Houle, "tweaks needed to be done."[345] "He is relatively easy to understand. He has a bit of a Parisian trill and his intonation goes up and down." The problem was Dion's slightly rising pitch. Houle explained that French is "more of a syllable-timed language while English is more of a stress-timed language." If the stress is placed incorrectly, "it sounds as if you are a little unsure of what you are saying [and] it could be difficult to be understood." Dion learned a mantra from Houle that he repeated before every speech and carried with him into Question Period in the House of Commons: "Slow and low … slow and low …"

But his hard work didn't appear to be paying off in Question Period. Deputy leader Michael Ignatieff sat on his left, and, not surprisingly, the former television pundit shone in the Commons format. And the better Ignatieff looked and sounded, the worse Dion appeared, almost as if he were psyched out by the presence of his one-time rival. Ignatieff's prominence did not go unnoticed by Prime Minister Stephen Harper across the aisle. In mid-February, Dion had left Ottawa to attend the funeral of two Winnipeg firefighters.[346] Ignatieff was pushing Harper to be clear on a question when Harper, looking pleased as punch, leaned across his desk and intoned: "What is clear is that the Honourable Member certainly has a plan to audition for a new role."[347]

Scuttlebutt grew that Ignatieff was using the deputy leader's position to build his own empire and steal Dion's job. Internal sniping increased, hurting morale in caucus. Attendance dropped and party whip Karen Redman sent out an advisory reminding Liberal MPs of their responsibilities. Dion's supporters complained that extra attention had to be devoted to "the care and feeding of the deputy leader" by the Opposition Leader's Office, and pointed to perceived slights of

Dion by Ignatieff. The deputy leader hadn't risen to join a standing ovation from Liberals for their leader one day in the House. Or Ignatieff had clapped only half-heartedly at a Dion speech somewhere else. They found fault with Ignatieff's approach to Question Period, pointing out a lack of judgement on this issue or that. "He's a whiner and a complainer," said one Liberal close to Dion. "But he complains because he is not in control."[348] It was an astute comment. At the heart of the matter, complaints and sniping were to be expected in a party that was out of power. And they were not against Ignatieff alone. Rae was not a team player, according to the opinion of some, and Kennedy was always imagining that key decisions were being taken behind his back. It had only been since January 2006 that Liberals had been pushed into the Official Opposition but they were ill suited to the role. Their discontent was the greatest threat to Dion's power, and the smart people around him knew that. They were well aware that a unity lunch at the Place d'Armes Hotel had not changed that essential dynamic.

At Liberal party headquarters, Jamie Carroll was running out of patience with Dion's former leadership rivals. He had felt Dion had done the right thing in sharing power, even in approving Ignatieff as deputy leader. But by March 2007, Carroll had begun to entertain a different thought: "I am starting to wonder if he may not have been a little too good to his former competitors."

It didn't help that Carroll understood what it meant to be Ignatieff, Rae, or Kennedy. "They are all in a tough spot. None of them has been in the habit of having to answer to others," he said. Moreover, Carroll agreed with Dion's argument that when Liberals "go down in the polls, people get antsy ... That doesn't mean the knives are out." Dion insisted that they stay on the high road and keep working to make his former opponents feel included. Carroll agreed and, yet, he worried. He lived in fear of an all-out drive against Dion. "All three of them have legitimate claims to being the next guy." And Carroll didn't censor his bluntest opinion: "What they do in public doesn't bother me. It's the shit they do behind the scenes—which I may not know they're doing—that keeps me up at night."

Still, what was too often forgotten with Stéphane Dion was what he had already gone through in his political career, the tough hacking through the jungle of the first decade. He had taken everything Lucien Bouchard could throw at him, been called a traitor in his own province, and survived exile in the political wilderness. And, as those who knew him pointed out, he was a fighter. What's more, many federal leaders had lived through rocky beginnings, among them Lester Pearson, Pierre Trudeau, Brian Mulroney, and Jean Chrétien. None other than Senator Grafstein, who hosted Dion's supposed bombing at the University Club, made that point. "I remember Trudeau's first couple of years. I was there," he said. "People forget. For the first year or so, all leaders have to get their feet wet and decide what issues are important." Grafstein characterized Dion as "a work in progress." He has "high expectations of himself," added Grafstein. "There's not an issue on which he's not restless to get all the facts ... and his wife is quite brilliant." The senator had squired Janine Krieber around at the University Club fund-raiser in December and couldn't help noticing that she'd been a hit. Grafstein had some advice for Liberals in the spring of 2007: give the new leader time and don't try to knock him off the high road.[349]

CHAPTER TWELVE

HE IS WHAT HE IS

A DAM CAMPBELL put down the telephone in his Alberta farm-house on a late autumn day and asked himself, "What the hell did I just say to the guy?"[350] He'd spent the last few minutes advising Stéphane Dion on the line from Ottawa about the need to speak clearly in English, and the inappropriateness of his advice washed over him. "Here I'm Scottish, I've got a thick accent, my English skills aren't so hot, and I'm saying that to him," recounted Campbell. "Luckily, he doesn't hold it against you."

Of all the friendships formed on the road during a political campaign, theirs was one of the oddest: the Jamestown, Fife, high-lander who was Liberal Party of Canada president in Alberta, and the Sillery, Quebec, academic who was running for the leadership. They had grown to like each other over the course of the 2006 campaign, with Campbell somewhat taking on the role of nurse-maid. "Adam looks after me," said Dion. In a political world that can be selfish and calculating, Dion appreciated somebody who seemed genuinely concerned if he looked tired or wasn't eating properly. They talked about their personal lives, Janine Krieber and Campbell's Thai-born wife, Chandra, and laughed at each other's idiosyncrasies and defects. Campbell learned by accident that Dion was colour-blind. He had helped Dion search for a brown folder he'd misplaced in Edmonton one afternoon until, at last, he opened the front door of the SUV they'd been driving and "sitting on the front seat is a red folder and Dion says, 'Aha! There's my folder.'"

Driving Dion through the back roads of Alberta during the leadership campaign, Campbell had become embarrassed that he was talking too much and asked if he should let Dion sleep. "No, I'm quite happy to listen to you," Dion had replied, telling Campbell that the conversation was interesting and to keep talking. He did, telling Dion about the problems of Alberta farmers, his fears that the Conservatives were going to dismantle the Canadian Wheat Board, and, later, the anger in Alberta over the federal government's decision to reverse tax policy on income trusts.[351] Campbell had been an immigrant to Alberta in 1996 (he'd been intending to go to Manitoba but felt "there were too many Scottish people there") and had become a grain farmer in Rosalind, thirty kilometres southeast of Camrose. It was lonely being a Liberal in Alberta, where all twenty-eight ridings had gone Conservative in 2006 and, before Campbell's time, Nick Taylor had gained a legendary reputation as the scrappy leader who'd soldiered on alone. Campbell extracted a promise from Dion: if he won the leadership, he would visit Alberta often and listen to what people had to say.

Dion kept his promise, and on January 11, 2007, he was guest speaker at an Edmonton town hall meeting organized by Campbell. It was the coldest night of the winter and yet more than four hundred people turned up to see Dion at the Ital-Canadian Seniors Association Centre, where they gave him a standing ovation after a speech and participated in a freewheeling question-and-answer session. Dion was relaxed, talking about his record as environment minister and reminding the crowd that he'd been out to Alberta five times during the past year, while Prime Minister Stephen Harper had come once—to a hockey game. That got a good laugh. There was already buzz that well-known consumer advocate Jim Wachowich was going to run in former cabinet minister Anne McLellan's riding of Edmonton Centre; maybe the Liberals could make gains in blue Alberta.

Earlier that day, Dion had met with the editorial board of the *Edmonton Journal* and enjoyed a good reception there, too. He had talked about the international carbon market he hoped would be established to help companies reduce their greenhouse gas emissions and stressed the opportunities for Alberta to become an innovator in environmental technology. "I thought he was intelligent and had thought things through," Allan Mayer, *Journal* editor in chief said later. "Plus, he was pretty funny. That surprised me because he doesn't come across that way on TV. He often had a clever turn of phrase."[352] The next day, the paper's columnist Alan Kellogg gave Dion a positive review, suggesting that perhaps Alberta voters weren't being smart giving all their votes to the Conservatives like "the goofy, oversized sheepdogs of the North American electoral process."[353] Kellogg praised Dion for having worn a suit to the town hall, instead of trying to dress all folksy and down home. "Dion seems to be telling us: This is who I am. I'm not a glamour puss and my English isn't great. But I'm honest, sincere, and have a vision for the future. Ready?"

Essentially, that had been Dion's message to Liberal delegates at the convention. It had been exciting for Liberals to watch him come out of the convention with an uptick in the polls, even in Quebec where a hostile reception had been predicted, and the party was seized with the notion that, come an election, their new leader would waltz over to 24 Sussex Drive without even having unpacked his bags at Stornoway.

Getting into a taxi late one December night in Ottawa, aide Gianluca Cairo turned to the driver and asked, "Do you know who this is?" Dion had already settled into the backseat, his knees drawn to his chest, his battered leather knapsack on the floor. The cab driver glanced at the passenger in the rearview mirror. "Nope," he said.

Cairo was happy to tell him. "This is Stéphane Dion and he's going to be the next prime minister of Canada." It was almost one in the morning and the driver remained silent, wheeling out onto the Airport Parkway and speeding into the blackness of downtown Ottawa.

Cairo's enthusiasm was understandable. A political science graduate, he was Dion's executive assistant and had begun working for him
two years earlier when it wasn't the popular thing to do. Earlier in
December 2006, they'd come off a bare-bones leadership campaign
and it was great being able to stay in actual hotels, instead of having
to bunk with friends. Other Liberals were equally enthusiastic. On
December 20, an editorial in *The Globe and Mail* mistakenly referred
to "Prime Minister Dion." His staffers were giddy; it was a sign.
Naturally, hubris set in. Within weeks, polls had plunged and the
pundits were talking about Dion in the past tense. Many analysts were
reminded that they'd thought his win was a mistake. Peter C. Newman,
the dean of political profilers, predicted he wouldn't last long.

But the reality was that once the intoxication of high expectations
had worn off, Stéphane Dion came into his own again in mid-March
of 2007. Dion was comfortable in the role of underdog; it was his
natural habitat and it was the best position in which to fight an
election when it came. He had been an underdog many times in his
political career and, before that, he'd been an iconoclast, even as a kid.
He was in it for the long haul—Adam Campbell and others knew
that about Dion, whether in the role of Opposition leader or, if the
stars aligned, prime minister.

There had been a brief and heady fling with the idea of coming to
power quickly and then everybody came back down to earth. Nobody
had even thought he was going to win the leadership three months
earlier; why should he be disappointed they didn't think he would be
prime minister? Moreover, the definition of an underdog was being
written off by the smart money. In March, Liberal strategists sent
Dion off on a cross-country tour in which he visited some seventeen
ridings in as many days, worked like a maniac, slept on airplanes, and
regained his equilibrium.[354] Campbell had always been an advocate
of having Dion out on the road, arguing in January that "the worst
mistake the team could make would be to isolate him and not allow

him to be in front of people." He told them, "You have to let him out there. It's the vulnerability thing." Campbell thought that Paul Martin's advisers had kept him in a box. It had worried Campbell watching Stephen Harper out flipping burgers on the barbecue circuit during the summer of 2005.

"The Liberal party had become a very elitist organization," said Campbell, "and that's what backfired in the end. There were lawyers, there were corporate people and, don't get me wrong, they did a good job. They piled money into the party and they'd done fund-raisers. But they'd lost the sense that the people we need to vote for us are working at Wal-Mart and Tim Hortons. We can have every lawyer and banker in Canada vote for a Liberal and we're not going to win the election in Canada. Normal people vote for politicians."

Normal people also contribute money to politicians. Lots of them, in small amounts. And how to get them to do it for Liberals was what Jamie Carroll was trying to figure out at party headquarters in Ottawa. In theory, there was no reason people wouldn't give money to Stéphane Dion because he was basically a normal kind of person. And if ordinary people didn't get that, senior Liberals knew it would be because his own party had allowed the Conservatives to define him for Canadians, rather than letting people see for themselves. Admittedly, he was a bit eccentric and absurdist in his humour. Sometimes he related to children like little adults. Denis Saint-Martin recounted how Dion gave his eight-year-old son a lecture on green-house gases. The boy's class had produced a project on the environment in 2005 and the teacher wanted the minister to sign it for them. Saint-Martin brought his son to Dion's townhouse on a Saturday morning. "Drinking a glass of orange juice in the kitchen, Stéphane asked my son, 'What is climate change?' And Jérémie said, 'It's pollution,' and Stéphane said, 'No, no! That's not it! Sit down. I'll explain it to you.'… Typical!"[355]

STÉPHANE DION had taken his lecture on greenhouse gases to delegates of the Liberal party, and he planned to take it to the Canadian electorate in time. It was the essential thing to understand about why he ran for the leadership and what he said he would do if elected prime minister. "It's not for the power, it's for what I can do with it," he said. It was a mindset for governing, rather than about changing an individual program or ministry. It was why Green party leader Elizabeth May held Dion in such high regard. He laid out his plan—ministry by ministry—one afternoon in an interview over the Christmas holidays in 2006. For him, it was a totally natural way to spend a holiday afternoon. As a preamble, Dion said that when he began campaigning for the leadership, he was advised not to make the environment his priority because it would look as if he were campaigning on his old portfolio. "You will not seem prime ministerial," he was told. "But I resisted that and said that I didn't want to be a candidate like the others. I have something different to say. It will not be the twenty-five pillars approach. It will be the three pillars approach."[356]

The environment wasn't like other issues; it was critical to survival on the planet. "I am confident that humankind will find solutions, and the countries that find the solutions will become rich. I want Canada to be among these countries, with their expertise, their know-how, their inventions, their innovations, everywhere in the world," Dion said. "We can miss the boat or we can take it; I want Canada to take it."

The criticism of Dion as environment minister was that greenhouse gas emissions had continued to rise; it wasn't fair to say that Canada hadn't met its Kyoto Protocol commitment because the first target period wouldn't begin until 2008. Nevertheless, Dion argued it wasn't the point. "What I was able to do as minister of the environment is nothing compared to what I will be able to do as a prime minister. Because when you are prime minister, you send this message everywhere and you shape your cabinet around it."

It was the same with the unity issue. "I didn't become unity minister because I was crying about Canada. I am not a classic nationalist. And I did not come to the environment because I wrote books … but above all because of my understanding of what the economy is about for the twenty-first century."

The unity question had once monopolized Stéphane Dion's life, and he could take some credit in March 2007 with the results of a provincial election in Quebec in which the Parti Québécois came third. While there were many factors at play in the campaign and vote (which returned Premier Jean Charest to power with a minority), Quebecers were showing even greater signs of referendum fatigue. Before Dion had waded into the unity struggle, separating from Canada had seemed relatively easy to do. That was the argument of the Parti Québécois. But his Clarity Act of 2000 had established the rules and shown just how long and tortuous negotiations to separate from Canada would be.[357]

Dion had thought intensely about how to approach the environment were he to become prime minister. Politicians talk about implementing one program or another, but he envisioned a paradigm shift in which each minister would be part of a larger vision. His goal in a sentence: "To be able to produce more with less waste."

He had worked out individual tasks. "When I phone my minister in public works, I will say, 'I want one megatonne less in emissions by 2012. We have three megatonnes of greenhouse gases in the atmosphere; it should be two, and if you are able to deliver it in your mandate in the next two or three years, I will be very pleased with you. That means that you need to have a green performance strategy—a real one. You have to not only talk about it, but deliver it. And you need to push your bureaucracy [and] if your bureaucracy is resisting, tell me.'"

Dion went on to include other front-line departments. "The minister of finance will have the mandate to come up with the greenest budget since Confederation and to come up with environmental tax reform. No GST cut can have a real transformative capacity for the economy. But a strong environmental tax reform can.... And the minister of the environment will have to deliver. And the minister of Treasury Board will have to come with the capacity to be sure that each department will respect their commitments regarding sustainability."

Under his plan, the minister of fisheries would be the "Minister of Oceans and Fisheries—not Fisheries and Oceans," with a clear mandate for sustainability. It would be the same for the minister of natural resources. The foreign minister and the minister responsible for the Canadian International Development Agency would represent a Canada that made clean water an essential issue in dealing with nations around the world. "My role will be to ensure that if we are a country that wants to help, we need to fix the water problem." The Foreign Affairs department would focus on the North and fight to give teeth to international laws that protect the frail ecological system of the Arctic.

His industry minister would be expected to fund research centres on clean air and water, as well as climate change. Scientists would be encouraged to work in Canada, thereby contributing to environmental technologies, and the trade minister would sell those Canadian advancements internationally. The prime minister would call in experts for private consultations (as any good academic might do), instead of listening only to traditional interest groups and lobbyists. On his Alberta trip in January 2007, Dion spent part of an afternoon listening to scientists, later taking business cards and asking his aides to follow up. Dion summarized his focus: "Nevermore will you have a report on the industrial strategy of Canada [in which] the environment is off the map." Growth had to be linked to the interests of the next generation, "to our children and our grandchildren. And Kyoto will be an incentive to do the right thing as soon as possible."

There was a final piece to his program. Dion would not cut the Goods and Services Tax (GST) by the further one percent promised by Prime Minister Harper. "That's $5 billion every year. When I think that some said my Kyoto plan was too costly—$10 billion over six budgets? If you compare it with the GST cut—$5.5 billion every year! And it's too costly when what I want to do is transform the economy, to have a strategy to make us more energy efficient? The GST [cut] gives nothing, completely nothing, to the economy!"

STÉPHANE DION KNEW he might not get the chance to implement his plan; he might remain as Opposition leader, and therein rested perilous implications for his survival. Many had told him he would be prime minister, including Adam Campbell in a telephone conversation in 2006 when he was running for leader. It was a gut feeling for Campbell, who said of Dion: "I think there is greatness there. But it's not a greatness like a Winston Churchill or a Roosevelt, or a Kennedy. It's not that. It's a very Canadian greatness." Campbell talked about Dion the night of his Edmonton town hall. "He's a very understated guy who, if he gets the chance, will change the way Canadians think and act and behave. You don't get that chance very often. But I think we saw it tonight. He spoke to a group of four hundred people and he had them, and I think they'll be back ... Dion won the leadership one person at a time."

Some argued that Dion should have a fair shot at winning the country. "He has earned the right to this election as leader," said Liberal emeritus David Peterson as election fever ramped up weekly during the winter and spring of 2007. It was whispered that Stephen Harper wanted to go to the polls; the Liberals would never be weaker than they were then; Harper was waiting only for the national polls to hold fast at forty percent to try and engineer a vote. Peterson, the former Ontario premier who had supported Michael Ignatieff, added that "the general theory" was that Dion had earned the right to take the party into two elections. Peterson said it would be unfair for anybody to challenge Dion. "The leader has been very, very good to all the front-runners and he has every right to expect loyalty." Besides, said Peterson, "he's a tough little son-of-a-gun." He thought Dion "ran quite a brilliant campaign. This was the greening of the party."[358]

(On the subject of his own loyalty, Dion said he had told Ignatieff, "If you win, Michael, you will not have a more loyal supporter, assistant, collaborator than me." And he had assured Paul Martin, "'Whatever people may tell you about me, don't have any doubts in your mind. I am very loyal to my leader.'" He said Martin replied that he knew.)

Life held no guarantees of fairness, of course. Within two months of his leadership win, the Conservatives were doing their job of negatively defining Dion to Canadians with their ad campaign. The Mike Harris Progressive Conservatives in Ontario had done the same thing to Dalton McGuinty after 1996. "They are dirty fighters; they play nasty," said Peterson. McGuinty had survived. But the attack ads against Dion were swift and effective. "Do you think it's easy to make priorities?" Dion was seen complaining to Ignatieff in one ad. Dion had meant that it was hard to fight for priority at the cabinet table, but that's not what he said. And the Conservatives had another purpose: to strip Dion of his green advantage in the public's mind. Harper was rolling out his own environment platform by 2007 and Elizabeth May worried about a repeat of the free-trade election strategy of 1988. It had served the Progressive Conservatives well. May believed Brian Mulroney won because the Progressive Conservatives muddied the issue of free trade for Canadians, just as Harper was doing with Dion and the environment. It would be one guy's three-point program versus another's five-point plan. What was the difference, really?

Ottawa veteran Peter Donolo thought Dion could survive. He remembered the first time he met him in Jean Chrétien's Langevin Block offices in Ottawa. Donolo was media director and was drafting the statement of Dion's appointment when an unassuming guy with a knapsack arrived to see Chrétien. "It was a difficult time. We were all kind of in shock from the referendum," said Donolo. "He was fearless in his own quiet way ... What's great about Dion is I don't think he's a complex guy. It's not that he doesn't know a lot. He knows himself, he's very disciplined, and there's a bit of the Boy Scout in him. But he's not like a Clinton or Nixon; there's not a lot of psychological motivation at play ... He is what he is."[359]

THERE IS A QUINTESSENTIAL IMAGE of Stéphane Dion. *Toronto Star* photographer Richard Lautens captured it in a photograph in August 2006 as Dion walked to André Lamarre's car at the airport in Quebec City. He was carrying his own bags as he always did, maybe because he'd worked as a bellhop when he was a student. Dion was an expert on China, having visited often and taught as part of a political science program in the early 1990s. Janine Krieber remembered one trip to China when, at the hotel, her husband had insisted on carrying everybody's bags. A hotel employee asked her if all Canadians were like that. In Lautens's photo, Dion is slightly stooped, his bony shoulder blades visible through his suit, his head down. There is a loneliness about it—and a sense of purpose.

NOTES

Prologue: "Hello, My Name Is Stéphane Dion"

1. Janine Krieber, interview, January 5, 2007.
2. Jamie Carroll, interview, January 26, 2007.
3. Stéphane Dion's riding was Saint-Laurent-Cartierville.
4. Buzzetti, Hélène, "Même Dion serait de la course," *Le Devoir,* January 25, 2006: A1.
5. Stéphane Dion, interview, January 14, 2007.
6. Mark Marissen, interview, January 12, 2007.
7. Ibid.
8. Adam Campbell, interview, January 11, 2007.
9. Goldenberg, Eddie, *The Way It Works: Inside Ottawa* (Toronto: McClelland & Stewart, 2006), 244.
10. André Lamarre, interview, January 24, 2007.
11. Stéphane Dion, interview, December 29, 2007.
12. Lamarre, interview, January 24, 2007.

Chapter One: The House on Liégeois

13. Records show Quebec West voted Liberal or Conservative provincially—mostly Liberal—with the exception of the election of Jean-Alphonse Savoie as a member of the National Assembly in 1948. The riding, which became Louis-Hébert in 1962, switched between Liberal and Parti Québécois in subsequent elections. From "Les membres de l'Assemblée nationale par circonscripton," *Informations historiques (Assemblée nationale du Québec),* www.assnat.qc.ca/fra/patrimoine/depcir/index.htm (accessed February 1, 2007).
14. Denyse Dion, interview, December 30, 2006. Unless otherwise indicated, quotes and personal recollections from Mrs. Dion are drawn from this interview.
15. Fraser, Graham, *PQ: René Lévesque and the Parti Québécois in Power* (Toronto: Macmillan, 1984), 7.
16. Ibid.

17. Diebel, Linda, "Can Stéphane Dion reel in the prize?" *Toronto Star*, August 8, 2006: A6.

18. John Meisel, interview, January 27, 2007.

19. Fraser, *PQ*, 9.

20. Ibid., 210.

21. Côté, Gabriel, "Visionnaire et homme de coeur," *Au fils des événements*, January 20, 2007, www.scom.ulaval.ca/Au.fil.des.evenements/2000/01.20/levesque.html (accessed February 1, 2007).

22. Stéphane Dion, interview, December 28–29, 2007.

23. Meisel, interview, January 27, 2007.

24. The skyline remains essentially uncontaminated, still the city of its founder Samuel de Champlain (c. 1570–1635), New France's governor-general Louis de Baude, Count of Frontenac (1622–97), its defender Marquis Louis-Joseph de Montcalm (1712–59), and its conqueror James Wolfe (1727–59).

25. His thesis was entitled *L'univers totalitaire: l'idéologie politique du nationale-socialism*. From l'Ordre national du Québec website, "Léon Dion," Ministère du Conseil exécutif, Gouvernement du Québec, www.ordre-national.gouv.qc.ca/recherche_details.asp?id=72 (accessed February 11, 2007).

26. Denyse Dion used the French term *chanoine*. I have taken liberty in translating this as "old cleric" to give the sense of the word. It's a term for someone in the ecclesiastical hierarchy and, in this context, carries a negative connotation. It might be translated as "bishop's stooge."

27. Lamontagne's career as a minister in Lester B. Pearson's government was disgraced in a scandal over furniture in the 1960s. Stéphane Dion called it a "stupid scandal of furniture he accepted from somebody" in an interview, January 5, 2007. Lamontagne was later appointed to the Senate of Canada.

28. Dion, Stéphane, "Le rôle moteur du gouvernement du Canada dans la Révolution tranquille," *La révolution tranquille 40 ans plus tard: un bilan*, Y. Bélanger, R. Comeau, and C. Métivier, eds. (Montreal: VLB Éditeur, 2000), 50–51.

29. Ibid., 51.

30. Dion, Léon, *Le Bill 60 et la société québécoise* (Montreal: Éditions HMH, 1967).

31. Two years later, in 1970, the school transferred over from the Jesuits to the secular system and was renamed Collège Saint-Charles-Garnier.

32. Laurent Arsenault, interview, February 6, 2007.

33. The Quebec system of CEGEP—*Collège d'enseignement général et professionnel*, meaning College of General and Professional Education—is different from other provinces. After finishing high school in secondary V (grade 11), students choose to follow either a two-year pre-university program, such as social sciences or commerce, or a three-year professional program similar to trade school. Quebec university students who have obtained a CEGEP diploma are required to complete only three years of undergraduate work in university.

34. Diebel, "Can Stéphane Dion reel in the prize?"

35. This theory was the subject of Max Weber's well-known book, *The Protestant Ethic and the Spirit of Capitalism*, first published in Germany as a two-part article in 1904–05.

36. Stéphane Dion, interview, December 21, 2006.

37. Francis Dion, interview, February 1, 2007.

38. "Palmarès," *La Presse*, December 31, 2006, "Rétro 2006": 1.

39. Stéphane Dion, interview, January 10–11, 2007.

40. Mark Marissen, interview, January 12, 2007.

Chapter Two: "We Cannot Betray Our Ancestors"

41. Stéphane Dion, interview, December 28–29, 2006.

42. Léon's approach to teaching is summarized as the result of several interviews, including sources who were happy to give their perspective without being named.

43. Janine Krieber, interview, December 28, 2006.

44. Léon Dion wasn't the only Canadian to feel outrage. There's a legendary story among media types about an Ottawa journalist who accompanied Prime Minister Brian Mulroney on a visit to Canadian war graves in Normandy in the 1980s. A *gendarme* was giving the Canadian press corps a hard time. *"Écoutez,"* said one reporter, *"nos soldats ont sacrifié leurs vies ici pour libérer votre pays pendant que votre mère se couchait avec les boches."* ("Listen, our soldiers sacrificed their lives here to liberate your country while your mother was sleeping with the Germans.") The officer had to be restrained.

45. "Enlèvement de Pierre Laporte" (audio recording of a television program), *Le Téléjournal,* October 10, 1970, updated July 6, 2006, found in "Octobre 70: le Québec en Crise," "Guerres et Conflits," Les Archives de Radio-Canada, Radio-Canada, archives.radio-canada.ca/IDC-0-9-81-323/ guerres_conflits/octobre_70/clip4 (accessed February 10, 2007).

46. Separate FLQ cells were involved in each kidnapping. In the immediate aftermath, members of the Cross cell were flown to Cuba. Ultimately, members of both FLQ cells involved were convicted and sentenced on a variety of charges, including kidnapping and, in Laporte's case, murder. Not everyone in each cell was convicted on the same charges. For example, Paul Rose and Francis Simard were convicted of murder in the death of Pierre Laporte. They received life sentences but have since been paroled.

47. Claude Laporte, interview, January 23, 2007.

48. Dion, Stéphane, "Explaining Québec Nationalism," *The Collapse of Canada?* R. Kent Weaver, editor (Washington, D.C.: The Brookings Institution, 1992), 80.

49. Peter Russell, interview, January 26, 2007.

50. École des hautes études commerciales de Montréal (HEC Montréal) is the prestigious business school at the University of Montreal.

51. Dion, "Explaining Quebec Nationalism," 97.

52. Vallières, Pierre, *White Niggers of America*, translated by Joan Pinkham (Toronto: McClelland & Stewart, 1971). The author wrote that the position of French Quebecers was about more than language. He saw it as a class struggle in which working-class Québécois were dominated by the Anglo bourgeoisie.

53. Fraser, Graham, *Sorry, I Don't Speak French: Confronting the Canadian Crisis That Won't Go Away* (Toronto: McClelland & Stewart, 2006), 30.

54. Ibid., 30. Fraser would become Canada's Official Languages Commissioner in 2006.

55. Peter Russell is referring to an extensive body of work by Léon Dion that includes *Le Bill 60 et la société québécoise* (1967), *La prochaine révolution* (1973), *Nationalismes et politique au Québec* (1975), and *Québec: 1945–2000* (1987).

56. The song title doesn't translate particularly well: "People of the Country"—more meaningfully, "us." The Gilles Vigneault song is heard everywhere at PQ gatherings in Quebec, telling people, in different words, that it's their time to pick up the torch; it's up to them. It's always very moving to hear *Gens du pays* because the melody is beautiful and everyone knows the words.

57. René Lévesque's comments were widely reported in the media. *"Je n'ai jamais pensé que je pourrais être aussi fier d'être Québécois que ce soir."*

58. Guy Lévesque, interview, December 30, 2006.

59. John Meisel, interview, January 27, 2007.

60. De Tocqueville, trained as a lawyer, is best known for *Democracy in America*, published in the United States in two volumes in 1840.

61. Dion, Stéphane, *La dimension temporelle de l'action partisane: l'étude d'un cas: le débat au sein du Parti Québécois sur les modalités d'accession à l'indépendance* (MA thesis, Laval University, 1979).

62. Ibid., 28–38.

63. Laurent Arsenault, interview, February 6, 2007. Unless otherwise indicated, comments from Mr. Arsenault in this chapter are from this interview.

64. A powerful industrialist in West Germany, Schleyer was kidnapped from his car in Cologne by the Baader-Meinhof Gang on September 5, 1977. His bodyguards were killed at the scene and Schleyer's body was found one month later in the trunk of a car. Beginning in the late 1960s, the Baader-Meinhof Gang, who referred to themselves as the Red Army Faction, killed more than thirty people during a campaign against elite Germans and United States military personnel.

65. Krieber, interview, January 6, 2006.

66. Jean-Philippe Thérien, interview, January 22, 2007. Unless otherwise indicated, his comments come from this interview.

67. Lucien Biroulès was president of *Les anciens combattants du 18ième arrondissement.*

68. An author's anecdote: I remember being subjected to a lecture on French grammar while shopping in a big Parisian department store called Galeries Lafayette. When asking the sales clerk where I could find the bathroom, I made the apparently grievous error of saying *"salle de bain."* For fifteen minutes she lectured me on how I should have said *"toilette"* instead, because the facilities did not include a *"bain"* (bathtub) and therefore could not be referred to as a *"salle de bain"* (bathroom). She "tsk-tsked" me and I reflected on how I had been trying to spend money in her store.

69. Crozier lay the foundation for his "strategic analysis of organizations" in this hugely popular book *Le phénomène bureaucratique: essai sur les tendances bureaucratiques des systèmes d'organisation modernes et sur leurs relations en France avec le système social et culturel* (Paris: Éditions du Seuil, 1963). The University of Chicago published an English version (Crozier's own translation) the following year.

70. Grémion, Pierre, "Michel Crozier's Long March: The Making of the Bureaucratic Phenomenon," *Political Studies* 40(1): 5–20.

71. Denis Saint-Martin, interview, January 23, 2007. Unless otherwise indicated, Saint-Martin's comments in this chapter are from this interview.

72. Dion, Stéphane, *La politisation des mairies* (Paris: Economica, 1986). This is the book version of Dion's doctoral thesis, which bore the title *La politisation des administrations publiques: l'exemple de l'administration communale française* (1984).

73. Crozier uses the term *"Clochemerles,"* which is a 1934 French satirical novel by Gabriel Chevallier describing a fictional village divided between its incumbent mayor, who opposes new technologies, and his challenger, who wants to install a urinal in the town. By invoking the image here, Crozier is conveying the over-politicization of an issue that makes little sense to outsiders but betrays the locals' fear of change and a strange conception of identity.

74. Crozier, "Preface," *La politisation des mairies,* Stéphane Dion (Paris: Economica, 1986), ii–iii.

75. Stéphane Dion, interview, February 14, 2007.

76. Dion, Léon, *Le Québec et le Canada: les voies de l'avenir* (Montreal: Éditions Quebecor, 1980).

Chapter Three: One Dion Was Enough

77. André Belanger, interview, January 25, 2007. Unless otherwise indicated, his comments in this chapter are from this interview.

78. Stéphane Dion, interviews, December 28–29, 2006. His comments in this chapter are from these interviews unless otherwise indicated.

79. Aubin, Benoit, "Ottawa's New Power Couple," *Maclean's*, January 22, 2007, 30.

80. Ibid.

81. Janine Krieber, interview, January 25, 2007.

82. Denis Saint-Martin, interview, January 23, 2007.

83. Graciela Ducatenzeiler, interview, February 1, 2007.

84. Blais, André, and Stéphane Dion, eds., *The Budget-Maximizing Bureaucrat: Appraisals and Evidence* (Pittsburgh: University of Pittsburgh Press, 1991).

Chapter Four: Finding His Religion

85. This program was called the *PBS NewsHour with Jim Lehrer* in 2007.

86. Stéphane Dion, interview, December 21, 2006. Unless otherwise noted, Dion's comments in this chapter come from that interview.

87. In 2007, Andrew Stark was professor of strategic management at the Rotman School of Management, University of Toronto. Keith G. Banting held the Queen's Research Chair in Public Policy at Queen's University and, during the 2006–07 school year, was on a research sabbatical at the University of Melbourne in Australia. Also in 2007, Thomas E. Mann was Senior Fellow in Governance Studies and the W. Averell Harriman Chair at The Brookings Institution in Washington, D.C.

88. Keith Banting, interview, February 26, 2007.

89. In 2007, R. Kent Weaver was Senior Fellow in Governance Studies at The Brookings Institution.

90. Weaver, R. Kent, editor, *The Collapse of Canada?* (Washington, D.C.: The Brookings Institution, 1992).

91. Andrew Stark, interview, February 23, 2007. He and his wife, Deborah, had had brunch with Stéphane Dion and Janine Krieber the previous Sunday in Toronto at the Royal Ontario Museum.

92. They are described in Sections 91 and 92, as any veteran journalist of the constitutional wars knows all too well. Section 93 left education in the hands of the provinces.

93. Dion, Stéphane, "The Decentralized Nature of the Canadian Federation," in *Straight Talk: Speeches and Writings on Canadian Unity,* Peter Russell, editor (Montreal and Kingston: McGill-Queen's University Press, 1999), 93.

94. Dion, Stéphane, "Explaining Quebec Nationalism" in *The Collapse of Canada?* 77.

95. Dion, Stéphane, "The Quebec Challenge to Canadian Unity," PS: *Political Science and Politics,* 26(1) (1993): 40.

96. Dion, Stéphane, "Explaining Quebec Nationalism," 79.

97. The Supreme Court of Canada would later rule that Quebec had never had a veto.

98. Constitutional scholars disagreed about whether Quebec's refusal to sign the Canada Act of 1982, which repatriated the BNA Act from Britain, meant its provisions didn't apply to the province. Meanwhile, talks were underway to try to achieve an accord with Quebec. The BNA Act was replaced by the Constitution Act, 1867.

99. John Buchanan compared the time for constitutional change as the "great wheel" in Act 2, Scene 4 of *King Lear:* "Let go thy hold when a great wheel runs down a hill, lest it break by neck with."

100. Dion, Stephane, "Explaining Quebec Nationalism," 112.

101. Bill 101, a law known officially as the Charter of the French Language, also denied English education to many Anglos as well. Anyone whose parents did not receive the majority of their education in English in Canada (at first it was limited to Quebec) was not eligible for English schooling. It was a thicket of Orwellian detail within the context of an understandable concept. The law faced a rocky road of court challenges until finally, in March 2005, the Supreme Court ruled in favour of Bill 101, with the stipulation that there had to be greater access to English schools for the children of English-speaking parents.

102. Dion, Stéphane, "Explaining Canadian Nationalism, 95.

103. Ibid., 94–95.

104. Ibid., 111. It's important to note that Dion wasn't saying he supported the Meech Lake Accord but, rather, analyzing the effects of its collapse on Quebec.

105. Ibid., 120.

106. Ibid., 121.

107. Stéphane Dion, interview, February 25, 2007.

108. Peter Russell, interview, January 26, 2007.

109. Stéphane Dion, interview, February 25, 2007.

110. Ibid.

111. The commission was chaired by Michel Bélanger, a federalist, and Jean Campeau, a separatist, and tabled its report on March 28, 1991.

112. Dion, Stéphane, "Le Canada malade de la politique," *La Presse,* February 26, 1992: B3.

113. Dion, Stéphane, "L'accord de Charlottetown et le ʃartage des pouvoirs," *Le Devoir,* October 16, 1992: B1.

114 Aubin, Benoît, "Ottawa's new power couple," *Maclean's,* January 22, 2007: 31.

115. Venne, Michel, "Léon Dion propose de donner une dernière chance au Canada." *Le Devoir,* December 13, 1990: A1.

116. Boivin, Gilles. "Léon Dion propose une dernière chance au Canada anglais." *Le Soleil,* December 13, 1990: A6.

117. Stéphane Dion, interview, February 25, 2007.

118. Adam, Marcel, "Au sujet du pretendu consensus québécois sur la question du partage des pouvoirs," *La Presse,* February 27, 1992: B2.

119. Gagnon, Lysiane, "Les pouvoirs? Mais pourquoi?" *La Presse,* March 14, 1992: B3.

120. The view obviously encompasses more than Marxist thought, touching on the ideas of Carl Jung, the philosophical examination of free will, even Leo Tolstoy or an interpretation of Mary Shelley. The flow of one of the best novels ever, *War and Peace,* is constantly interrupted so Tolstoy can lecture readers on his rivers-of-history theory, often using the example of Napoleon.

121. Denis Saint-Martin, interview, January 23, 2007.

122. Ibid.

123. Voyager á titre canadien (video clip), "Discussions avec Dion," leadership campaign website www.stephanedion.ca/?q+fr/Conversation (accessed February 25, 2007).

124. His 1972 film *Le charme discrète de la bourgeoisie* comes to mind.

125. Stéphane Dion, interview, January 10–11, 2007.

126. Marissal, Vincent, "Le politicologue Stéphane Dion semonce les liberaux," *Le Soleil,* January 30, 1995: A4.

127. David, Michel, "L'impertinent," *Le Soleil,* January 31, 1995: A12.

128. Graveline, Pierre, "Ce peuple obsède de constitution," *Le Devoir,* February 2, 1995: A6.

129. Diebel, Linda, "Can Stéphane Dion reel in the prize?"

130. Keith Banting, interview, February 27, 2007.

131. Leishman, Rory, "Parizeau's odious allegations are based on a bad translation," *The Gazette,* March 23, 1995: B3. Leishman, who was at the conference, wrote there had been an error in translation in a report by the Presse Canadienne. A statement by Hartt saying Prime Minister Jean Chrétien should "let Quebec suffer" was translated as Chrétien having a duty "to make Quebec suffer."

132. Hartt, Stanley, "C.D. Howe meeting didn't plot a Quebec recession," *The Gazette,* March 23, 1885: B3.

133. Presse Canadienne, "Le politicologue Dion se défend de vouloir faire souffrir les Québécois," *Le Devoir,* March 18, 1995: A8.

134. Stéphane Dion, interview, February 9, 2007.

135. Dion, Stéphane, "Rester dans le Canada," *La Presse,* September 21, 1995: B3.

136. François Vaillancourt, interview, January 5, 2007.

137. Dion, Stéphane, and François Vaillancourt, "Le choix référendaire résume en douze propositions fondamentales," *La Presse,* October 14, 1995: B3.

138. Geoffroi Montpetit, interview, February 22, 2007.

139. Picard, André, Rheal Seguin, and Richard Mackie, "No knockouts in Quebec debate," *The Globe and Mail,* August 30, 1994: A1.

Chapter Five: A Walk in the Snow

140. Yakabuski, Konrad, "King of the Hill," *The Globe and Mail,* January 20, 2007: F1.

141. Stéphane Dion, interview, December 21, 2007. Unless otherwise indicated, material in this chapter comes from this interview.

142. Jean Chrétien, interview, January 25, 2007.

143. Stéphane Dion, interview, December 21, 2007.

Chapter Six: The Minister of Unity

144. The National Capital Commission has a brief interactive history of Queen Victoria's decision on its website. See "1857—A Capital Choice" in "Discover the Capital," National Capital Commission, updated January 18, 2007, www.canadascapital.gc.ca/bins/ncc_web_content_page.asp?cid=16297-58245-59585&lang=1 (accessed March 3, 2007).

145. "New unity minister says Quebec can be split up if it separates," Canadian Press NewsWire, January 26, 1996.

146. In English, Trudeau, Marchand, and Pelletier were called "the three wise men."

147. Stéphane Dion, interview, December 21, 2006.

148. Goldenberg, Eddie, *The Way It Works,* 244.

149. Jean Chrétien, interview, January 25, 2007. Unless otherwise indicated, Chrétien quotes in this chapter come from this interview.

150. Stéphane Dion, interview, December 21, 2006.

151. Goldenberg, 244.

152. Geoffroi Montpetit, interview, February 19, 2007.

153. Janine Krieber, interview, January 6, 2007.

154. By 1996, George Anderson had held senior positions in the Department of Finance, among other departments, and had been a fellow at Harvard University's Center for Intergovernmental Affairs. He had studied at Queen's, Oxford University, and the École nationale d'administration in Paris. In 2006, he was president and chief executive officer of the Forum of Federations, an organization that encourages the practice of federalism internationally. Anderson became Dion's deputy minister in March 1996, serving in the first weeks as a deputy secretary reporting to Ron Bilodeau.

155. George Anderson, interview, February 9, 2007. Any uncited comments from Anderson in this chapter originate in this interview.

156. Stéphane Dion, interview, December 10–11, 2006. Uncited Dion quotes in this chapter come from this interview.

157. Eddie Goldenberg, interview, January 31, 2007.

158. Stéphane Dion had also been appointed president of the Privy Council, a largely ceremonial role. For real policy wonks there is delicious reading about

traditional functions of the Privy Council in *The Government of Canada* by R. MacGregor Dawson (Toronto: University of Toronto Press, 1947). The author's copy is the fifth edition, revised by Norman Ward in 1970. Membership in the Privy Council was expanded greatly to accommodate all those who wished to be part of the official Canadian delegation to the coronation of Her Majesty Queen Elizabeth II at Westminster in 1952. Such uses for the Privy Council may well still exist, but the author's research regrettably did not encompass its uses and functions. Also, it's worth mentioning that the secretary to the cabinet is more commonly referred to in Ottawa as the clerk of the Privy Council.

159. Anderson, interview, February 9, 2007.

160. Stéphane Dion, interview, December 21, 2006.

161. Goldenberg, 233.

162. Goldenberg, interview, January 31, 2007.

163. Stéphane Dion, interview, January 10–11, 2007.

164. Anderson, interview, February 9, 2007.

165. Gaboury, Paul, "Sauveur ou messager?" *Le Droit,* January 27, 1996: 24.

166. Marissal, Vincent, "Remaniement ministériel à Ottawa," *Le Soleil,* January 26, 1996: A7.

167. Gomery Commission, *Commission of Inquiry into the Sponsorship Program and Advertising Activities,* Hearings on January 25, 2005, Vol. 62, English translation, 10878–10880. See the Gomery Commission website: www.gomerycommission.ca/documents/transcripts/en/2005/02/2005221370. pdf (accessed March 6, 2007).

168. Ibid.

169. Quebec was not alone. The country was divided into five regions, Quebec being one of them, with veto powers applying to all of them.

170. Delacourt, Susan, "Liberals ponder the unthinkable." *The Globe and Mail,* January 27, 1996: A1.

171. Gagnon, Lysiane, "Danger à l'horizon," *La Presse,* February 1, 1996: B3.

172. Dion, Jean, "Chrétien contredit Dion," *Le Devoir,* February 23, 1996: A1.

173. Stéphane Dion, interview, January 10–11, 2007.

174. Bill 1 died without ever having been put to a vote.

175. Stéphane Dion, interview, January 10–11, 2007.

176. The Federal Justice Department website at www.justice.gc.ca/en/ news/nr/1996/bertBack.html (accessed March 6, 2007).

177. Duffy, Andrew, "Separatism: The end of the myth." *Ottawa Citizen,* August 19, 1998: A1.

178. Came, Barry, "Taking on separatism," *Maclean's,* May 27, 1996: 14.

179. Anderson, interview, February 9, 2007.

180. Picard, André, "Bouchard rejects election option," *The Globe and Mail,* May 14, 1996: A1.

181. Dion, Stéphane, "Speech on a Motion by the Opposition, House of Commons, Ottawa, May 16, 1996," in *Straight Talk,* 187.

182. Dion, Stéphane, "Canada's Communities and the Hope for Canadian Unity," in *Straight Talk*, 9.

183. Dion, Stéphane, "The Ethic of Federalism," in *Straight Talk*, 31.

184. Montpetit, interview, February 19, 2007.

185. Geoffroi Montpetit recounted the phone call, saying that Dion arrived at his Montreal townhouse at the end of a very long day and found a thick briefing binder from Anderson awaiting him. He was tired and upset. "George should know my schedule," he complained to Montpetit, who was travelling with him, before sitting down to read everything. By the time he had annotated everything, it was close to 3:00 A.M. "Now I am ready to call George," Dion told Montpetit. He wanted to go over specific points with his deputy. "Mr. Minister, look at the time. It's 3:00 A.M.," said Montpetit. Dion replied that he didn't care about that. Thought Montpetit: "This is really going to be fun!" Montpetit had to place the call to the deputy's home in Ottawa, chirping brightly to the sleepy Anderson: "Hi George, sorry to bother you but ..." The next morning, Montpetit asked Anderson if he even remembered the conversation. Anderson, ever the professional, didn't let on that the call had even bothered him.

186. Russell, Peter, "Preface," *Straight Talk*, vii–viii.

187. Krieber, interview, January 6, 2007.

188. Stéphane Dion, interview, January 5, 2007.

189. The Federal Justice Department website.

190. Reference re Secession of Quebec, [1998] 2 S.C.R. 217, 1998 CanLII 793 (S.C.C.).

191. Johnson, William, "Separatists are still dreaming the impossible dream," *The Globe and Mail*, January 17, 2001: A13.

192. Fraser, Graham, "New Brunswick premier maintains he was merely expressing support for unity," *The Globe and Mail*, August 7, 1997: A6.

193. Ibid.

194. Ibid.

195. Ibid.

196. *Breaking Point*, dir. Jacqueline Dubé-Corkery and Pierre Béliveau, DVD, Radio-Canada Television, original broadcast 2005.

197. Dion, Stéphane, "Letter to Mr. Lucien Bouchard, August 11, 1997," in *Straight Talk*, 89. Dion preferred the French edition for this particular letter because of an error mixing up two paragraphs in the English text.

198. Dion, Denyse, "Un homme constamment à la recherche de la verité," *La Presse*, August 28, 1997: B2.

199. Robitaille, Antoine, "Dion contre Dion," LeDevoir.com, December 9–10, 2006, www.ledevoir.com/2006/2/09/124521.html (accessed March 6, 2007).

200. Dion, Stéphane, "Letter to Mr. Bernard Landry" in *Straight Talk*, 194.

201. Greenspon, Edward, "Landry scoffs at Dion letter," *The Globe and Mail*, August 28, 1997: A1.

202. Dion, Stéphane, "Letter to Mr. Bernard Landry, August 28, 1997" in *Straight Talk*, 198–99.

203. Stéphane Dion, interview, January 10–11, 2007.

204. Dion, Stéphane, "Letter to Mr. Claude Ryan," in *Straight Talk*, 223.

205. Reference re Secession of Quebec [1998]2 S.C.R. 217, 1998 CanII 793 (S.C.C.).

206. Ibid.

207. Stéphane Dion, interview, January 10–11, 2007.

208. Thompson, Elizabeth, and Philip Authier, "After the ruling, we win, both claim," *The Gazette*, August 22, 1998: A1.

209. Ibid.

Chapter Seven: Clarity

210. Macpherson, Don, "Prudent course for Ottawa," *The Gazette*, November 3, 1999: B3.

211. Stéphane Dion, interview, January 10–11, 2007. Unless otherwise indicated, Dion's comments in this chapter come from this interview.

212. Dion, Stéphane, "Anti-Nationalism and Constitutional Obsession in the Quebec Referendum Debate," *Inroads*, April 1995: 14–16.

213. Jean Chrétien inherited a $42 billion deficit when he became prime minister in 1993. The elimination of that deficit under the stewardship of Finance Minister Paul Martin has been praised as a hallmark of the Chrétien government. However, critics have blamed Martin for contributing to the decline of social programs in the provinces, particularly his 1995 budget that cut $25 billion over three years, eliminated 45,000 government jobs, and decreased spending to the provinces by $7 billion.

214. Dion, Stéphane, "Zero Deficit: Our Common Objective" in *Straight Talk*, 107.

215. Lucien Bouchard was seventeen years older than Dion and a product of the Collège de Jonquière, later Cégep de Jonquière, in Quebec's Saguenay-Lac-Saint-Jean region. It had been founded by the Oblate order, which had also educated Dion. As well, Bouchard attended Laval University, which had been founded as a Jesuit seminary and retained the rigour of the order.

216. Marcel Massé, interview, January 25, 2007. Before his time in the Chrétien cabinet, Massé had worked in the administrative and economics division of the World Bank, Washington, D.C., and in several senior public service positions in Ottawa, including secretary to the cabinet and clerk of the Privy Council. In 1999, he became executive director for Canada at the Inter-American Development Bank in Washington and, in 2002, executive director for Canada at the World Bank, also representing a number of Caribbean nations.

217. Dion, Stéphane, "Identité collective et idéologie," *Le Devoir*, June 5, 1999: A11.

218. Ibid.

219. Ibid.

220. Jean Chrétien, interview, January 25, 2007. Unless otherwise indicated, Chrétien quotes in this chapter come from this interview.

221. Eddie Goldenberg, *The Way It Works*, 150.

222. George Anderson, interview, February 9, 2007.

223. Goldenberg, 151. Quotes following in this paragraph are from Goldenberg, 151–52.

224. Clarity Act [S.C. 2000, c.26].

225. Aubin, Benoît, "Ottawa's new power couple," *Maclean's*, January 22, 2007: 32.

226. Editorial, "Demonizing federalists," *Toronto Star*, February 4, 2000: A24.

227. Gagné, Jean-Simon, "Le poison constitutionnel," *Le Soleil*, November 28, 1999: A4.

228. Gagné, Jean-Simon, "Les blues du vendeur d'assurances" *Le Soleil*, December 12, 1999: A1.

229. Loïc Tassé, interview, January 22, 2007.

230. Don Macpherson, interview, March 11, 2007.

231. Ibid.

232. François Goulet, interview, January 25, 2007.

233. Linda Diebel, "Can Stéphane Dion reel in the prize?"

234. Dion, Stéphane, et al., "The Clarity Act Debate in the House of Commons," *Canadian Parliamentary Review*, 23.2 (2000): 20, www.parl.gc.ca/InfoParl/english/issue.htm?param=75&art=174 (accessed March 27, 2007).

235. Ibid.

236. Ibid.

237. Ibid.

238. Ibid.

239. Ibid.

240. Ibid.

241. Ibid.

242. Ibid.

243. Ibid.

244. Lisée, Jean-François, "J'accuse Stéphane Dion," *L'actualité*, February 2007: 28–30. A former journalist who reported from Washington, D.C., and Paris for French and Quebec media in the 1980s, Lisée became former Quebec premier Jacques Parizeau's special policy adviser in 1994 and played a key role in the 1995 referendum Yes side strategy. He continued as an adviser under Bouchard until 1999. In 2007, he was executive director of the University of Montreal's Centre d'études et de recherches internationales (CÉRIUM).

245. Stéphane Dion, interview, March 13, 2007.

246. Marcel Massé, interview, January 25, 2007.

247. Ibid.

248. Goldenberg, *The Way It Works,* 255.

249. In 2007, Bouchard would be with the law firm Davies Ward Phillips & Vineberg.

250. Thompson, Elizabeth, et al., "Bouchard to step down as premier, PQ leader," *The Gazette,* January 11, 2001: A1.

251. McKenzie, Robert, "Bouchard to stay until new premier is chosen," *Toronto Star,* January 12, 2001: A1.

252. Marissal, Vincent, "Bonne nouvelle pour le Canada," *La Presse,* January 12, 2001: A9.

253. Stéphane Dion, interview, March 23, 2007.

Chapter Eight: Dead Man Walking

254. Stéphane Dion, interview, January 5, 2007. Unless otherwise indicated, quotes from Dion come from this interview.

255. Geoffroi Montpetit, interview, February 19, 2007. Unless otherwise indicated, information from Montpetit comes from this interview.

256. André Lamarre, interviews, January 5, and January 18, 2007. Unless otherwise indicated, material from André Lamarre comes from these two interviews. Neither André Lamarre nor Stéphane Dion wanted to name the people who had spoken to them. Dion said he preferred to leave it in the past.

257. Johnston, David, "Stéphane Dion finds his way on the campaign trail," *Ottawa Citizen,* May 23, 2004: B4.

258. Patricia Bittar, interview, February 8, 2007. Unless otherwise indicated, material from Bittar comes from this interview.

259. "Text of letter by Stéphane Dion, sent to Premier Ralph Klein," *Canadian Press NewsWire,* February 21, 2003. The text contained Dion's letter to Klein and Klein's response to Prime Minister Jean Chrétien.

260. Ibid.

261. Stéphane Dion, interview, March 12, 2007.

262. Stéphane Dion, interview, December 28–29, 2006.

263. In 2007, Dalton McGuinty was premier of Ontario, Stephen Harper prime minister of Canada, Sam Sullivan mayor of Vancouver, and Gordon Campbell premier of British Columbia.

264. Mark Marissen, interview, January 12, 2007. Unless otherwise specified, quotes from Marissen come from this interview.

265. Susan Delacourt best described those years of struggle in the juicy pages of *Juggernaut: Paul Martin's Campaign for Chrétien's Crown* (Toronto: McClelland & Stewart, 2003).

266. Bryden, Joan, "PM's failure to defend Dion," Canadian Press, February 15, 2004.

267. Jean Lapierre would successfully run in Outremont and Pablo Rodriguez in Honoré-Mercier, both Montreal ridings.

268. Janine Krieber, interview, January 6, 2007.

269. Jean Chrétien, interview, January 25, 2007.

270. Diebel, Linda, "Two men who would be king," *Toronto Star*, June 26, 2004: A1.

Chapter Nine: Project Green

271. Senator David Smith, interview, March 15, 2007.

272. Gorrie, Peter, "In search of a softer, more inclusive Kyoto Climate Conference," *Toronto Star*, November 26, 2007: A1.

273. May, Elizabeth, "Clearing the Air on Climate Change," speech presented to Manitoba Wildlands, Winnipeg, June 20, 2006. In her answer to a question from the floor, May recounted the drama that unfolded during the last twenty-four hours of the conference in Montreal and provided a transcript of her answer to the author. Material from the transcript is included in this chapter as noted.

274. Elizabeth May, interview, March 2, 2007.

275. John Bennet, interview, March 2, 2007. By 2007, Bennett would be Canadian executive director of the Climate Action Network, a global network of nongovernmental organizations.

276. Peter Gorrie, interview, February 22, 2007.

277. Peter Gorrie, "Cooling warming climate change preoccupied UN delegates in Montreal for two weeks," *Toronto Star*, December 12, 2005: A4.

278. Ibid.

279. Watson, Harlan L., "U.S. Climate Change Policy," transcript of digital video conference from Washington, D.C., February 18, 2004, Bureau of Oceans and International Environment and Scientific Affairs, Under Secretary for Democracy and Global Affairs, U.S. Department of State website, updated February 20, 2004, www.state.gov/g/oes/rls/rm/2004/29641.htm (accessed March 17, 2007).

280. May, "Clearing the Air on Climate Change."

281. Ibid.

282. Stéphane Dion, through aide Gianluca Cairo, in answer to an email question, March 17, 2007.

283. May, interview, March 15, 2007.

284. May, interview, March 16, 2007.

285. Clinton's comment may be true about climate change, but Al Gore made it clear in *An Inconvenient Truth* that his concern for the environment dated from his student days.

286. Clinton, William J., "Remarks by President William J. Clinton," transcript of speech presented at the United Nations Climate Change Conference (COP-11/MOP-1), Montreal, December 8, 2005, Sierra Club of Canada website, www.sierraclub.ca/national/postings/clinton-speech-12-2005.html (accessed March 17, 2007). This website lists the speech as a "side event."

287. Martin, Paul, "Address by Prime Minister Paul Martin at the UN Conference on Climate Change," Montreal, December 7, 2005, Privy Council Office online archives, Government of Canada, www.pco-bcp.gc.ca/default.asp? Language=E&Page=archivemartin&Sub=speechesdiscours&Doc=speech_20051 207_666e.htm. (accessed March 17, 2007).

288. Russo, Robert, "Canadian politicians rip apart U.S. to build up Canada's image: U.S. envoy," Canadian Press, December 9, 2005.

289. Ibid.

290. Stéphane Dion, interview, December 28–29, 2006. Unless otherwise indicated, the quotes from Dion in the remainder of this chapter come from the December 28–29 interviews.

291. Ibid.

292. Gordon, James, "Liberals under pressure to produce Kyoto plan," *National Post,* February 17, 2005: A1.

293. Corcoran, Terence, "Kyoto plan an exercise in collective insanity that will never work," *National Post,* April 14, 2005: FP23.

294. May, "Clearing the Air on Climate Change."

295. Ibid. It is also worth pointing out that under one of the more controversial sections of the North American Free Trade Agreement of 1987, Canada is bound to maintain its level of energy exports to the United States in times of shortage, such as in wartime. When Mexico signed on as a NAFTA partner in 1994, the Mexican government of President Carlos Salinas had refused to accept such conditions.

296. John Bennett, interview, March 8, 2007.

297. May, "Clearing the Air on Climate Change."

298. Ibid.

299. Ibid.

300. André Lamarre, interview, February 15, 2007.

301. Lamarre, interview, March 18, 2007.

302. May, "Clearing the Air on Climate Change."

303. Ibid.

304. Ibid.

Chapter Ten: Politics Is an Art

305. Stéphane Dion, interview, December 21, 2006. Unless otherwise indicated, Dion's comments in this chapter come from this interview.

306. Gerard Kennedy, interview, January 15, 2007. Unless otherwise indicated, Kennedy's comments in this chapter come from this interview.

307. MPs Maurizio Bevilacqua (North York), Carolyn Bennett (St. Paul's), and Hedy Fry (Vancouver Centre) had already dropped out, all going to Bob Rae.

308. Diebel, Linda, "Calling Mr. Kennedy," *Toronto Star,* October 8, 2006: A6.

309. "Auditor General's Report 2004," *CBC News Indepth,* February 11,

2004, www.cbc.ca/news/background/auditorgeneral/report2004.html (accessed March 3, 2007).

310. In separate criminal trials, advertising executives Paul Coffin and Jean Brault, as well as bureaucrat Chuck Guité, who oversaw the Sponsorship Program from 1996 to 1999, were convicted of a total of twenty-six fraud-related charges and sentenced to prison. Coffin and Brault were released after serving partial sentences and, in 2007, Guité was free pending an appeal. Gagliano was kicked out of the Liberal party and left politics after Martin fired him from his Denmark ambassadorship. He did not face a criminal trial but said he accepted political responsibility for what happened. In September 2006, he published an autobiography in French, *Les corridors du pouvoir* (Montreal: Les Éditions du Méridien, 2006), which included his version of the sponsorship scandal and criticized the way Martin handled it. Gagliano argued the matter should have been referred to police for investigation.

311. Commission of Inquiry into the Sponsorship Program and Advertising Activities, Hearings on January 25, 2005, English translation, vol. 62,10882. www.commissiongomery.ca/documents/transcripts/en/2005/02/20052213 107.pdf (accessed March 6, 2007).

312. Gomery Commission, 10904.

313. Gomery Commission, 10908.

314. Adam Campbell, interview, January 11, 2007.

315. Pratte, André, "La réhabilitation de Stéphane Dion," *La Presse,* April 9, 2006: A27.

316. Peter Donolo, interview, February 22, 2007.

317. Denis Saint-Martin, interview, January 23, 2007.

318. Loïc Tassé, interview, January 22, 2007. By 2007, Tassé was a lecturer in the political science department of the University of Montreal, specializing in international relations and Asia, with special emphasis on the political economy of China.

319. Saint-Martin, interview, January 23, 2007.

320. Janine Krieber, interview, January 6, 2007. Krieber's comments in this chapter come from this interview.

321. In 2007 Janine Krieber was a member of l'Institut des hautes études internationales at Laval University.

322. Marta Wale, interview, December 29, 2007. This was a joint interview with Marta and Norman Wale.

323. In 2007, Megan Meltzer was director of development for the Canadian Jewish Political Affairs Committee.

324. Jean Chrétien, interview, January 25, 2007.

325. Norman Wale, interview, December 29, 2006. Wale was a retired civil servant who had also been a long-time vice-president at Canadian Pacific and had taught at Concordia University and Haute études commerciales (HEC) in Montreal.

326. Megan Meltzer, interview, March 22, 2007.

327. Wells, Paul, et al., "Stéphane Dion's wild ride," *Maclean's,* December 18, 2006: 32.

328. Denise Brunsdon, interview, March 2, 2007. Unless otherwise indicated, Brundson's comments come from this interview.

329. Rob Silver, interview, January 18, 2007.

Chapter 11: Let's Have Lunch

330. Herb Metcalfe, interview, January 30, 2007. Metcalfe's comments in this chapter come from this interview.

331. Stéphane Dion, interview, December 21, 2006.

332. Martha Hall Findlay, interview, January 4, 2007, and Bob Rae, interview, January 15, 2007. Unless otherwise indicated, comments from Hall Findlay and Rae come from these separate interviews.

333. Gerard Kennedy, interview, January 15, 2007.

334. Paul Wells et al., "Stéphane Dion's wild rise," 46.

335. Dubé, Audrey, "The Suite of the Leader of the Opposition," Curatorial Services, House of Commons (provided January 5, 2007).

336. Stéphane Dion started out on Parliament Hill in 1996 with an old blue nylon knapsack. Soon afterwards, however, Bryon Wilfert, from the Federation of Canadian Municipalities, presented him with the leather knapsack he was still carrying in 2007. By then, Wilfert was Liberal MP for Oak Ridges.

337. Stéphane Dion, interview, December 28–29, 2006. Unless otherwise indicated, Dion's comments in this chapter come from this interview.

338. Mark Marissen, interview, January 12, 2007.

339. Taber, Jane, "He cut a deal, then danced the night away," *The Globe and Mail,* December 19, 2006: A1.

340. Ray Heard sent two emails to the author, one on January 8, 2007, and the other on March 4, 2007. Heard had supported Gerard Kennedy for the leadership until he disagreed with his position against the recognition of Quebec as a nation and switched to Dion. Heard asked Peter C. Newman if he had any problem with the anecdote being told. Newman replied in a March 25, 2007, email: "Of course you can go on the record ... but you should also point out my columns on him for the *Globe:* First, predicting his victory six months into the race; 2) predicting his downfall, six days after he won—and noting the fact that he is a mouth-breather."

341. Hébert, Chantal, "How soon will PM move in for kill on Dion?" *Toronto Star,* March 5, 2007: A13.

342. Stéphane Dion, interview, February 9, 2007.

343. Stéphane Dion, interview, March 4, 2007.

344. Jamie Carroll, interview, March 3, 2007. Unless otherwise indicated, Carroll's comments in this chapter come from this interview.

345. Mary Houle, interview, March 3, 2007.

346. The two firemen, both in their fifties, were Captain Harold Lessard and Captain Thomas Nichols. They died fighting a fire.

347. Taber, Jane, "Ignatieff back in the spotlight," *The Globe and Mail,* February 17, 2007: A15.

348. While most people spoke openly, a few preferred to express their opinions to the author, or provide information, privately.

349. Senator Jerry Grafstein, interview, March 25, 2007.

Chapter 12: He Is What He Is

350. Adam Campbell, interview, January 12, 2007. Campbell's comments in this chapter are from this interview.

351. In the fall of 2006, federal Finance Minister Jim Flaherty had announced that Ottawa was removing tax benefits for income trusts, which allowed Canadian corporations to shield billions of dollars from Revenue Canada. He said the changes to tax law would be phased in during the next four years. Critics attacked the Conservative government for having broken a campaign promise not to do so.

352. Allan Mayer, interview, March 15, 2007.

353. Kellogg, Alan, "Dion showing signs he's got human touch," *Edmonton Journal,* January 13, 2007: A2.

354. Things also seemed to be slipping into place for Dion's former leadership rivals by the spring of 2007. Gerard Kennedy won the Liberal nomination for the next election in Parkdale-High Park and Bob Rae won in Toronto Centre. Martha Hall Findlay was appointed as Liberal candidate in Willowdale. Hall Findlay would say that Rae had been "professional" in his dealings with her on party policy issues.

355. Denis Saint-Martin, interview, January 23, 2007.

356. Stéphane Dion, interview, December 29, 2007. Unless otherwise indicated, comments from Dion in this chapter come from this interview.

357. The campaign had not been fought over a referendum but, rather, on Premier Charest's record. But while Parti Québécois leader André Boisclair supported calling another referendum, Mario Dumont, from the Action démocratique du Québec, had moved away from the separation issue. (As ADQ leader in 1995, Dumont had signed the pre-referendum Bill 1, which said the province would separate in one year if negotiations failed with Canada.) There was a united front against a referendum that seemed to show a generational shift in Quebec, but Dion, better than most, understood the mercurial nature of Quebec's relationship to Canada. He said he was pleased to see there would not be a referendum—"for the time being."

358. David Peterson, interview, March 21, 2007.

359. Peter Donolo, interview, January 17, 2007.

SELECTED BIBLIOGRAPHY

Blais, André, and Stéphane Dion, eds. *The Budget-Maximizing Bureaucrat: Appraisals and Evidence.* Pittsburgh: University of Pittsburgh Press, 1991.

Dawson, MacGregor R. *The Government of Canada.* 1947. Reprint, Toronto and Buffalo: University of Toronto Press, 1977.

Delacourt, Susan. *Juggernaut: Paul Martin's Campaign for Chrétien's Crown.* Toronto: McClelland & Stewart, 2003.

De Tocqueville, Alexis. *Democracy in America.* 2 vols. 1839. Reprint, New York: Random House, 1990.

Dion, Léon. *Le Bill 60 et la société québécoise.* Montreal: Éditions HMH, 1967.

———. *Le Québec et le Canada: les voies de l'avenir.* Montreal: Éditions Quebecor, 1980.

Dion, Stéphane. *La politisation des mairies.* Paris: Economica, 1986.

———. *The Collapse of Canada?* Ed. R. Kent Weaver. Washington, D.C.: The Brookings Institution, 1992.

———. *Straight Talk: Speeches and Writings on Canadian Unity.* Montreal and Kingston: McGill-Queen's University Press, 1999.

Fraser, Graham. *PQ: René Lévesque and the Parti Québécois in Power.* Toronto: Macmillan, 1984.

———. *Sorry, I Don't Speak French: Confronting the Canadian Crisis that Won't Go Away.* Toronto: McClelland & Stewart, 2006.

Goldenberg, Eddie. *The Way It Works: Inside Ottawa.* Toronto: McClelland & Stewart, 2006.

Johnson, William. *Stephen Harper and the Future of Canada.* 2005. Reprint, Toronto: McClelland & Stewart, 2006.

Mann Trofimenkoff, Susan. *The Dream of Nation: A Social and Intellectual History of Quebec.* Toronto: Macmillan, 1982.

Plamondon, Bob. *Full Circle: Death and Resurrection in Canadian Conservative Politics.* Toronto: Key Porter, 2006.

Rae, Bob. *From Protest to Power: Personal Reflections on a Life in Politics.* Toronto: McClelland & Stewart, 2006.

———. *The Three Questions: Prosperity and the Public Good.* 1998. Reprint, Toronto: McClelland & Stewart, 2006.

Regush, Nicholas M. *Pierre Vallières: The Revolutionary Process in Quebec.* New York: Dial Press, 1973.

Schull, Joseph. *Laurier: The First Canadian.* Toronto: Macmillan, 1965.

Vallières, Pierre. *White Niggers of America.* Trans. Joan Pinkham. Toronto: McClelland & Stewart, 1971.

Wells, Paul. *Right Side Up: The Fall of Paul Martin and the Rise of Stephen Harper's New Conservatism.* Toronto: McClelland & Stewart, 2006.

ACKNOWLEDGEMENTS

Never has a book owed so much to a margarita. When Natasha Daneman and I met to have a drink and catch up last December, we brainstormed about book projects. The idea of a book about Stéphane Dion, to be written for a spring release date, appealed to Bruce Westwood, my agent and Natasha's boss at Westwood Creative Artists. Although limping from a sports injury, Bruce moved with impressive speed to arrange meetings during the holiday season. He showed why he's the best in the business. I was swept along by their enthusiasm before my own doubts about the deadline had time to surface, and I am indebted to Bruce and Natasha.

At Penguin Canada, David Davidar signed off on the project on the eve of his Christmas holidays. The entire Penguin team was terrific throughout what would be a wild ride. Although we had only three months, my brilliant editor, Diane Turbide, made me feel as if I had all the time in the world, as did her assistant, Elizabeth McKay, and Martha Sharpe, who edited swiftly under intense pressure. Shima Aoki pulled off a miracle in production, and her fact-checkers and proofreaders have saved me from certain embarrassment. Publicity director Yvonne Hunter brought enthusiasm and originality to the project, and I am grateful for the ideas and hard work of my publicist, Stephen Myers. At Penguin, I must thank as well, Lorraine Kelly and Christine Gambin. I am also indebted to Quebec agent Luc Jutras and to Erwan Leseul and his team at Les Éditions de l'Homme for quickly turning this book around for publication in Quebec. Translator Marie-Luce Constant felt like an old friend within days.

I could have written this book without my research assistant, Joanna Smith, but not in three months. I owe her a huge debt of gratitude for her hard work, high spirits, and wise advice, including suggesting the title. Joanna will excel both in her journalism career and (when she chooses) as an author. Her friend Christian Beare provided the invaluable service of improving my computer work site.

I would also like to thank Yolande Buono, from the Collection nationale at the Bibliothèque et Archives nationales du Québec, for granting special permission for extended use of the multimedia computer, and to the staff at the Inter-Library Loans Department of the Toronto Reference Library, a branch of the Toronto Public Library, who went beyond the call of duty in having documents shipped to Toronto from other libraries.

Many people very kindly agreed to be interviewed, and their names appear throughout the book. I am indebted to all of them, especially to those who made themselves available time after time. There is very little in this book that comes from "off the record" sources. That was an important point for me. However, some people in the political arena chose to speak to me on a background basis and their interviews added to my depth of understanding.

I am grateful to my colleagues and friends at the *Toronto Star*. John Honderich has been an inspiration and is responsible for the high points in my career. Jagoda Pike made this project possible, Rob Pritchard encouraged me on this book, and Fred Kuntz was unfailing in both his support and his refusal to take my projected return dates seriously. My longtime editor John Ferri is in a class by himself. Lynn McAuley, with the best ideas, has been endlessly patient with me. I am also indebted to Joe Hall, David Olive, Carol Goar, Richard Lautens, Peter Power, Peter Gorrie, Thomas Walkom, Pat Strain, Michelle Shephard, Jim Rankin, Mark Trensch, Bart

LeDrew, Joan Sweeny-Marsh and her team in the library, and the *Star*'s incredible switchboard operators. David Walmsley and Sean Stanleigh guided my coverage during the Liberal leadership with gusto. And I owe a special thanks to Duncan Boyce of Editorial Systems.

I think I understand how Stéphane Dion came to see me over the course of my research: as a student of his life. Even a good student doesn't necessarily agree with the professor. He was brave, in my view, to give such broad access to his life without conditions, and was exceedingly generous with his time. I thank André Lamarre for opening the door. I am also grateful to Mr. Dion's family, particularly Janine Krieber and Denyse Dion, who are not, themselves, public figures, but were, nevertheless, unfailingly open with me and imposed no restrictions. Ms. Krieber even agreed to see a writer who, through a chain of circumstances, showed up the first time in a Hummer. And thank you to Norman and Marta Wale for their hospitality.

Writing a book is like living in a cave, and I am indebted to friends who threw me a lifeline whenever they felt I'd been incommunicado for too long: Don Macpherson (also my esteemed Quebec colleague); Vera Santos; Noreen McAneney; Audrey Smith, Jim Smith, Karen Smith, and Deborah Flom; Lynne Provencher and Steve Castellano; Joe Modeste; and Ruth Valancius. As always, my friend Linda McQuaig was a constant source of support and late-night laughter. My friendship with Kelly Toughill has been a mainstay of my life for a very long time, through thick and thin as they say, and she is very dear to me. My last debt of appreciation is to my mentor, Dr. Sheila Grossman.

INDEX